PRINCE CHARMING

THE JOHN F. KENNEDY, JR.

STORY

WENDY LEIGH

PRINCE CHARMING

THE
JOHN F. KENNEDY, JR.
STORY

RESEARCH ASSISTANCE BY STEPHEN KARTEN

A DUTTON BOOK

DUTTON

Published by the Penguin Group

Penguin Books USA Inc., 375 Hudson Street, New York, New York 10014, U.S.A.

Penguin Books Ltd, 27 Wrights Lane, London W8 5TZ, England

Penguin Books Australia Ltd, Ringwood, Victoria, Australia

Penguin Books Canada Ltd, 10 Alcorn Avenue, Toronto, Ontario, Canada M4V 3B2

Penguin Books (N.Z.) Ltd, 182–190 Wairau Road, Auckland 10, New Zealand

Penguin Books Ltd, Registered Offices:
Harmondsworth, Middlesex, England

First published by Dutton, an imprint of Dutton Signet,
a division of Penguin Books USA Inc.
Distributed in Canada by McClelland & Stewart Inc.

First Printing, November, 1993

1   3   5   7   9   10   8   6   4   2

 REGISTERED TRADEMARK—MARCA REGISTRADA

LIBRARY OF CONGRESS CATALOGING IN PUBLICATION DATA:
Leigh, Wendy.
Prince Charming : the John F. Kennedy Jr. story / by Wendy Leigh:
research assistance by Stephen Karten.
p.   cm.
ISBN 0-525-93712-9 : $22.00
1. Kennedy, John F. (John Fitzgerald), 1960– . 2. Children of
presidents—United States—Biography. I. Karten, Stephen.
E843.K42L45 1993
973.922′092—dc20

[B]

93-20800
CIP

Printed in the United States of America
Set in Centaur

DESIGNED BY STEVEN N. STATHAKIS

For Steven Gaines,
with thanks

Acknowledgments

Prince Charming could not have been written without the interviewing, editorial, and research skills of my husband, Stephen Karten. To say that I'm indebted to my agent, John Hawkins, is an understatement. His guidance, friendship, encouragement, and publishing expertise have been invaluable. Many thanks also to Sharon Friedman at John Hawkins & Associates, Inc., for her legal counsel. Special thanks are due to Warren Frazier for his good-natured patience, and to Moses Cardona and Gladys Guadalupe at John Hawkins & Associates, Inc.

I am especially grateful to Christopher Schelling, my editor at Dutton, without whose confidence this book would not have been possible. I would like to thank publicists Lynn Goldberg, Becky Simpson, and Camille McDuffie of Lynn Goldberg Communications,

Acknowledgments

and Lisa Johnson and Jennifer Marcus of Dutton publicity for their enthusiasm and commitment.

Gail Gabert was a miracle worker in transcribing hours and hours of interview tapes.

Thanks also to Doreen Alfaro and her staff at Christafaro's catering in West Palm Beach for their mouthwatering food.

Countless researchers, librarians, journalists, and editors contributed immensely to the book. I am grateful to researcher Martha Trachtenberg in New York; Christopher Donnelly of *The Boston Herald;* Melody Blake of the *Washington Post;* Maureen O'Sullivan of *The Palm Beach Daily News;* Nancy Edwards of the *New York Daily News;* Nancy Halloran at the *Cape Cod Times;* the staff of the *Providence Journal;* Sandra Burke of the *Irish Times,* Dublin; Greg Retsinas at the *Brown Daily Herald;* the staff of the *Phillipian,* Andover; Ruth Quattlebaum, archivist at Phillips Andover Academy; Chris Bowen at the *Star;* Sharon Churcher, coauthor of *Obsession: The Unauthorized Biography of Calvin Klein;* Karen Phaneuf of the Palm Beach County Library; Claudia Anderson, archivist at the Lyndon Baines Johnson Library; Susan Naulty of the Richard M. Nixon Library and Birthplace; Alan Goodrich, Susan Duntroment, Maura Porter, June Payne, and Ron Whelan of the John F. Kennedy Library, Boston; Marilyn Wurzberger of the Peter Lawford Collection, University of Arizona; Melvin Laska, Department of the Treasury, United States Secret Service; Hans Tasiemka Archives, London; the staff of the London Sunday *Times* Library, London; the staff of the New York Public Library; the tourist office of St. Barthélemy, French West Indies; *Publishers Weekly* Library; Noreen Taylor, the *Daily Mirror,* London; Richard Lay in New York; Bill Lowther in Washington, D.C.; Richard Kaplan, editor, the *Star;* John Connolly, *Spy* magazine; Joanna Elm; Beverly Ecker; Lydia Encinas; Ayesha Attari in Hyderabad, India; Richard Chalfin of "The Better Book Getter"; and Joel Selvin of the *San Francisco Chronicle.*

While many friends and associates of John F. Kennedy, Jr., were eager to provide information for the book, they were also unwilling to be quoted for attribution. I am grateful for their insightful contributions and have naturally respected their request for anonymity. The following individuals gave interviews, checked facts, or provided sources or additional information. I am immensely grateful to Rebecca Michael of Compliments Catering, London; Ingrid DeVita of *Inside Edition;* Leo Damore, author of *Senatorial Privilege;* Stephen Birmingham, author of *Jacqueline Bouvier Kennedy Onassis;* Chris Andersen, author of *Madonna Unauthorized;* Stuart Schectman; Russell Turiak; Angie Coqueran; Jack Anderson; Erika Belle; Leticia Baldridge; Agnes Ashe; Dr. Denis Murphy; Raoul Felder; Zsa Zsa Gabor; David Horowitz, coauthor of *The Kennedys;* Couri Hay; Victor Malafante; Nora Lawlor; Richard Wiese; Betty MacMahon; Rita Dallas; Jenny Christian; Larry Newman; Barry Clifford; Senator George Smathers; Ben Bradlee; Dick Gallagher; William Haddad; Jim Seymore of *Entertainment Weekly;* Carol Wallace of *People* magazine; Hugh "Yusha" Auchincloss III; Jamie Auchincloss; George Plimpton; Paul Smadbeck; Carol Rosenwald; Majorie Dobkin; Paul Fay; Janet Travell; Peter Burrow; Dickie Thieras; Stanley and Barbara Hirsch of Camp Androscoggin; Bob Cramer; Creon Brown; Barbara Gibson; Sylvia Whitehouse Blake; Harold "Holly" Owen; Mark Kamins; Rick Burke; Dave Powers; Liz Rosenberg, publicist for Madonna; Jane Conway; Larry Conway; Patricia Seaton Lawford Stewart; John Kessanis at Olympic Airways; Lynn Alpha Smith; Mary Gallagher; Evelyn Lincoln; Skip Owen; Christie Orr; Wilson McCray; Rose Ganguzza; Barry Landau; Stephen Harvey; Steven Gaines, author of *Obsession: The Unauthorized Biography of Calvin Klein;* Cathy Griffin; Helen Thomas of UPI; Tim Carroll; Aaron Latham; Paul Steiner; Arianna Stassinopoulos Huffington; James Spada, author of *Peter Lawford, The Man Who Kept the Secrets;* Lilly Fallah Lawrence; Sally Bitterman; Kitty Kelley; the producers of *Seinfeld;* Sugar Rautbord; Karla Kincaid and Paul Irving at Manatt, Phelps & Phillips; the office of Oliver Stone; Gary Patterson at the Robert Stigwood Organisation; Cathy Morse at the Kahala Hilton, Ha-

Acknowledgments

waii; John Spierling; Sarah Fargo at Ambrosio & Mortimer (agent to Christina Haag); Jeremy Spiegel at *A Current Affair;* Jay Schadler at *Prime Time Live;* George Dix; Brewster Connant, Jr.; Ron Czarnetsky; Christine Thomson; Gordon Donald; Toni Bradlee; Peter Cohan; Eleanor Lambert; Jim Connors; Elizabeth Melaragno; Andrew Gibbon Nyhart; Brian Crull; Mark Bego, author of *Madonna;* Heather Trim; Douglas Creedon; John Dabney; Peter Burrow; Chris Harty; Lenny McGurr (a.k.a. Futura 2000); Joseph Daly; Detective Joe Keenan; Joanne Bon Giorno at the Drake Hotel in Chicago; Susan Vaughn.

Prologue

Dateline: Spring, 1988, Time-Life Building, Manhattan

It was the kind of informal brainstorming session the editors of *People* magazine relish. As arbiters of popular taste in America, six of the magazine's best and brightest gathered in the conference room on the twenty-ninth floor to select the 1988 candidate for Sexiest Man Alive.

Their feet propped on chairs, they sipped coffee and tossed out names drawn from lists of famous stars.

Each name bandied about had merit, but none completely filled the bill. There were two years left in a decade marked by eight years of greed under an actor-president. The country was shifting out of the superficial *me* mood and into the more stringent, less indulgent mode that would approach with the nineties. In years previous, physical beauty and theatrical presence had been enough—every winner thus far had been an actor. This was not simply the male version of a beauty pageant—the right name could help elevate the award.

Senior editor Carol Wallace mentally sifted through the accumulated list of names of hunky stars. Not one of them had the right combination of looks, charisma, and image. The perfect candidate should have a certain magic, some legendary aspect that would make their choice indisputable. He would have to come out of the era of the New Frontier yet still be a part of the generation that would take America into the twenty-first century. Ideally, he would also—

She sat up with a start and turned to face assistant managing editor Jim Seymore, whose instinct for true celebrity is considered second to none.

"John F. Kennedy, Jr.," Wallace said.

"Yes!" Seymore snapped his fingers.

"I realized this was the right moment," Jim Seymore remembers. "John's public image had been growing while he grew—from a little boy who saluted his father's coffin into a movie-star-handsome grown-up with an incredible background. If that's not celebrity, I don't know what is."

People's decision to proclaim John F. Kennedy, Jr., the Sexiest Man Alive did more than remind the country that America's favorite little boy had grown into a handsome, desirable man. It reminded America of the vision of the future that his father had so forcefully and eloquently expressed before his death.

In the decades that followed the death of the President and of his dream for the nation, the shimmering kaleidoscope that was Camelot had been shattered, leaving the glittering Kennedy mystique obscured by the shadows and the whispers of a corruption so deeply rooted that the controversy eclipsed even the legend.

Jackie fell from her pedestal. Bobby was murdered. Teddy was disgraced. Jack's womanizing had been revealed. In the eyes of the public, only two Kennedys escaped demythification relatively unscathed: the dead President's children.

And despite the passing years, the image of John's salute never receded. He was part of history, an indelible reminder of what the country had lost, of what might have been. Through John, every American was an heir to Camelot.

"John grew up with the baby boomers. They all remember him saluting his father's coffin. And I think he is a god on feet," Carol Wallace of *People* said.

The decision was made. In a country where no man can be king, the royal image of JFK's son was about to rise from the ashes of Camelot.

The John F. Kennedy, Jr., "Sexiest Man Alive" issue of *People* hit the stands on September 12, 1988, the thirty-fifth wedding anniversary of his parents, John and Jacqueline Kennedy. At the tender age of twenty-seven their son had been dubbed not a knight of Camelot, but a prince.

CHAPTER ONE

A Touch
of Magic

Legend has it—and legend is, after all, the fabric of which the Kennedy era was woven—that on February 15, 1960, the young and beautiful wife of the senator from Massachusetts was in Fort Atkinson, Wisconsin, campaigning ardently for her husband in a key primary, when a minor miracle transpired.

"Go forth and multiply" was a Kennedy motto, and at that point in their marriage Jackie was the mother of just one child, Caroline. After two miscarriages, she knew that bearing a son was virtually mandatory.

Crowds thronged the pavement outside the town's Blackhawk Hotel waving "I Like Kennedy" placards and chanting the campaign slogan: "Action—Courage—Integrity." One of the earliest primaries, Wisconsin would be a launching pad toward the presidency. John Kennedy campaigned with gusto. He shook hands, flashing his infectious smile and radiating charisma while Jacqueline in her whispery voice cajoled the townspeople, "Please vote for my husband."

Jackie worked her way along one side of the main street; Jack progressed along the other side. She was fairly far away from him when his trusty political aide Dave Powers rushed up with a message that Jack wanted her to cross the street to join him. Jackie allowed Powers to escort her to her husband's side.

There she found Jack posing for pictures with the wife of the local Lutheran minister. Her job was to charm additional voters on her husband's behalf—why had she been summoned from that task?

Jack introduced her to the minister's wife.

"She's the proud mother of no less than thirteen children," he said in his clear, ringing voice. "Shake hands with this lady, Jackie. Maybe it will rub off on you."

Jackie did as she was told. Within a month, she was pregnant.

The news that Jackie was again pregnant came out later during the primaries. The country sat up and took new notice of the dashing senator, his beautiful wife, and their seemingly idyllic marriage.

Seven years had passed since the young senator from Massachusetts, one of the country's most eligible bachelors, had married one of the country's loveliest debutantes. Jacqueline Bouvier Kennedy's illustrious French pedigree and European allure had only enhanced her husband's political appeal and furthered his quest for power. But once the misty romanticism of courtship, a wedding ceremony cheered by three thousand well-wishers, and a honeymoon in Acapulco had faded into the past, it was clear that although they each claimed Irish roots (he on both sides, she on her mother's), Jacqueline and Jack Kennedy came from different worlds.

Jack Bouvier was a notorious rake whose alcoholism caused him to miss his beloved daughter's wedding. The rest of the Bouviers were far more subdued, and more cultured, than the Kennedys. Jackie had grown up steeped in art, literature, drama, and music. A protracted stay in France had made her sophisticated beyond her years.

Jack Kennedy, too, had spent time in Europe, but had lived a privileged life fueled by unlimited money and an unquenchable hedonism. An inveterate womanizer like his father (who remained married to the pious Rose while carrying on a torrid affair with the actress Gloria Swanson), he had seemed destined to live out his years as a playboy and dilettante.

It took the death of his older brother, Joe Jr., combined with his father's unstoppable ambition to thrust Jack into politics. With his brothers' and sisters' support, his father's millions and ferocious will to win, and his own drive for power, Jack became invincible. Jackie had been prepared for that, but not, perhaps, for the power, the coarseness, or the ruthlessness of his family. The Kennedys saw winning as their divine right, granted by a loving and lenient God who condoned all.

Carrying Jack's second child should have solidified Jackie's status in the family. But even had she been willing or able to produce as many children as Bobby's wife, Ethel, Jackie would have remained an outsider, cast in a more delicate mold than her more coarse-grained in-laws.

Bobby had never posed a problem; nor had Teddy, who would always adore her. Jackie's chief adversaries would always be Eunice (Jack's favorite sister) and sister-in-law Ethel, who prided herself on being more Kennedy than Kennedy. To Eunice and Ethel, Jackie was "Jacleen, whose name rhymes with Queen"; to Jacqueline, they were "the rah-rah girls."

Observing Jackie at dinner *chez* Kennedy, close friend Dorothy Turbridy had noted the competitive atmosphere at the table. A Kennedy who didn't contribute to the conversation would be pounced on:

"Why haven't you read today's *Wall Street Journal?*" Obsessed by sports, the members of the clan had tremendous energy, excelled in sarcasm, avoided real intimacy, and had little respect for literature, culture, contemplation—all dear to Jacqueline.

Dinah Bridge, a long-standing Kennedy family friend, pointedly evaluated the differences between Jackie and the Kennedys.

"She was rather a gentle, quiet character, and suddenly to be bowled into the Kennedy family, you really had to do a bit of shouting to keep up. Meals were fun, never dull and never quiet. They'd drink gallons of milk and talk and talk, and you might hear Jackie trying to say something at the end of the table. She hardly ever got it out, though. Didn't have a chance."

Jackie did not share the Kennedy appetite for escapades and malicious practical jokes. At times the family exhibited a loutishness almost bordering on cruelty; at other times they showed a recklessness about other people's lives and sensibilities that seemed to be based on a sense of *droit du seigneur.*

In the summer of 1960, journalist Clark Mollenhoff, Washington editor of *The Des Moines Register,* received a telephone call from his friend Bobby Kennedy inviting him to come over for a swim. Mollenhoff, who was still wearing a neck brace after a car accident, refused the invitation. He told Bobby why he couldn't come; Bobby repeated the invitation, and Mollenhoff agreed to visit later that afternoon.

As Mollenhoff was walking across a gangplank leading from the pool to the outdoors, Bobby rose from the water like a dolphin and pushed him into the pool. Miraculously, Mollenhoff survived unhurt. But journalist Fletcher Knebel, who saw what happened, later said, "This is his good friend with a broken neck. That just confirms the ruthlessness of Bobby and all that. He's not only ruthless, he's idiotic." At the time, Knebel thought the incident was "liable to cost

Jack the nomination, but people are skeptical of the Kennedys anyway around the country."

Knebel's editor refused to run his eyewitness account; the story was suppressed, and the Kennedy reputation survived intact.

If the public remained unaware of the incipient sadism inherent in the fabled Kennedy sense of humor, Jackie, with her acute sensitivity and ability to slice below the surface, definitely did not. Instead of succumbing to the lure of the group, by 1960 she had already begun to carve out her own domain.

"In her own way, she's much more talented, I think, than most of the Kennedys, so she's survived because of her interests," said Dorothy Turbridy. "She cares about ballet, art, music—all those things the Kennedy sisters aren't particularly interested in. So she followed her own interests and created this atmosphere about herself. Through all the years, she had her own life."

Pregnant with her second child, Jackie bent her strong will to the goal of making her husband President. She might have been terrified of losing her baby, but she still campaigned in Kentucky, Delaware, Tennessee, Maine, North Carolina, and New York, where she charmed voters by making speeches in their native Spanish, Italian, Polish, and, of course, French.

Traveling with Jack in the converted twin-engine Corvair named *Caroline,* which Joe Kennedy had bought for $350,000, Jackie worked tirelessly. She not only gave speeches but also corresponded with thousands of Kennedy supporters across the country, meticulously answering letters by hand. With her Vassar poise and her Parisian charm, Jackie was wildly telegenic. Her husband was quick to capitalize on her assets on television and radio shows all over America. Jackie answered questions in her breathy, light voice, her eyes never leaving the interviewer's face, her personality captivating millions of viewers and listeners. She appeared on *The Today Show,* acted as "receptionist" on a

TV show monitoring viewers' questions to the senator, and in general did everything possible to advance her husband's career.

During the last days of the election she defied her doctor's orders and campaigned for Jack in New York, again winning hearts and votes by speaking fluent Spanish, Italian, and French. The besotted crowds that followed her everywhere only foreshadowed the adulation to come. After the homespun matriarchs Eleanor Roosevelt, Bess Truman, and Mamie Eisenhower, America was ready to lay itself at the feet of a glamorous goddess.

But though he might soon be elevated to godlike status, Jack Kennedy was not ready for sainthood. He courted a variety of women, including Sophia Loren and Jean Simmons—both of whom surprisingly remained immune to his charms. But there was one Hollywood woman-about-town who didn't: statuesque twenty-six-year-old Judith Campbell, whose lovers included Chicago crime boss Sam Giancana.

On November 8, 1960, when Jackie was almost nine months pregnant, Jack Kennedy was elected President. The First Family-elect was living at 3307 N Street NW in Georgetown. Jack had picked the charming house because he liked the door knocker, but Jackie had redecorated four times in their first three months there. She looked forward to spending their last Thanksgiving in Georgetown before moving to the White House after the Inauguration.

With the baby due on December 12, the family enjoyed a day-before-Thanksgiving dinner before Jack flew back to Palm Beach, where Bobby and Teddy were waiting for him. Jackie, condemned to what was left of a cold Washington autumn, was not pleased that Jack was deserting her, and their farewell was not particularly cordial.

About an hour after Jack's departure, Jackie began to scream for Maud Shaw, Caroline's English nanny, who immediately telephoned Jackie's doctor, John Walsh. At exactly 10:35 P.M., ambulance driver

William Baucom of the Hospital Emergency Oxygen and Equipment Company received the call to transport Jackie along the twelve-block route from N Street to Georgetown University Hospital. She spent the six-minute trip, while the aides tried to reassure her, worrying about what would happen to the baby if she fell off the stretcher.

By now, the President-elect had taken off from Washington, bound for Palm Beach in a chartered American Airlines plane. He was discussing his prospective Cabinet choices with aide Kenny O'Donnell when a radio message came through: Jackie had been rushed to the hospital and was about to give birth.

The minute Jack landed in Florida he telephoned Walsh, who told him Jackie was undergoing a cesarean. Jack hung up the phone and arranged to fly back to Washington on the press plane that had just landed—complete with the press corps sent to cover his visit to Palm Beach. Once on board the DC-6, Jack listened intently to the radio through earphones, desperate for news.

At 1:17 A.M. on November 25, Thanksgiving morning, the news came through that Jackie had given birth to a boy. Jack took off his earphones and smiled. Press secretary Pierre Salinger announced the birth over the loudspeaker system, and the press corps congratulated the President-elect, applauding as he bowed and waved.

That moment and the circumstance of his birth symbolized what the future would bring for the first child ever born to an American President-elect and his wife: applause and adulation all the way.

John F. Kennedy, Jr., was the most famous baby in the United States, if not the world. Born on the seventy-ninth birthday of Pope John XXIII, the son of America's first Catholic President weighed six pounds, three ounces and spent the first few days of his life in an incubator. His premature birth left him with a mild version of the lung condition that would later kill his infant brother, Patrick.

While John struggled to survive, the world paid homage to his arrival. The Queen of England and Prince Philip sent warm congratulations; the august *Times* of London commented, "Press coverage of the event has been so enthusiastic that one could get the impression that this was a royal birth and the dynasty had been saved."

Jack's Vice President-elect, Lyndon Johnson, in Paris for a NATO Parliamentarian meeting, sent a telegram: "Name that boy Lyndon, and a heifer calf will be his."

Gifts and flowers poured in: a large arrangement of birds of paradise from Frank Sinatra, a bouquet of roses and snapdragons from Senator George Smathers, and a two-hundred-year-old christening cup delivered personally by an Irish airline hostess named Margaret Ryan, from the Kennedy ancestral home in New Ross, County Wexford.

Two schoolchildren, Betty Jean Mastrandrea and her brother Victor, wrote from Rochester, New York, "We love your new baby. All of us in our school will be watching you on TV during classes. We all wish you the best of luck while you are President and keep us safe from the Reds."

Presidential assistant Ralph A. Dugan answered the letter, "The President asked me to thank you and Betty Jean for your beautiful card congratulating him and Mrs. Kennedy on the birth of their son. They were pleased by your thoughtfulness. The good wishes you express are also appreciated. You may be sure, Victor, that the President shares your desire that America be kept safe. He will work very hard so that you and all other boys and girls can grow up in a world at peace."

The new baby elicited extravagant compliments before he was even out of the incubator. Maud Shaw, Caroline's usually crisp nanny, who would be John's nanny as well, described him as "the tiniest, sweetest little mite you ever saw." And Dr. Walsh pronounced John Jr., good-looking and healthy.

Jack arrived at Georgetown Hospital at 4:18 A.M., surrounded by a small detail of Secret Service agents and trailed by reporters. Gazing at the new baby, the President-elect pronounced, "That's about the most beautiful baby boy I've ever seen. Maybe I'll name him Abraham Lincoln."

Kennedy family nurse Luella Hennessy, who had known Jack since he was twenty, watched over Jackie during her hospital stay and was touched by the reaction of the hospital staff and patients every time the President-elect arrived for a visit. "Everybody gathered around in the corridors and he was so kind to them all. He would come down the corridor and stop at each door and shake hands with any patient who was at the door to greet him or wave to him. They just all fell in love with him every time he came to see his wife."

On his third visit to Jackie's room, Jack commented that he wasn't sure whom the baby resembled. "I'll have to study him some more," he said. Asked about his wife's condition, he said, "Jackie's a little sick but she's getting along all right. She seemed very happy. I guess she's been worried about the baby."

Back on N Street, Caroline also was worried. "Mummy is bringing back a new baby brother for your birthday," Jack told her. Maud Shaw, too, did her utmost to prepare Caroline for her new sibling, helping her pick out a silver brush and comb set as a present for John. Caroline afterward insisted that only her comb and brush be used on her brother's hair.

On the morning of November 29, the baby was judged strong enough not to need oxygen pumped into his incubator, and his formula was decreased. On December 1, while Jack was finalizing his Cabinet appointments, Jackie held the baby for the first time and fed him his bottle. When he was eight days old, he was taken out of the incubator for good and placed in a bassinet. Outside the hospital, the crowds watching for a glimpse of the proud father increased daily, as did the droves of reporters. When Jackie ventured into the corridor, a photographer jumped out at her. Although he was quickly thrown out, Jackie sensed that this was only the beginning of the unwavering media focus that would be trained on her and her family for the rest of their lives.

The baby was baptized John F. Kennedy, Jr., at 4 P.M. on December 8, 1960. Jackie was fiercely proud of her first son and the celebrated name she had given him, though later she would wish passionately that she had given him another.

Jackie's intense pride and joy were momentarily shaken when Jack pushed her wheelchair into Georgetown University Hospital's Roman Catholic Chapel and a group of reporters and photographers came into view. Instinctively she recoiled.

"Oh, God. Don't stop, Jack. Just keep going."

He kept going, ignoring the reporters' requests for a comment.

Jackie's black wool broadcloth suit made a dramatic contrast against her tiny son's white batiste christening gown and matching carrying shawl which his father had worn at his own christening in 1917. A religious medallion—a gift from the baby's godfather, Prince Stanislaus Radziwill, who was married to Jackie's sister, Lee—was pinned to the christening gown. On his head the baby wore a ruffled lace bonnet that his mother had worn as a child.

Once inside the small chapel, the Reverend Martin Casey of Holy Trinity Church in Georgetown began the brief ceremony: "John Fitzgerald Kennedy, Jr., wilt thou be baptized?" The baby gave a subdued cry. Father Casey ended the service with the blessing, "John Fitzgerald Kennedy, Jr., go in peace, and may the Lord be with you."

As they left the chapel, Jackie glanced down at the baby in her arms and said, "Look at those pretty eyes! Isn't he sweet?"

Jack nodded, preoccupied. During the ceremony he and Bobby had had a whispered argument. Jack wanted to make William Fulbright secretary of state; Bobby insisted Fulbright was a racist. The debate raged on, with the debaters oblivious to the mother and her newly baptized baby. For her part, Jackie had done her duty. She had delivered the heir to the throne.

The day after the baptism, Jackie made an extensive tour of the White House, escorted by her predecessor, Mamie Eisenhower. Not long after, Jackie described her new home as resembling "a hotel that had been decorated by a wholesale furniture store during a January clearance." Tired and dispirited, she returned to the sanctuary of the Georgetown town house she had furnished and refurnished so painstakingly and now dreaded leaving. Feeling depressed and ill, she made a snap decision to fly immediately to Palm Beach, taking John Jr., Caroline, and nurse Elsie Philips with her.

The President-elect flew to Florida with them, smoking a cigar en route. Jackie saw the cigar smoke whirling above John's bassinet and demanded that Jack move to the front of the plane. Caroline, however, wouldn't be moved from the pink and white bassinet in which her new baby brother slept despite the bumpiness of the flight.

Jackie and the children would stay in Palm Beach until after Christmas. And so it was that John spent the first few weeks of his life in an oceanside nursery at the Kennedy family's winter compound.

The six-bedroom house at 1095 North Ocean Boulevard is far less imposing than the phrase "Kennedy compound" suggests. Although it was designed by Palm Beach's renowned architectural father, Addison Mizner, and was built in 1923 for a little less than $50,000, the house is not as grand as most of Mizner's other palatial mansions on Ocean Boulevard.

Joe Kennedy had purchased the property for around $100,000 from Rodman Wanamaker of Philadelphia, and for years afterward the Kennedy compound was still known as the Wanamaker estate among Palm Beach's ruling bluebloods.

The Kennedys would never become a part of the Palm Beach social whirl. Initially Joe Kennedy did apply to join the two private clubs, the Everglades and Bath and Tennis clubs, but his applications were summarily rejected. In a characteristic act of defiance, the ex-bootlegging patriarch joined forces with Palm Beach's Jewish community, and in 1953 cofounded the Palm Beach Country Club. This was the same isolationist with strong anti-Semitic tendencies who before World War II had complained that "Roosevelt and the kikes are taking us into war."

Joe, who had enjoyed gambling at Bradley's Beach Club, said "the zipperoo had gone out of the place" when Bradley's closed in 1946. In any case, the Kennedys avoided most of the Palm Beach social extravaganzas that are still the focal point of this playground of the rich and risqué.

The Kennedys valued their Palm Beach interludes for the climate and the privacy the compound afforded. The house may have been grim and oppressive (until 1993, it had no central air-conditioning), but here the Kennedys could luxuriate in their self-created universe. The compound boasted a tennis court, a pool, and a tunnel leading to the beach. Joe Kennedy in particular favored the white enclosure near the swimming pool, where he could sunbathe in the buff while making calls to direct the management of his empire.

In 1960, the same Palm Beach which had once rejected the Kennedy family now waited to bask in the prestige of being the newly elected President's Winter White House. Rose would not entertain at the compound; the house, she proclaimed quite correctly, was far too shabby for receiving visitors. As usual, Rose ruled, and the Kennedy compound was reserved for family alone.

Family was Rose Kennedy's raison d'être. When she first set eyes on the newest addition to her dynasty, Rose worried that John Jr. might catch a cold, but was careful not to issue instructions about the new baby's care without consulting her daughter-in-law.

Rose was the kind of mother-in-law who accepted her sons' wives uncomplainingly, treating them as family members as soon as the wedding ceremony was over. And although Jackie had been known to mimic her mother-in-law's idiosyncratic speech behind Rose's back, there was little outward sign of conflict between mother-in-law and daughter.

A natural diplomat and the daughter of Boston's former mayor, John "Honey Fitz" Fitzgerald, Rose understood the politics of family and worshipped the edicts of the Catholic Church. Rose was so pious that when her daughter Kathleen married out of the faith in 1944, Rose checked into the New England Baptist Hospital and issued a statement to reporters that she was "too sick to discuss the marriage."

Nevertheless, Rose possessed a vibrant streak of vanity; she ordered countless haute couture gowns at the Paris collections each year and religiously applied what she described as "frownies"— skin-colored adhesive patches intended to smooth out wrinkles.

None of these measures kept Joe Kennedy from straying repeatedly, not only with Gloria Swanson but with Marlene Dietrich and other sultry cinematic beauties. Through it all, Rose maintained a dignified silence, never alluding to her husband's infidelities or even admitting that they took place. But according to Jack's old friend, Senator George Smathers, "Rose finally put a curtain wall up in the living room. Joe was on one side and she was on the other."

Since only family and a few close friends were ever invited home to the compound, outsiders were no more aware of the details of Rose's suffering than of the curtain she had erected to shield her from the husband who humiliated her. As Joe Kennedy's wife during his meteoric career, spanning Wall Street and the ambassadorship to the Court of St. James, and now as mother of the soon-to-be thirty-fifth President of the United States, Rose had always been aware that she and her family could never truly escape the limelight for any length of time. Eternally conscious of her dignity and that of her family, she never confided in outsiders, could sometimes be cold and distant, and was careful never to show emotion in public. She was also an avid social climber.

"Rose spent the entire lunch at the Ritz-Carlton trying to impress me," remembered a woman who, as a seventeen-year-old girl, dated Joe Jr. "I can't imagine why. I was so young, yet she kept saying things like, 'You have no idea how important I am. All the Ladies' Clubs want me to talk to them.'"

With John Jr. and her legion of other grandchildren, Rose dedicated herself to forming their minds and morals. Having raised nine children with the efficiency of a five-star general, Rose applied the same approach from afar to her grandchildren. She sent memos imprinted with "Mrs. Joseph P. Kennedy" to instruct them on a variety of subjects, advising them to watch certain educational television programs, to speak grammatically, and to drink more milk in the interest of preserving their distinctive Kennedy teeth.

On the all-important religious front, she encouraged her children to subscribe to Catholic magazines and dispatched prayers, rosary beads, and religious artifacts to all her grandchildren.

If Rose's style of grandmothering was didactic, it was also well-meant. In later years, John Jr. consistently viewed his grandmother through a prism of happy memories. Rose encouraged her grandchildren to put pen to paper, and when he was twelve, John composed a testament to his grandmother, writing of how much she had taught him, of how bad his father had been as a little boy, how much they laughed together—and how much he enjoyed her Boston cream pie.

By the age of forty, Joseph P. Kennedy was already a multimillionaire. With his instinct for speculation and his thirst for drama and excitement, after Prohibition Joe turned his attention to Hollywood, terming the new motion picture industry "a gold mine." Once in Hollywood, he not only increased his fortune, but also satiated both his libido and his considerable vanity.

In her autobiography, Gloria Swanson recalled Joe's foreplay as being "like a roped horse, rough, arduous, rearing to be free"; she described his lovemaking as brief—a charge that would one day be leveled at his equally libidinous son, Jack.

Despite the steamy affair with Swanson and briefer liaisons with other actresses, Joe ultimately favored the role of patriarch over that of Casanova. On the rare occasions when he spent time with his family, he concentrated on developing their competitiveness, honing it during sporting events, exhorting them always, "We want winners. We don't want losers around here."

Joe had been the victor in every arena he had entered except one: politics. All his life, he had craved the power of the highest office in the land. He had won the favor of Franklin Roosevelt, who had appointed him ambassador to the Court of St. James; but with his bluntly stated policy of appeasement and his passionately voiced anti-Semitism, Joe had destroyed his own chances of ever attaining real political power. Admitting defeat, he resolved to channel his ruthless determination and his genius for publicity into ensuring that one of his children ascended to the presidency.

His eldest son, also named Joe, was naturally the child he had in mind. Jack was frail in comparison. The pecking order in the family was immutable, as far as Joe was concerned: Joe Jr. came first, followed by Jack, Bobby, and, lastly, the baby of the family, Teddy.

No father could have had more power within a family, but all that power gave Joe no control over the destiny of his children. Kathleen was killed in a 1948 plane crash; Joe died during World War II. Rosemary was born retarded, underwent a lobotomy that went disastrously wrong, and was committed by her father to a Wisconsin mental facility. Jean married Steve Smith, who had risen to prominence in the Kennedy political machine, raising funds for Jack's 1960 campaign. Eunice, the most aggressive and competitive of the sisters, married Sargent Shriver, who managed the family's Merchandise Mart in Chicago until Jack made him director of the Peace Corps in 1961. Patricia made an unconventional choice by marrying British actor Peter Lawford, thus setting the stage for a dramatic chain of events that began when Peter introduced Jack to Marilyn Monroe and ended with the star's death.

Jack had become Joe's last hope for immortality. One of the twelve richest men in America, Joe had poured into Jack's campaign not only millions of dollars, but also the power of his Mafia ties from the old bootlegging days. He used Mafia muscle to buy and cajole valuable political support for the son whose presidency he was masterminding. Money, power, ruthlessness, and a genius for public relations had been transformed into weapons skillfully wielded by Joe in quest of the White House for his son. Jack Kennedy himself was given no option—he was "drafted" into politics, as he would later say, by a father who brooked no refusal.

Joe always made great use of his nine children in furthering his public image and saw to it that the family came off as attractive, radiantly healthy, and quintessentially American. His Hollywood showmanship inspired what is perhaps his most often quoted pronouncement: "It doesn't matter what you are, it only matters what people think you are."

The Kennedy clan was uniquely American, eerily star-crossed, and, thanks to Joe's public relations tactics, consistently immortalized by both the still and the motion picture camera. It would be no different for John Jr., now an eminently photogenic addition to the Kennedy image. He had been in Palm Beach for a short while, cared for by Elsie Philips and kept in diapers by an enterprising woman named Marjorie Griffiths. She had buttonholed a Kennedy Secret Service agent and won an eight-week contract to include John on her diaper route.

The new father, having learned his lesson well from his own father, was scheduled for a session with renowned photographer Richard Avedon. Jack flew to Palm Beach for the occasion, January 4, 1961. The President-elect looked particularly handsome and well groomed. Caroline followed him, decked out in a white organdy dress with a pink ribbon in her curly blond hair.

Jackie, still physically under par, was as always a photographer's dream. Kenneth did her hair. Her clothes were designed by her self-appointed couturier, Oleg Cassini, and showed her figure off to the best advantage. However, the *pièce de résistance* was definitely John Jr., who, according to his fond grandmother, "looked infinitely adorable."

The public was already captivated by the President-elect's son, deluging Jack's office with gifts for John. All offerings were vetted by the Secret Service before being passed on. Apart from a vast collection of toys, the gifts included a rose plant named after John Jr., proffered by the grower, Mrs. Emma Anderson of St. Louis, and a football signed by all the members of the Navy and Missouri teams and presented to the President-elect at the Orange Bowl in Miami.

Meanwhile, back in Washington, the White House was being readied for the arrival of the President-elect and his wife and children—an event all Washington awaited with mounting excitement and sentimental expectations. They would not be disappointed.

CHAPTER TWO

The White House Years

Leaving Caroline and John Jr. in Palm Beach until the whirlwind of the Inauguration subsided, Jackie flew back to Washington on January 16 to prepare for her new role as First Lady. Still weak after the cesarean, she braced herself for the arduous but glamorous galas ahead of her.

Galas and glamour were now her life. Jackie relished the attention; she enjoyed matching a Cassini gown with the appropriate accessories or topping an understated velvet suit with a jaunty pillbox hat. She did not relish the prospect of having her clothes reviewed (and their prices revealed) by the media. Living in the strobe-lit public eye was seriously at odds with her innate desire for independence and privacy.

During the campaign, she had stuck stubbornly to her own style, despite the angry letters she received from time to time.

"Why does Jackie wear slacks to the grocery store?" wrote one woman.

"Why does she wear her hair in that wild style?" came from another part of the country.

But the moment her husband had become President-elect, all criticism ceased. Jackie was canny enough to understand that she had won her own kind of election.

"I am absolutely the same now as I was before," she told her mother. "Before they hated it and now they love it."

Ten thousand guests—each of whom donated $1,000 to aid the Democratic party's campaign fund—flocked to the Inauguration Eve Gala. They loved Jackie, watching star-struck as she arrived at the National Guard Armory on Jack's arm. Swathed in gossamer white organza, she laced through the blizzard that was pelting Washington. They idolized her, crowning her Queen of America.

In principle, it was Jack's night, a star-studded gala arranged in his honor by Peter Lawford and produced by Frank Sinatra, then an ardent Kennedy disciple. Two Broadway shows and countless Hollywood sets had been closed down so that their stars could participate in this show-business night of nights.

It was the kind of night relished by Joe Kennedy, the magician whose fortune and bulldog tenacity had helped elevate his second son to the presidency. There was ritual, drama, comedy, and glitter. But no matter how high the glamour, how compelling the drama, none of it could compete with the evening's true stars: Jackie, Jack, and the entire Kennedy clan.

Along with Rose, Joe, Teddy, and his wife Joan, Jack and Jackie watched spellbound as the gala began with Mahalia Jackson's heartfelt singing of the national anthem. Sinatra followed with an equally stirring rendition of "The House I Live In."

"We see a great nation and we are happy and confident that they have picked a great man for the job," said Sir Laurence Olivier, who had traveled from England for the Inaugural.

Ella Fitzgerald, Nat King Cole, Harry Belafonte, Gene Kelly, and Jimmy Durante dazzled the audience. Durante sang a crusty version of "September Song," a number Jack often intoned as the last guests were slipping away. Sinatra belted out his own version of "That Old Black Magic," changing the words to "That old Jack magic that he weaves so well." His performance was reminiscent of the campaign song he had sung for Jack: "High Hopes" re-jiggered as "Everyone's pulling for Jack/Everyone wants to back Jack/Jack is on the right track."

At the time, Sinatra symbolized the hip Hollywoody-ness, the trendiness, the "swinging" quality of the Kennedy administration. In keeping with his status, at the end of the evening Sinatra gave his blessing to the new administration: "I hope no one will think it presumptuous for some of us in the entertainment world to come here to pay tribute to the President-elect of the greatest nation in the world. We hope he's a smash, we wish him good luck, and may God be with him."

Like the great impresario he was, on Inauguration Day Joe Kennedy worried that his star's first lines might lack impact. His fears vanished when Jack ascended the podium.

"Let the word go forth from this time and place," the new President said, "to friend and foe alike, that the torch has been passed to a new generation of Americans, born in this century. . . ."

One of his sons was now President. Joe could relax and drink in the solemn ceremony heralding the fulfillment of his dreams.

At the end of the speech, Jack looked up and with a few brief words sent the challenge that would define his presidency.

"And so, my fellow Americans, ask not what your country can do for you; ask what you can do for your country."

During the parade along Pennsylvania Avenue toward the White House, Jack acknowledged that it had been his father who had made this day possible. As he passed the reviewing stand where Joe, Rose, and the rest of the family were watching, he took off his top hat and saluted his father. It seemed a small gesture, a son's tipping his hat to his father, but that was the only time Jack removed the hat during the entire parade.

The Inauguration over, Jacqueline Kennedy was now mistress of the White House. Her first concern was for her children's comfort and pleasure: she summoned famed decorator "Sister" Parrish to Washington. Caroline's nursery was designed in pink; John was given a large second-floor nursery with white walls and pale blue molding just above the Grand Entrance Hall. The room had a hot plate so that Maud Shaw could conveniently prepare his formula and solids.

The nanny was a trifle displeased when she saw her new charge for the first time since his departure for Palm Beach. According to her strict standards, John was a little underweight and more than a little discontent. Unimpressed with his new surroundings, including his white wicker crib with its long organdy skirt, he spent his first few weeks at the White House crying with alarming regularity every afternoon.

The ever resourceful Miss Shaw quickly took action, switching John's meal of beef extract from late morning to lunch-time and increasing his formula. Soon the new First Son's emotional equilibrium was reestablished. By March 16 John napped peacefully, and dined on strained meats, soup, vegetables, cereals, and fruit. He weighed a sturdy twelve pounds, twelve and a half ounces.

Cecil Stoughton, JFK's official photographer at the time, characterized the appeal of the White House for the Kennedy children by describing it as "a transplanted New England village." It seemed designed for children. Their father's office would become the most photographed children's play area in history. It was only a short walk away, and they were kept out only when the most serious business was in progress.

It had pictures of ships on the walls. Scrimshawed whale teeth decorated the mammoth desk, which had a secret compartment. Daddy's secretary, Evelyn Lincoln, was always waiting with pink and white rock candy, reserved for good children who might drop into their father's office.

Jackie designed a play yard around a tree house outside the President's West Wing office window. The tree house proved a great temptation for the mischievous Caroline, who, although she adored her baby brother, had to be dissuaded from pushing him down the slide in his baby carriage.

The play yard housed a great variety of pets during the Kennedy years in the White House. An animal lover herself, Jackie firmly believed in bringing as many creatures as possible into her children's lives—even buying ducks for the South Fountain. When one of the many family dogs tormented them, the ducks reacted by feasting on the tulip beds. Eventually Jackie was forced to send them into exile.

The Kennedys had only a Welsh terrier, Charlie, when they first arrived at the White House. Premier Khrushchev of Russia then sent the children the gift of a puppy named Pushinka. Although the Cold War was not yet at its frostiest, the advent of Pushinka concerned the Secret Service, who harbored suspicions that Pushinka might be a Trojan dog, with a bug implanted in her lustrous fur.

Joe Kennedy gave Jackie a German shepherd named Clipper; a priest from Dublin sent the President a wolfhound with the unoriginal name of Wolf, and President Eamon De Valera of Ireland sent a cocker spaniel named Shannon. Jack's willingness to give dogs the run of the White House attested to his eagerness to be a good father— when he was around them, his eyes and face swelled and he could barely breathe. John Jr. would prove to be allergic to horses, and although he liked riding his pony, Leprechaun, his eyes grew puffy whenever he went riding. His mother, hoping that John would become an accomplished horseman, resolutely ignored his allergy.

The children owned at least fifteen pets at any given time, including Zsa Zsa (a beer-drinking rabbit that could play the trumpet), Macaroni (Caroline's pony, whose name soon became known in every American household), Tom Kitten, Caroline's cat (eventually given away because the President also had an allergy to cat hair), and Robin (Caroline's canary, buried in the Rose Garden when she died). The children's hamsters, Marybell and Bluebell, made news when one of them died in the President's bathtub. Jackie drew the line when it came to the gifts of an Indian tiger cub and an Indian elephant.

But even with such a menagerie, life in this paradise had its price for the children.

"It was difficult on them at first," Jackie recalled later, "especially during the first three months when we barely saw them. It almost broke my heart. And you could see it in Caroline. This sad little face. And to have to live in an office building." However, the office building did have more than fifty rooms and was surrounded by eighteen acres of lawns and gardens.

Not long after the Inauguration, Jackie sent a memo to her press secretary, Pamela Turnure: "I feel strongly that publicity in this era has gotten completely out of hand and you must really protect the privacy of me and my children."

The fact that Jackie's only previously paid work had been as the *Washington Times-Herald's* Inquiring Photographer did not mitigate her growing hatred of the press. When asked by journalists what she planned to feed her new dog, Clipper, Jackie said, "Reporters."

Much of the burden of maintaining the delicate balance between Jack's obvious willingness to use his children as publicity tools (following in the footsteps of his father) and Jackie's reluctance to expose them to any publicity whatsoever fell on White House press secretary Pierre Salinger.

"The President understood the political advantages of having the children photographed," Cecil Stoughton said, "whereas Jackie saw it as an invasion of their privacy."

Jack made it eminently clear that his children were not out of bounds for the media. In Palm Beach, during a press conference held on the compound's patio, Caroline teetered out dressed in a nightgown and her mother's high heels. Well into the press conference, Jack continued undeterred.

Cute photos were one thing, but image maker Salinger couldn't always control what the children might say. A persistent journalist once approached Caroline in the West Lobby of the White House and asked the little girl what her father was doing.

"Oh, he's upstairs with his shoes and socks off," she said. "He's not doing anything."

In the face of Jack's easy familiarity with the press—he regarded some as friends, others as tools to be used in romanticizing his administration—Jackie often took matters into her own hands. When the "White House Guide Book" was being assembled, she fought to prevent a picture of John's bedroom from being included.

"Even at the age of two, one's bedroom should be private," she said.

Jack's attitude remained easygoing—based, as Evelyn Lincoln put it, on "his feeling that the whole world should be allowed to enjoy his kids within limits." But Jackie felt an ever growing fear that her children were becoming products, readily available for the press to consume. "I'm determined that Caroline and John should be able to get in and out of the White House without being pestered by photographers, or being made constantly aware of their position," she confided to Princess Grace of Monaco.

On another occasion, she told White House usher J. B. West, "I don't want them to think they are 'official children.' When I go out with them or when they go out with their nurses, please ask the doormen not to hover around to open the doors for them."

Always a realist, Jackie finally had to accept that her new position required the occasional compromise. She tried planting large rhododendrons around the fence surrounding the children's playgrounds, but eventually acknowledged that she couldn't shut out the public completely.

"I guess you can't block off any more than that," she said. "People are entitled to some view of the White House. But I'm sick and tired of starring in everybody's home movies."

There was no way to ban photographers from shooting through the White House fences with telescopic lenses, so they produced a constant stream of candid pictures of the Kennedy children at play. In his attempt to preserve some degree of privacy, which even the President occasionally required for his children, Pierre Salinger faced a Catch-22. At times he would make an agreement with press photographers that they would stop shooting the children for a while, only to have a candid pose snapped by an enterprising tourist who then sold it to a newspaper or wire service—whereupon Jackie would explode, accusing Salinger of failing in his duty.

"I thought you had made an arrangement with the fotogs not to take the children playing at WH," she wrote in one memorandum. "They have had all the pictures of Macaroni they need. I want no more—I mean this—and if you are firm and will take the time, you can stop it. So please do. What is a press secretary for—to help the press, yes—but also to protect us."

The problem didn't exist just in the White House, but anywhere Jack, Jackie, and the children traveled. When the family went cruising near Palm Beach on Joe's boat, the *Honey Fitz*, an armada of press boats carrying photographers with telescopic lenses followed close behind, recording every second of the President's day at sea with his family.

The same situation arose at Glen Ora, the Virginia farm where the family often spent their weekends. A mere thirty-five miles from Washington, the estate was accessible to enterprising photographers.

The Kennedys were safe from photographers only at Camp David, the mountain estate run by the Navy and named after President Eisenhower's grandson. Because Camp David was a military establishment, it was out of bounds for the press, and the family could relax in privacy.

Despite her attempts to elude the press, Jackie knew perfectly well that publicity had helped win the presidency for Jack. She eventually learned to exercise control over her children's exposure to the media in a subtle way. A former journalist herself, she knew she had to give the press something of her children or they would turn and start writing articles she didn't want. She began conjuring up little stories and agreeing to certain photographs and filtering them to the press. "What the public didn't realize," one newsman said, "was that Mrs. Kennedy carefully planned and directed most of the publicity her children received."

At four months, John made his second trip to Palm Beach, where Maud Shaw took him to a birthday party. His father was in the midst of the maneuvers that would lead to covert American involvement in the Bay of Pigs invasion of Cuba. Later the President joined his family for an Easter celebration, reeling from the failure of the mission.

By May, the consequences of the Bay of Pigs crisis had begun to recede, and the President's popularity skyrocketed. John at six months was described by the White House as "a really happy little character. Quite plump, wonderful-looking and always sunny. The bright and smiling child hasn't had so much as a cold since leaving the hospital incubator. His diet is just like that of most babies his age—milk from a bottle and baby foods including cereal, fruit, vegetables and cottage cheese. He weighs eighteen pounds." There was a collective sigh from millions of American mothers who were monitoring the progress of baby Kennedy as if he were their own.

Jackie, meanwhile, flew with the President to Paris, the city she had always considered her spiritual home. When studying there at the Sorbonne, long before she met Jack, Jackie had been tempted to settle in Paris forever. Now, arriving at Orly Airport, she was greeted with a 101-gun salute and feted by an adoring French public who felt they had a proprietary interest in the American First Lady. She smiled and waved to the crowds chanting, *"Vive* Jackie!"

Whether consciously or unconsciously, she upstaged Jack with her spectacular Parisian performance—and it *was* a performance, executed by a skillful actress. More beautiful than Judith Campbell, more alluring than Marilyn Monroe or Angie Dickinson, Jackie was at the height of her splendor.

At a candlelit state dinner held at the Palace of Versailles for 150 guests, she wore a magnificent Givenchy gown. Months later when Jack met Princess Grace of Monaco, he asked if she, too, was wearing a Givenchy. Back in America, *Time* magazine summed up Jackie's conquest of Paris: "From the moment of her smiling arrival at Orly Airport, the radiant young First Lady was the Kennedy who really mattered."

Even the imposing President De Gaulle seemed to agree. While deeply impressed with her mastery of French language, literature, and history, he stressed her beauty above all, pronouncing with Gallic eloquence that Jackie was "a charming and ravishing woman with extraordinary hair and eyes."

Rose was in Paris, too. Determined to be on hand for her son's triumph, she witnessed Jackie's stupendous reception at Orly.

With his talent for showmanship, Jack quickly and easily took up the role of straight man, making a remark that went around the world:

"I am the man who accompanied Jacqueline Kennedy to Paris and I have enjoyed it."

Jackie's triumphal procession continued through Austria; in Vienna, bedazzled crowds cheered her wildly. Then it was on to London, where the normally staid British aristocrats were bowled over by her poise and charm at the christening of her niece, Christina Radziwill, at Westminster Abbey.

The Palace of Versailles made a deep impression on Jackie, and she swore to duplicate its grandeur in the White House. Returning to America, she instantly put some of her plans into operation.

With her flair for drama, Jackie broke with tradition. Most kings, queens, and dignitaries who visited the President were met at Washington Airport, where the sound of planes drowned out the ceremony. Instead, Jackie arranged to have them arrive on the South Lawn of the White House, which afforded a stellar view of the Washington and Jefferson monuments. Both monuments were now bathed in lights to ensure that the scene would be unforgettable for the distinguished White House visitors.

Like a great theatrical designer, Jackie fashioned her new set to display herself, her family, and the seat of the nation to maximum advantage. Jack, professing that he was "trying to give this administration a semblance of class," allowed Jackie free rein in embellishing the White House. Hiring the best French chef money could buy and printing state dinner menus in French, Jackie simultaneously eliminated receiving lines and the formality that had stultified past White House functions.

The sixty-six state receptions held at the White House by Jackie and the President during his administration received glowing press coverage around the world. This clearly enhanced the growing image of the Kennedy White House as a utopia of grace, charm, elegance, and sophistication.

Although Jack was far more interested in politics and current affairs than in the arts, he bowed to his wife's discriminating tastes, which he secretly admired. Although he found ballets, operas, and concerts boring, he happily welcomed to the White House Pablo Casals, Isaac Stern, Igor Stravinsky, Nobel prize winners, and poet laureates.

One of Jackie's first state dinners was held at Mount Vernon, George Washington's plantation, for President Mohammad Ayub Khan of Pakistan. The 132 venerable guests were transported along the Potomac from Washington in the *Honey Fitz* and three Navy vessels borrowed for the event. The highlight of the evening for John Jr., however, was the two silver rattles, which doubled as whistles, presented to him by the Pakistani president himself.

The world watched fearfully as the Wall was erected in Berlin and Jack Kennedy battled the specter of the Cold War after his nearly abortive meeting with Khrushchev in Vienna. He later confided that the Russian premier's manner reminded him of the intractability of his own father. Meanwhile, John Jr. spent the first summer of his life at the Kennedy family home at Hyannis Port, Cape Cod.

The family had been coming to Hyannis Port since the summer of 1925, when Joe initially rented the fifteen-room house facing Nantucket Sound on Cape Cod's southern shore. Buying the house in 1928, he remodeled it so that it ultimately comprised eleven rooms, nine bathrooms, a tennis court, a projection room, and an indoor swimming pool. Far less gloomy than the Palm Beach compound, the Hyannis Port compound was also more deserving of its title. Bobby and Ethel owned the house next door, and now Jackie and Jack bought the house behind.

With its two and a half acres, its ocean view, large lawn, and airy porch encircling the house, Hyannis Port would be an idyllic setting for John's summers. During that first season, he spent nine weeks at

Hyannis, with his father flying in to spend Saturdays and Sundays with the entire family.

The President would leave Andrews Air Force Base on a Friday afternoon, landing at Otis Air Force Base in Falmouth at 4:32, and from there would fly to Hyannis by helicopter. By the time the President's helicopter began its descent outside the compound, the driveway would be blocked off by fire trucks, with all the children, dogs, maids, and friends standing by to welcome the President. In later years, when Joe Sr. had been paralyzed by a stroke, the whirring of the presidential helicopter would serve as a signal for him to be wheeled out onto the porch. The helicopter would land in front of his wheelchair, as if before the throne of some ancient king.

Years later, remembering those halcyon summers at Hyannis, Rose re-created the next moment as clearly as if she had just seen it. The door of the helicopter opened and the President stepped out.

"Caroline and John would run and jump into his arms," Rose remembered. "He would lean over ever so affectionately and hug and embrace them. I always realized he was a little wary as to how he bent, so as not to hurt his back. Of course, he never lifted them up into his arms."

After the initial greeting, the family dispersed and then met again for a lively dinner, which invariably began with fish chowder. During the weekend, there would be golf, tennis, and the inevitable game of touch football. Jackie, who had once broken her ankle during an early attempt at mastering the sacred Kennedy sport, resolutely avoided the roughhousing.

For Jack, the highlight of his weekends at Hyannis would be cruising on the *Honey Fitz.* Relaxing in his leather swivel chair in the stern of the boat, he loved racing through the Cape Cod waters. Sometimes he'd read the newspapers, savoring the trivia of the week that might have gotten past him. In contrast, Jackie preferred water-skiing or sunbathing, never quite relaxing in case her fierce foes, the press, might snap a picture of her at leisure.

Described by a close relative as a dream baby who laughed all the time but already seemed to have a will of his own, John was now nearly a year old. He had two front teeth, weighed twenty-two pounds, and crawled all over the White House, exploring his surroundings.

Called on to substitute for Maud Shaw one evening, White House maid Cordenia Thaxton baby-sat for John. He spent the first hour or two crying bitterly because he missed Maud Shaw. Finally Thaxton found a jack-in-the-box that popped up to the tune of "Pop Goes the Weasel." John was captivated and, distracted from his grief, fell silent while she played the tune over and over. Then the door opened and the President walked in singing "Pop Goes the Weasel."

At the time, given John's age, Jack was giving more of his attention to Caroline. But his son was beginning to intrigue and confuse him. Although John could say "ma ma" and "da da" when he saw his parents, Jack was puzzled at what he considered his son's late development.

"When is John going to talk?" he asked Miss Shaw.

"Oh, but he does talk, Mr. President," said Miss Shaw, adding, "it's just that you can't understand him."

"That's right, Daddy," interjected Caroline. "He does talk to me."

"I guess you'd better interpret for me," said the President, laughing.

John celebrated his first birthday on November 25, 1961. A week earlier, the White House released two official birthday portraits. The first showed John nestled in Jackie's arms, smiling broadly at the camera. The second showed him sitting on a gold rug amid a collection of colored balls, playing with a toy rooster (a gift from his mother's admirer General De Gaulle). While they were delightful, not everyone was satisfied with the First Son's official birthday pictures. UPI sent an irate letter to Pierre Salinger.

"Needless to say, we are quite disappointed that we cannot take our own birthday pictures of Baby Kennedy, and that all we will get will be one black and white which the White House will distribute. Can we at least get two different shots—one for the a.m. papers and a different one for the afternoons? Also, is there no chance that color pictures could be made for distribution at the same time?"

Although John Jr. was clearly big news, his birthday party was memorable in that the star attraction proved to be not the birthday boy, but a chimpanzee named Suzie. The chimp was brought in for the event from the Baltimore zoo, wearing a child's dress—and made the national news. Jackie, not amused that her son had been upstaged by a monkey, refused all pleas from the children to allow Suzie to entertain them again.

Not that John-John, as he was now known outside the family, lacked for attention. Birthday cards had been flooding into the White House at a rate of seventy-five a day since November 9, further evidence that America loved its First Family, wished them well, and prayed for their continuing health and happiness.

CHAPTER THREE

Father
and
Son

Joe Kennedy suffered a near-fatal stroke on December 19, 1961, and although it was suggested to the family that life for the architect of the family's fame and fortune would hardly be worth living, they rejected all suggestions that they switch off the life-support machine and let the seventy-three-year-old patriarch die without further suffering.

Refusing to accept defeat for the father who had so long dominated their every thought and action, they kept Joe alive. But despite their will to make him whole again, it was obvious that their father was now paralyzed and capable only of saying the word no—a cruel irony for the man who had made yes his byword.

Joe's family determined that life would go on as usual. Adhering to the time-honored Kennedy cycles, John Jr., Caroline, Jack, and

Jackie flew to Palm Beach to celebrate Christmas, and on January 3 Jackie took John Jr. to see Joe in St. Mary's Hospital. Later that day Jack, too, went to see his father, sandwiching the visit between meetings with Defense Department officials.

On January 5 John, wearing rompers, took his first steps in public as he accompanied his father to Palm Beach airport to see him off to Washington. A few weeks later, on January 25, John and Caroline flew up to join their father in the White House. During the flight, John garnered a great deal of attention from the reporters by crawling up and down the aisle.

He was a born scene stealer, and Caroline was not always delighted with him. On February 5 she wrote a description of a sleigh ride in the snow to Rose, ending with the words "John is a bad squeaky boy who tries to spit in his mother's Coca Cola and who has a very bad temper."

John's strong will surfaced without respect for situation or rank. During a state visit to the White House on April 12, the Empress Farah Diba of Iran tried to present him with a daffodil in the White House gardens; he recoiled and shouted no with great conviction.

John's willfulness, however, was the least of Jackie's problems. On May 19, 1962, Jackie took John Jr. and Caroline to Virginia, where she was riding in a horse show. She was a fearless rider, mounting the wildest stallion without concern for her safety. While some of her relatives were sometimes afraid of the more spirited horses, Jackie was not. She dazzled them with her horsemanship and courage. She loved to ride, but this weekend there was a deeper reason for accompanying her children to Virginia.

Aware that Jack was due to be feted at an early birthday party in Madison Square Garden and that Marilyn Monroe was scheduled to be the star attraction, Jackie divorced herself entirely from the proceedings. By going away, Jackie executed a classic emotional checkmate, leaving her husband to make the next move.

In the decades since then, Marilyn Monroe's appearance at Madison Square Garden has grown to near-mythic proportions. This was, in many ways, her public declaration of her passion for Jack and enmity toward Jackie.

In a transparent $12,000 dress whose 6,000 hand-sewn beads barely covered her extraordinary body, Monroe sang "Happy Birthday, Mr. President" in a voice as breathy and babyish as Jackie's. In her seven-minute, electrically charged performance, she not only figuratively seduced the screaming crowd of twenty thousand people packed into Madison Square Garden but threw down a glittering sexual gauntlet at Jack Kennedy's feet as well.

Jack met the challenge with his famous wit. "I can now retire from politics after having 'Happy Birthday' sung to me in such a sweet wholesome way."

In the end, in attempting to make public her relationship with the President, Marilyn Monroe had overlooked an important truth of American politics: Quite simply, sex and politics don't mix. No matter what John F. Kennedy felt for her, he was an Irish Catholic who loved his family—and the Presidency—above all. Imagine bringing Marilyn Monroe home to meet Rose Kennedy!

Apart from a brief post-party encounter, Jack never had sex with Monroe again.

While Jack's birthday quip about retiring after Marilyn's song might have satisfied the public, Jackie was not above exacting her own form of revenge. During August—the month when Marilyn died—Jackie traveled to Ravello, Italy, to visit her sister, Lee, and Lee's husband, Prince Radziwill. To Jack, it appeared that Jackie was spending an inordinate amount of time in the company of a fellow house guest, millionaire Fiat boss Gianni Agnelli. And while Agnelli's accomplished wife, Mariella, was also staying in the nine-hundred-year-old palazzo with the Radziwills, on seeing published photos of Gianni and Jackie swimming, Jack took what for him was an extraordinary step. He sent a cable to Jackie: "A little more Caroline and less Agnelli."

He might have been prompted by a sense that the American public, enthralled as it was by its First Lady, might not welcome seeing her cavort with Agnelli. But in the eyes of those close to Jackie—for example, her personal designer, Oleg Cassini—other, stronger emotions might well have come into play.

"I think JFK, so to say, 'fell in love' with his wife a second time after they reached the White House and she was able to demonstrate her gifts and abilities," Cassini said.

The President was also falling more and more in love with his young son. While Jackie and Caroline were away in Italy, he spent two weekends with John at Hammersmith Farm, in Newport, Rhode Island, where John was staying with Janet Auchincloss.

"The Secret Service appeared and ninety-nine telephones were pulled in and out, the Newport police went into a tailspin and put little booths up here and there, and the Coast Guard whizzed around the dock," said Auchincloss, noting the chaos inherent in having the President of the United States as a weekend guest. "I don't think he was particularly conscious of all of this—he was an extraordinarily unpretentious man."

Once all the fuss surrounding his arrival had died down, the President was able to relax and enjoy being with his son, playing with him at the shore and taking him to a pool near Bailey's Beach. Until now, Caroline had been the sole apple of his eye, but during those unusually lazy days in Newport, Jack Kennedy had the chance truly to discover his son.

His own father had been remote, cold, not inclined to show physical affection. Senator George Smathers, recalling Joe's character as a father, compared it to what he saw Jack Kennedy aspiring to be. "There wasn't a great affection for Jack. He and his father weren't close at all. I don't think Joe was close with any of his children— perhaps to his daughters, but other than that, he was a dictator who ran his family.

"Jack talked to me about his father all the time and he liked him, admired him greatly, and knew his father was no great family man. Joe was tough and Jack was basically a really sweet, tender guy."

The White House abounded with witnesses to Kennedy's tenderness toward his son. "He was enjoying his kids," said Cecil Stoughton, who immortalized some of the President's gentle moments with John. "There weren't so many in his family as there were in his own, so I think it was even more enjoyable to him than he thought it would be. But he really came to understand them and he played with them in that marvelous way that some people have and others don't."

Jack, who wanted to see as much of them as possible, allowed Caroline and John the run of the White House, to the extent that the Oval Office soon became as familiar to them as their nurseries. He had developed a ritual that became as sacred as any other in the White House. Each morning, John and Caroline would accompany him on the short walk to the Oval Office, where secretary Evelyn Lincoln would be waiting, armed with candy. Then they would spend five or ten minutes with their father before Miss Shaw arrived to whisk them back to their own domain.

Often, while Caroline was at nursery school, Jack would allow John to stay with him longer, letting him hide in his favorite place behind the secret panel in the desk, which opened like a door. Made from the timbers of the British warship H.M.S. *Resolute*, the desk had been presented to President Rutherford Hayes in 1878. Later, President Roosevelt sat behind it while giving his stirring fireside radio chats. Still later, Jackie found it in the White House cellar and had it sanded, refinished, and moved into the Oval Office.

White House staff, politicians, and visiting dignitaries soon became accustomed to John's jumping out from inside his hiding place. Aide Dave Powers was present during a discussion between the President and Randolph Churchill in which they were intently analyzing the current political prospects of the British Labour Party.

The desk panel swung open and John emerged. "I'm a big bear and I'm hungry!"

Without skipping a beat, the President of the most powerful nation on earth countered, "And I'm a great big bear and I'm going to eat you up in one bite!"

Seeing Churchill's expression as John rolled around the floor and giggled, Jack said, "You may think this is strange behavior in the office of the President of the United States, but in addition to being the President, I also happen to be a father."

Contrary to the media myth, the President never called John Jr. "John-John." Dave Powers remembers that the nickname was jumped on mistakenly by the press when they heard Jack call for his son so eagerly that the words ran together. Also, Jack refused to use baby talk with either John or Caroline. Although he read to them often, he also regaled them for hours with stories about a bear called Bruin, a giant named Lobo, and a little girl named Maybelle—all characters of his own invention.

Once, while Jack was in the midst of dealing with various political matters, Caroline demanded that he tell her a story about precisely five bears.

"Caroline," the President said, momentarily preoccupied, "why don't I tell you about five governors instead?"

His daughter frowned, less than pleased.

Compromising, he began, "Five bears were the governors of five states."

By September 1961, Jack began to feel a tremendous anxiety about his long absences from his family.

"John sees so little of his father," the President told a Naval aide. "How can he ever know me?"

Father and son had just spent a happy few days together in Newport, where the President watched the America's Cup yacht race from the deck of the U.S.S. *Joseph P. Kennedy, Jr.* Occasionally lost in thought, he followed the race through his binoculars, smoking a cigar.

He had spent much of the time at Bailey's Beach, the waterfront club frequented by Newport's elite. Arriving there at eleven o'clock with Caroline and John, he used Hugh Auchincloss's cabana (Auchincloss was Jackie's stepfather) and spent two hours playing in the sand with the children. Leaving them with their maternal grandparents, Jack found it difficult to say good-bye to the children after such a happy interlude.

He was determined to sustain his role as a father no matter how grave the political situation in the world outside his children's protected universe. In the heat and pressure of the Cuban missile crisis, on October 24, 1962, the President took the time to carve a Halloween jack-o'-lantern—complete with different faces on each side of the pumpkin. He and Caroline then posed next to their masterpiece for a photograph.

Once the crisis passed, Jackie planned a joint party in the private Presidential Suite to celebrate John's second and Caroline's fifth birthday. Along with twenty-eight young guests, John—who was noted for his singing, dancing, and high-octane curiosity—gorged himself on creamed chicken, ice cream, and cake, all washed down with milk, before watching a cartoon in the White House film theater.

In November 1962, Konrad Adenauer visited the White House. Later that night, the President showed Ben Bradlee a Polaroid snapshot of the eighty-six-year-old German chancellor throwing John up into the air. Jack marveled over and over at Adenauer's strength and agility. Jackie, who normally went on at great length about the wonderful relationship Jack had with his son, noted that this was the first time anyone had ever thrown John Jr. into the air.

Bradlee later described the comment as "an unfair dig," given the President's total inability to throw his son up over his head. He loved roughhousing with his son and felt that his back problems cramped his style as a father.

When a relative innocently made the mistake of saying, "He can barely pick up his own son," Jack was so upset that the White House finally issued a response: "The President's back is improving but his son is getting heavier."

Eventually, though, Jack devised a solution. Concluding that there would be less strain if he lay on the floor and then lifted John, he managed to incorporate the "lifting John into the air" exercise into his ritual so satisfactorily that John never forgot it.

On November 30, the President of Honduras, Ramon Villedo Morales, made a state visit to the White House. John wore a bright red snowsuit and was allowed to watch the welcoming ceremonies from a White House balcony. Miss Shaw stood next to him as he watched, mesmerized by the flags furling and troops marching below. When the twenty-one-gun salute boomed across the White House lawn, John did not flinch, enthralled by all the military pageantry, the marching, the colors, the music, and the saluting.

As always, the family flew to Palm Beach to celebrate Christmas at the compound with Rose, Joe, and the rest of the family. On December 17, Jackie, rejecting the opulent toys displayed in Worth

Avenue's most extravagant shops, took John and Caroline to the far more modest Burdine's in West Palm Beach. Given that Palm Beach is an island whose inhabitants consider West Palm Beach across the water utterly beyond the pale, shoppers in the Burdine's toy department were shocked to discover the First Lady in their midst.

Stepping back and making sure not to crowd the First Family, the shoppers watched in awe as John sat on the toy department floor playing with a model helicopter while his sister sat on Santa's knee and delivered her Christmas list.

Whatever Caroline's Christmas wishes, anyone aware of the principles Jackie applied to bringing up her children knew that many of them would remain unfulfilled. Determined that John Jr. and Caroline would not be spoiled, Jackie continually emphasized values other than materialism. Whenever she went away, she wrote and addressed postcards for each of them, asking the White House usher to mail a card every morning so that the children had daily news of her. Aiming to put more emphasis on communication, she also took care not to shower them with gifts on her return to Washington.

Presents for the children flooded into the White House every day, but unless they came from old friends, most were sent back. Jackie was so firmly resolved not to spoil the children that even close family members were told to limit their gifts to Caroline and John. At birthday parties, she stressed playing games over getting presents, and when it came to bestowing gifts, she decreed that the children make something instead of buying it at a store.

She also stuck rigidly to the children's prescribed bedtimes. Films were very much part of Kennedy life, with a movie theater at their disposal in the White House and private projection rooms at Hyannis, Palm Beach, and Camp David. Although the President thoroughly enjoyed his cinematic evenings with the children, going so far as to have a popcorn machine installed at the Palm Beach house, their bedtime was eight o'clock. No matter how thrilling the film, even if the climactic ending was just ten minutes away, Caroline and John were still dispatched into bed at eight exactly.

Jackie was a strict mother, and Maud Shaw was with her every step of the way, respecting Jackie's edicts and adding a few of her own.

"It isn't fair to children in the limelight to leave them in the care of others and then expect that they will turn out all right," Jackie said. "They need their mother's affection and guidance and long periods of time with her. That's what gives them security in an often confusing new world."

Despite their mother's philosophy of personal involvement, much of the children's upbringing was left in the capable hands of Miss Shaw.

Finding John, with his voracious curiosity and incessant questions, a little tiring, Miss Shaw nevertheless felt sorry for him. She knew the effect of living in the White House and never being able to venture out without a Secret Service detail in tow, drawing attention to his every move.

Whenever possible, Miss Shaw kept the agents at a safe distance and hidden from public view. One afternoon the three went to the beach in Florida, with the Secret Service out of sight. Suddenly Miss Shaw, Caroline, and John were approached by a strange woman.

"Say, I hear the Kennedy children are coming down here today," she said, patting John's tousled hair. "I guess they must be real nice kids."

As she walked away, Miss Shaw breathed a sigh of relief. Recently John had taken to thrusting his hand toward strangers, drawing himself up to his full height, and declaring with pride, "I'm John F. Kennedy, Jr."

Miss Shaw taught the children a traditional English child's prayer: "Thank you for the world so sweet./Thank you for the food we eat./Thank you for the birds that sing./Thank you, God, for everything."

She started on hearing a voice from the doorway.

"That's a lovely prayer, Miss Shaw," the President said. "Is it an English one?"

He and Jackie trusted Miss Shaw completely and respected her tactics for dealing with the sometimes unruly John. An intelligent child who responded to reason, John took to telling Miss Shaw, "I'm your big boy," when he had been particularly good or clever. He would obediently follow any instructions attached to the concept that if he behaved, he would be acting like Miss Shaw's big boy.

Though she anticipated the normal sibling rivalry, Miss Shaw never detected any jealousy between brother and sister. Always proud of John, Caroline never appeared to resent him. For his part, John strove desperately to keep up with his older sister, trying hard to match her brightness during one craze in which Caroline obsessively badgered everyone for answers to riddles.

"I know a riddle, too," John would say.

"Oh, really?" Miss Shaw said, continuing her work. "And what would that be?"

"Um ... apples, giraffes—and alligators."

Miss Shaw looked at him.

"I'm afraid you've stumped me again," she would say.

John wandered away chuckling whenever she failed to come up with what he considered the correct answer for one of his nonsensical riddles. She never pursued his logic, recognizing that he was simply happy to be acting like Caroline.

The children diverged when it came to sports. Like his father, John Jr. was instinctively drawn to the sea. Never afraid of the water, John plunged into the ocean at an early age, often with all his clothes on.

"I can swim, Miss Shaw, can't I?"

"Yes, John. You swim very well."

Horses, however, were quite another matter. Given Caroline's natural ability and her own genuine love of horses, Jackie was bent on his starting to ride as soon as possible despite his allergy. But once mounted on his pony, Leprechaun, John became extremely glum and demanded, "I wanna get off!"

Comparing John and Caroline with their other Kennedy cousins, Miss Shaw noted the differences and was proud of her part in their development.

"All the other Kennedy children were allowed to do pretty much as they pleased," she said. "What people did not expect, though, was that Caroline and John would be such unspoiled, nice kids. There was nothing 'bratty' about them."

Miss Shaw's and Jackie's efforts to make sure the children weren't spoiled didn't keep John from occasionally playing "prince in the palace." For although Miss Shaw had instructed both John and Caroline to address their three Secret Service agents as "Mister," the agents had all pledged to lay down their lives for the Kennedy children and would refuse them nothing.

If John demanded candy before lunch, Miss Shaw refused. But he knew that all he needed to do was ask one of the Secret Service men for a sweet and it would be given to him. While Miss Shaw's word mostly remained law, John occasionally tested the power of his name and exalted position. At one point, Secretary of Defense Robert McNamara's chauffeur, West, was reading in his limousine while McNamara was finishing a meeting. Suddenly John appeared, interrupted the chauffeur's reading, and demanded that West drive him around the South Ground Circle.

"I can't," West said. "I'm waiting for Robert McNamara."

"You'd better do it," John said, "or my daddy will make you."

Had his father witnessed this display, the President would probably have smiled without comment. Jackie and Miss Shaw frowned on anything but the best behavior, but to Jack his son's very existence was all that mattered. And although John was only two, the President and the First Lady were rapidly discovering that they had very different ideas indeed about bringing up their son.

"Jackie was so adamant about not spoiling John, but Jack wanted to spoil him to death," Senator Smathers said. "While Jackie tried to keep him under control, Jack would let John break into meetings, interrupt his schedule, and give him whatever he wanted. Jack adored him, thought he was perfect, and wanted to be with him all the time."

Jackie did everything possible to ensure that the official White House celebrations would run smoothly for her second Christmas as First Lady. Before leaving for Palm Beach, she made certain mistletoe was hung over the vast doorways at both ends of the entrance hall. Green garlands were draped over the mirrors, portraits, and chandeliers; lovely red and white flowers bloomed in each room.

Again breaking with tradition, Jackie had ordered the eighteen-foot Christmas tree erected in the Blue Room. Decorated with ornaments inspired by *The Nutcracker,* the tree also bore gingerbread cookies, candy canes, and miniature musical instruments on every available branch.

Beautifully adorned to symbolize the joy and hope of Christmas, the White House by now had become home to Jackie. When she had first moved into the White House, Jackie had been afraid that she would fail to re-create the cozy surroundings she had so enjoyed in Georgetown. Now, though, the White House felt more like home.

"It was filled with small, unrecorded rituals of special meaning," Cecil Stoughton said. "She brought the children to their father at times when it meant the most to him. She planned recreation to give the President needed interludes in the daily grind. There were quiet weekend dinners with friends and family. Jackie was fiercely protective of the world she created for her children and her husband within the White House."

Protective and, as 1962 was drawing to a close, relatively secure.

On February 6, 1963, just as President Kennedy was delivering his State of the Union address, John Jr. tripped and fell, banging his front tooth on a White House step. The bloody tooth fell out, and John lay on the ground crying. Maud Shaw rushed to his side and comforted him. Within minutes his tears subsided, and he darted away into the shrubbery. He returned with the missing tooth and proudly presented it to his nanny.

Both Jackie and the President were unnerved by the large gap in John's normally engaging smile. Perplexed, Jack approached Miss Shaw wanting to know every detail of the accident. Miss Shaw obliged, and the event was even immortalized by Cecil Stoughton. When he asked John where his tooth was, the boy smiled such an infectious toothless grin that Stoughton felt compelled to take a photograph.

The incident of the missing tooth turned into a game. The next day John rushed up to Kenneth Burke of the White House Police Force, who was patrolling the Diplomatic Reception Room. Tugging on Burke's coattail, John pointed to his mouth and showed off the gap. He proceeded to spend much of the day smiling at everyone as a way of demonstrating his recent loss.

At times the White House seemed like a grand playground, equipped with every kind of amusement available for a growing boy. Camp David, too, was exciting, with long weekends out of the sight of prying photographers. The highlight of many a stay was a visit to the local snake farm, where John always exhibited a ghoulish delight in playing with George, the farm's tame cobra.

Although he was growing up quickly, in the spring of 1963 John was still not far from babyhood and the sweet, unspoiled emotions of early childhood. On April 30, 1963, Grand Duchess Charlotte of Luxembourg was invited to the White House for a special state reception, and as usual John and Caroline were to be presented to the dignitaries.

Maud Shaw had taught them well. Caroline knew how to curtsy and John to bow, just like a little English gentleman. The evening was an important one to Jackie, who had arranged for the British actor Sir Basil Rathbone to declaim Shakespearean verses, accompanied by an ensemble of Elizabethan musicians and singers. Miss Shaw waited with trepidation outside the reception for her little charges to return after fulfilling their social duties.

Inside, John watched as the adults shook hands and greeted each other. His eyes soon wandered to the table, which was spread with all manner of treats. Everyone was being so polite; he knew better than to interrupt to remind them that he hadn't received his cookie and ginger ale yet. It didn't seem fair. He was being good.

Finally he'd had enough.

"John, I'd like you to meet—"

Before Jackie could finish, John threw himself on the floor, rigid with anger.

"John, get up this minute."

He refused to move.

"Would you ask Miss Shaw to come in?" Jackie said.

Mortified, Miss Shaw saw John on the floor and quickly pulled him out of the room.

"What on earth did you do that for?" she asked once they were upstairs. "That's not being my big boy, is it?"

"But Miss Shaw," John said tearfully, "they didn't give me my cookie."

She sighed, knowing the breach of etiquette could not be repeated, and gave him a stern lecture. John drank in every word and took her warning to heart.

This meant reserving his high spirits for more private

moments—except once, when the Cold War blocked access to his father's office. After being barred from entering because Soviet Foreign Minister Gromyko was meeting with the President, John stood outside the door shouting, "Gromyko, Gromyko."

On March 26, 1963, Ben Bradlee had dinner with the Kennedys. "John-John—now two and a half years old—has a big thing about coming up to you and whispering a lot of gibberish in your ear," he wrote in his diary. "If you throw your head back and act surprised, John-John roars with laughter until he drools."

Later, on the ever sensitive subject of not being able to lift his son, the President said, "He doesn't know it yet but he's going to carry me before I carry him."

The refreshing effect of having young children around the White House, interwoven with the important politics of the time, was not lost on observers.

"The Kennedys seem remarkably good with their children considering what would appear to be the almost insuperable barriers of formality imposed on that relationship by the Presidency," Bradlee wrote in his diary. "They see less of their children, obviously, but that doesn't seem to have interfered with the normal gaiety that attractive children express in themselves and produce in their parents."

Bradlee recognized that both Jack and Jackie were appalled by the "national hunger" for pictures and news of the First Family and were terrified that the children would not emerge unspoiled. But he also recognized that Jack Kennedy did not let formality impinge on his enjoyment of his son, even when the astronauts and their wives arrived for a White House reception.

Right in the middle of the festivities, the President dropped to his hands and knees to grab John.

"I'm going to get you, John," he cried, tickling the boy until he wet his pants from excitement. The group all smiled.

As always, Jack, Jackie, and the children spent that Easter in Palm Beach. Caroline and John raced around the living room, unaware of Joe's advanced paralysis; in his exuberance, John rushed into the table next to Joe, spilling his drink all over him.

Jack spent his Palm Beach days as he loved to do, sailing or relaxing in the pool, where he found it easier to play with the children without straining his back. He deliberately chose a furry monkey puppet over a squirt gun when he played with John in the pool. Very quietly, the President was becoming aware that his son's life in the White House was having its effects. Jack had relished watching his son trying on the hats of visiting generals, saluting, waiting eagerly for each and every White House parade; but he was beginning to worry.

"I'm concerned about John's fascination with military things," Jack told Cecil Stoughton. "He's right there whenever he sees guns, swords, or anyone wearing a uniform."

"Why don't you just stop letting him watch the parades?" Stoughton asked.

Jack looked at Stoughton. To do so would break his son's heart. "I guess we all go through that phase. John just sees more of the real thing."

Without a thought, he also continued to indulge his son's passion for helicopters. A newly talking toddler, John called them "la-pa-cas." Whenever he heard the sound of his father's helicopter landing on the White House lawn, John would dance with delight, and once he had learned the proper pronunciation, he would shriek, "The chopper's coming! The chopper's coming!"

Joy at the helicopter's arrival was replaced with dismay whenever the President prepared to lift off without him. On hearing the whir of the chopper from inside the Oval Office, John would weep bitterly, clinging to his father's pant leg, crying, "Don't leave me."

Seeing his small son in tears, Jack would relent. It didn't matter that John was sometimes dressed only in his pajamas and bathrobe. "Come on, John," the President would say. "Let's go to work." Eyes drying, John would trot happily after his father to the helicopter. The President would allow John to fly to Andrews Air Force Base with him in the helicopter, then arrange for a Secret Service agent to fly back with him to the White House.

John's tears seemed to be prompted as much by his love of the aircraft as his ever increasing devotion to his father. The idea of disappointing his young son or depriving him of a moment's happiness was unthinkable to the President, who let John fly with him on the helicopter as often as possible. On May 11 he took John with him when he flew to Andrews Air Force Base en route for Cape Cod for a meeting with the prime minister of Canada, Lester Pearson. As soon as the President boarded the plane at Andrews, John started to cry, and a distressed Miss Shaw whisked him back in the helicopter to the White House as quickly as possible.

John was in a sunnier mood on the afternoon of May 21, when Jackie took the children to Glen Echo Amusement Park. Secret Service men helped steady John's rifle at the shooting range while he pulled the trigger, knocking over a moving metal duck. Jackie helped him fire a water pistol into a hole, and a young woman with the improbable name of Kelly Green, whose job it was to guess the weight of fairgoers, correctly guessed his weight at 33 pounds.

In June, the President left for a European tour that started in Berlin, where he made his landmark "Ich bin ein Berliner" speech. Next stop was Dublin, to visit his Irish relatives, and to stand solemnly before the graves of the men who took part in the 1916 Easter uprising. He brought a hand-carved boat home for John before heading off to Rome, where the Pope granted him an audience and presented him with a medallion for John. Italy's president, Antonio Segni, gave Jack a little Amstead two-sail boat, also for John.

By July 4, the President was back in the United States, and he and Jackie and the children spent the weekend in Cape Cod, where they had rented the $1,000-a-month Brambletide Cottage for the summer. Although the cottage stood just a few miles from the Kennedy compound by road and a short walk along the beach at low tide, this was the first time Jack had rented a place just for his own family that was not under the direct control of his mother.

Jackie's pregnancy was well advanced, and she and Jack spent an idyllic weekend cruising Nantucket Sound on the *Honey Fitz,* walking on the beach, and playing golf. At one point, watching John frolicking on the beach, Jack turned to aide Kenny O'Donnell and commented warmly, "John has grown up to develop a colorful personality."

The following weekend, the President flew into Otis Air Force Base to be met by John (who had been driven there by a Secret Service agent) and a crowd of two thousand well-wishers. Seeing John eagerly waiting for him at the end of the ramp, Jack bowed to his son with exaggerated formality and patted his head, then took him by the hand and led him toward the waiting Marine Corps helicopter.

Having grown more and more involved with his two children, Jack was elated at the idea of having another. Although he adored Caroline, calling her "Buttons," and had a great deal of fun with her, there was little doubt which gender he was rooting for.

"Although he never said so," Jackie said later, "I know he wanted another boy. John was his real kin spirit."

At 11 A.M. on August 7, 1963, almost eight months pregnant, Jackie arrived with the children at the Cape Cod stables where they kept their horses, looking forward to a ride. Just as she was about to get out of the car, she felt a sharp pain. In agony, she turned to the Secret Service agent and asked him to telephone John Walsh, her trusted obstetrician, who was on call in Cape Cod in case of emergency. By 11:20, Jackie, Walsh, and a Secret Service man were in a helicopter bound for Otis Air Force Base Hospital, twenty miles away.

Jackie had planned to have the baby at Walter Reed Hospital in Washington, but there was no time to get there. Otis Air Force Base Hospital was put on alert; three officers, all with Jackie's AI Rh-positive blood type, stood ready and waiting to give blood for transfusion. By noon, one pint had already been taken.

Exactly twenty minutes after he first received the call from White House physician Janet Travell, also on call in Massachusetts, the President was on his way to Cape Cod. He flew in a twin-engine, eight-passenger Jet Star; none of the presidential Boeing 707s was available.

By the time he arrived at the hospital, a ten-member military team led by Walsh had delivered Jackie of a baby boy who weighed four pounds, ten ounces. Minutes after the birth, Air Force chaplain Father John Cahill baptized the baby Patrick Bouvier Kennedy. At 2:30 P.M., President Kennedy saw his newborn son for the first time.

Lying in an incubator like the one that had sustained John, Patrick was suffering from a similar lung ailment—hyaline membrane disease. It was clear that the small Air Force hospital could not provide the special treatment needed to save the life of the President's tiny son.

Swaddled in a blue blanket inside the incubator, Patrick was readied for the one-hour dash by ambulance to Children's Medical Center in Boston. Before he left, the President wheeled the incubator up to Jackie's bed so that, drowsy as she was, she could take one look at her new son.

In Boston the baby was put into a huge hyperbaric pressure chamber that would force oxygen into his lungs.

"Nothing must happen to Patrick," Jack said to Janet Auchincloss. "I just can't bear to think of the effect it might have on Jackie."

Back at Otis, Jackie was sleeping peacefully, unaware of her son's fight for life. After thirty-nine hours and twelve minutes, Patrick Bouvier Kennedy lost the fight; he died at 4:04 A.M. on August 9, 1963. Pierre Salinger made the announcement to the press.

"The struggle of the baby boy to keep breathing was too much for his heart."

The President's son was the first Kennedy to be buried in the new family plot at Holyrood cemetery in Brookline, just outside Boston.

"That's where I would like to be buried when my time comes," Jack told his close friend Charles Bartlett. "McNamara says I should be buried at Arlington National Cemetery, but I think I'd rather be with my family."

Afterward Jackie told close friends the President was inconsolable after Patrick's death.

"As shocking as it was for me, it was worse for him," she said. "Jack nearly collapsed."

Patrick's death had a profound and shattering effect on them both. Jack, not prone to displays of emotion, wept bitterly. He held Jackie in his arms and she clung to him far more than at any time during their marriage.

"You know, we mustn't create an atmosphere of sadness in the White House," he said, "because that wouldn't be good for anyone— not for the country and not for the work we have to do."

He was not normally very sensitive to her feelings, but now he expressed great concern. "It's so hard for Jackie," he said. "She wanted so to have another child. Then, after all the difficulties she has in bearing a child, to lose him is doubly hard."

After bringing Caroline to Otis Air Force Base Hospital earlier in the day, Jack brought John Jr. to see his mother for the first time since the birth and death of Patrick. Dressed in yellow and white rompers, John ate a bowl of peach ice cream during the visit. His presence left Jackie less despondent.

When she returned to Brambletide Cottage to convalesce, Caroline and John and their nine dogs were waiting on the patio to greet her. Jack had planned it that way, hoping that the sight of her family might help her rally physically and emotionally.

Her sister, Lee, had come from London to lend moral support, and Jackie spent the next few weeks sailing and reading *Civilization of Rome* by Pierre Grimal. Europe continued to lure her, and the two sisters talked of taking a trip to help her recuperate. The best choice seemed to be Greece, where Lee had been invited for a cruise by shipping tycoon Aristotle Onassis.

Jackie and Jack planned to celebrate their tenth wedding anniversary on September 12, 1963. Together for a decade, they had accomplished more than either had ever imagined. Their marriage had survived not only the pressures of public life but also the internal pressures exerted by two strong individuals attempting to face the world as one. They would also survive Patrick's death, though their emotions were excruciating.

As Jack flew to Point Naval Air Station, he thought about his ten years with Jackie and his two and a half years as President. Who could have foreseen the Cuban missile crisis and the Bay of Pigs debacle? He had used both to vanquish his political enemies. The specter of his Mafia connections had momentarily faded as his sureness in making decisions and standing behind them rose to the forefront. His "Ich bin ein Berliner" speech was still resonating throughout the world, and the limited Nuclear Test-Ban Treaty created new hope for a thaw in the Cold War. His introduction of sweeping civil rights legislation expressed the depth of his commitment to acting on his beliefs. All in all, he seemed poised for an effortless election to a second term as President.

He was bound that night for Hammersmith Farm in Newport, Rhode Island, the Auchincloss family estate. Jacqueline had made her debut at Hammersmith Farm, and they had held their wedding reception there. Jack had grown to love the farm and often described it as just about as beautiful as any place on the Atlantic coast.

Tonight promised to be an intimate evening, a small family dinner with only five couples: Jackie's mother, Janet, and stepfather, her half brother, Yusha; Sylvia Whitehouse Blake, who had been one of Jackie's bridesmaids; Jackie's half sister, Janet Auchincloss, and her stepbrother, Jamie; and Benjamin Bradlee and his wife, Toni. None of Jackie's raucous Kennedy in-laws were present, so Jackie could relax.

The President landed at Point Naval Air Station, where he was met by the governor of Rhode Island. Television cameras were on hand but broke down in the middle of recording the moment. The cameraman asked the President to re-create the meeting. Dubbing the request "cheeky," Jack nevertheless complied, mindful of the importance of television in immortalizing every aspect of his administration.

With the Bradlees, the President flew in a helicopter to Hammersmith Farm, landing on the lawn in front of the Deck Room, which commanded a spectacular view of the bay. Jackie ran out to the helicopter and, as Ben Bradlee observed, "Jackie greeted JFK with by far the most affectionate embrace I had ever seen them give each other."

Inside the house, Yusha Auchincloss mixed Jack his own special daiquiri made with three kinds of rum and fresh lemon, lime, and orange juice.

It was just over a month since Patrick's death, and Jack was aware that his wife was still reeling. To distract her, he brought with him an array of precious artifacts from which she could choose her anniversary gift.

"You can only keep one. You have to choose." He spread his treasures at her feet all around the Deck Room, where they lay sparkling in the twilight. She gazed at the exotic display—glistening gold, burnished silver, blue-white diamonds, glowing emeralds, an ancient Egyptian bust depicting the god Osiris, a gold bracelet in the shape of a serpent, a pair of ornate gold sixteenth-century earrings, an Italian bracelet carved in the fourth century B.C..

After telling her about each treasure, Jack reminded her, "Now, don't forget, you can only keep one."

"Can I wait and select one later?" she asked.

Jack smiled and bowed to her wishes.

Characteristically, Jackie had invested more of herself in her gift to him, a red leather, gold-embossed scrapbook of photographs of the White House Rose Gardens, whose restoration she had initiated. She had captioned each picture herself with a quotation from Bartlett's. The gift was typical of Jackie, involving more effort, artistry, and grace than money. She also presented Jack with a gold St. Christopher's medal to replace the one he had so lovingly placed in the coffin by Patrick's side.

As he gently fingered the medal, tears sprang to their eyes.

"Jack normally didn't show emotions," said Jamie Auchincloss. "There was more eye contact between Jack and Jackie than I ever saw before. They looked at each other as if to say, 'Isn't it a wonderful life?' Before, Jack would have been embarrassed."

Jack was notably attentive to Jackie that night at Hammersmith Farm, and as she watched the evening unfold, Jackie's mother, too, believed that the two had achieved a new closeness.

"They'd certainly been through as much as people can go through together in ten years," she said. "Tragedy and joy with their children's births and deaths; then Jack's illnesses and Jackie's cesarean operations; mixed in with all the campaigning and finally occupying the highest office in the world. I can't think of two people who had packed more into ten years of marriage than they had.

"And I felt that all their strains and stresses, which any sensitive people have in a marriage, had eased to a point where they were terribly close to each other. They were very, very, very close to each other and understood each other wonderfully. He appreciated her gifts and she worshipped him and appreciated his humor and kindness."

Janet Auchincloss truly believed that the phoenix of her daughter's marriage had been reborn out of the ashes of Patrick's death and that a new era had dawned for John and Jacqueline Kennedy. The dinner guests toasted the anniversary couple, wishing them all the happiness the universe could muster on their behalf. The party truly seemed to herald a new dawn for the First Couple's marriage.

When Lee telephoned Jackie from London, again suggesting that she cruise the Mediterranean on *Christina*, Aristotle Onassis's yacht, Jackie accepted.

Jackie was back in America on October 17, after a sixteen-day trip that had taken her to Europe and North Africa. She had flown home via Paris to New York and from there to Washington on *Caroline*. At National Airport, John, Caroline, and the President welcomed her, eager to hear her tales about life on the high seas with the tycoon, whom she later tellingly described as "an alive and vital person who has come up from nowhere."

In Jack's mind, Aristotle Socrates Onassis was romantically linked to opera diva Maria Callas and, according to gossip, might well have tangled romantically with his sister-in-law Lee. With Jackie on the cruise were Lee, her husband, Prince Radziwill, dress designer Princess Irene Galitzine, Artemis and Theodore Garofalides, Lee's friend Accardi Gurney, and Jack's under secretary of commerce, Franklin D. Roosevelt, Jr., who with his wife, Suzanne, had volunteered to act as chaperone.

The day of Jackie's arrival back in America had been an eventful one for John as well. President Tito of Yugoslavia had visited the White House, and John had stood on the White House balcony enjoying the parade below.

"We want Kennedy, we want Kennedy!" he shrieked. All dressed up with two toy six-shooters stuck defiantly in his belt, John could hardly stand still with all the excitement.

John's antics made the evening news after a sharp-eyed photographer caught him accidentally dropping his gun from the balcony to the ground by Tito's feet. Journalists subsequently reported that John had dropped his gun on President Tito's head.

The President called Maud Shaw to his office the next day, troubled about his son's lack of discipline. There was hope, however. John would soon join Caroline at the White House nursery school, and there was every chance that daily lessons would help control his exuberance. Held in the White House Solarium, which was light and airy, with magnificent views to the south, the school was Jackie's solution to the dilemma over John's and Caroline's education. Not wishing them to be educated outside the White House, she nevertheless did not want them to be deprived of the company of other children.

She arranged for eight children of White House staff members (including Avery Hatcher, the son of Associate White House Press Secretary Andrew Hatcher) to attend lessons at the school given by two teachers, who were paid from the nominal tuition fees.

Jackie's routine was strict. She started the day with a brisk one-hour walk around the White House grounds, had lunch with the children in what was known as the High Chair Room, spent the afternoon with the children, and sat with them while they ate their dinner.

Jack often deviated from his working schedule to spend spontaneous time with them. Able to see the White House schoolchildren playing in the sand behind his office during their recess, the President occasionally dropped everything and walked out to watch them making mud pies. The children would cry out, "Oh, look, here's Caroline's Daddy!"

In December 1962, *Look* photographer Stanley Tretick had suggested a photo essay for the magazine titled "The President and His Son." Although three years had passed since they had moved into the White House, Jackie still loathed the thought of Caroline's and John's being photographed in their home.

But John had grown accustomed to being photographed by Cecil Stoughton, pestering him constantly to "take my picture, Taptain Toughton." Both John and Caroline turned being photographed into a game, an everyday distraction that was as familiar to them as going swimming or riding their ponies.

Jack delayed the *Look* session for more than eighteen months, until on October 9, when Jackie was away in Greece, he summoned Tretick to the White House.

"You know we better get this out of the way pretty quick," he said. "Things get pretty sticky when Jackie is around."

Tretick spent five days photographing the President with his son. When the photographs were finally published, they would be heartbreakingly revealing.

Jack's father had rarely touched him or expressed affection, and those who knew the President often commented on his own discomfort with physical contact. But with John, it was a different matter.

"John was sitting on the floor of his office that first night, talking to him," said Stanley Tretick, "and he was saying something to the President and the President was looking down and talking to him. And then he just kind of reached for him, pulling his pajama up—you know, bathrobe and pajama—and he kind of rubbed his bare skin, right above his rear end. He wanted to touch him.

"Another time when he was sitting outside with him, he put him over his knee like he was going to spank him but you could see the way that he was feeling him and he was having fun with him. He'd always kind of feel at him. And you know, it was a genuine thing between the two of them."

Throughout the session, Tretick afterward recalled, the President "was more concerned with what I thought about the child than he was about my pictures. He kept saying, 'What do you think of him? Isn't he a charge?' " To Tretick, the President of the United States was just another proud father showing off his son, saying, "This is my boy, do you like him?"

Jack and John were together almost continuously now, almost as if the President somehow knew what lay ahead. On October 1, while Jackie was away, he had taken John with him in the White House limousine to the Sheraton Park Hotel, where he was attending an international monetary conference. As they walked together, the President took a white handkerchief out of his pocket and gently wiped John's nose with it.

He teased his son lovingly. On Halloween, when John was dressed up and ready for trick-or-treating, Jack called him "Sam" and pretended not to recognize him. John couldn't stop laughing at the simple joke.

On October 27, John went with his father, Caroline, and Jackie to the Roman Catholic Church of St. Stephen the Martyr in Middleburg, Virginia, for his first Mass. For Veterans Day, November 11, 1963, father and son went to Arlington National Cemetery, where they stood side by side. For a brief moment during the ceremonies, John became captivated by all the spectacle and moved away from his father, whereupon the President, surveying the great expanse of Arlington National Cemetery, instructed a Secret Service agent, "Go get John. I think he'll be lonely out there."

Father and Son

He was the least lonely child in the world, that November of 1963. His father's military aide, General Chester V. Clifton, was teaching him to march and salute like a soldier. Cecil Stoughton had taken a picture of him playing soldier, carrying a rifle, about to salute. The First Family spent the weekend together at their farm in Atoka, Virginia, where John marched some more and his father played their favorite game with him. When it came time for lunch, Maud Shaw knew exactly where to look for the two of them.

"I had a good idea where John would be, down in the helicopter hangar. Sure enough, he was. And so was the President. Both of them were sitting at the controls of the helicopter with flying helmets on. The President was playing the game seriously with his son, taking orders from Flight Captain John, thoroughly absorbed in the whole thing. I retreated quietly and left father and son very happy together."

On November 21, 1963, John F. Kennedy left the White House by helicopter, bound for Dallas.

CHAPTER FOUR

Life
After
Death

On November 22, 1963, at 1:45 P.M., Eastern Standard Time, the sky outside the White House was dark, gloomy, heavy with rain; but inside the nursery the atmosphere was bright and happy. Cousins Kara and Teddy Kennedy, Jr., had come for lunch with their nurse, Miss Dowd, and John and Caroline were chattering away merrily about their upcoming birthdays.

At that moment, Jacqueline Kennedy was racing in the open limousine to Parkland Memorial Hospital, her husband's unconscious body by her side.

"They've killed my husband and I have his brains in my hands," she kept saying. "They've killed my husband and I have his brains in my hands."

Meanwhile, John Jr. and Caroline were still in blissful ignorance of a place called Dallas and a man named Lee Harvey Oswald.

A call came through from Jackie's secretary, Nancy Tuckerman, while the dessert dishes were being cleared away. In keeping with her strict routine, the ever vigilant Miss Shaw was readying John and Caroline for their afternoon rest and was bidding the guests good-bye.

Tuckerman told Maud Shaw the news. Drawing on every grain of self-control, Miss Shaw impassively instructed the children to go into their bedrooms for their afternoon nap. Without a word of protest, they obeyed. Once in their rooms, John fell fast asleep, while Caroline lay on top of the bedcovers reading a fairy tale.

Caroline was still reading and John still sleeping when a message was transmitted from *Air Force One*, carrying Jackie and the body of the dead President back to Washington. The children were to be taken immediately to the house of Jackie's mother, where they were to stay until morning.

Bundled up against the chill Washington weather, they left the White House at 5:30 P.M., excited and happy. Dinners at Grandmere's house in Georgetown were rare, and they hardly ever spent the night there. Despite her tear-stained face, Janet Auchincloss scurried around to make John and Caroline welcome, asking her cook, Marie Steinmetz, to prepare supper for them and then bring a crib down from the attic for John.

It was only when Janet finally talked to Jackie that she discovered her daughter hadn't sent the original message. She wanted the children to be at home in the White House, reasoning in the midst of her grief, "I think the best thing for them to do would be to stay in their own rooms with their own things so their lives will be as normal as possible."

A silent crowd had gathered outside the White House, along

with the photographers, whose flashbulbs popped as the limousine bearing John, Caroline, and Maud Shaw sped through the White House gates.

"Why are all those people there?" asked Caroline brightly.

"To see you," Miss Shaw answered, hurrying her charges into the White House.

At Jackie's request, Maud Shaw was to break the news to Caroline just before she went to sleep early that evening. John, it was decided, would be told the news by his uncle, Bobby Kennedy.

As she tucked the little girl under the covers, Miss Shaw told her that her father had gone to heaven. Caroline cried and cried, gasping as if she were about to choke.

By the early evening of November 22, Rose Kennedy had seen the news of her son's death on television. Bobby had gotten it from J. Edgar Hoover, who telephoned him at home in Virginia, and Teddy had been told while he presided over the Senate.

Jack was the third of Joe Kennedy's children to meet with a violent death. None of those who ministered to Joe really knew when—or if—he grasped the news of the tragedy.

Eunice had come to him, knelt beside his wheelchair, and put her head in his lap. "Dad, Jack's been shot," she whispered. "Jack's in heaven, so he's all right."

But when Joe's nurse, Rita Dallas, showed him the morning paper, with Jack's picture outlined in black, a flicker of comprehension lit his normally lifeless eyes. For a moment he seemed to be reading the headlines, to understand, even to accept the truth. There was a long silence; then Joe Kennedy, the man who had forbidden his children to cry, shed his own tears.

In shock, yet refusing sedatives because she wanted to be fully with her husband at the moment of death, Jacqueline had kissed his eyes, his fingers, and his hands, and then, tearing her wedding ring off her trembling finger, had placed it on his.

Bobby, who would spend most of the night sobbing and asking God why He had wrought such misery on the family, choked back his tears and went to Andrews Air Force Base, where he met Jackie at the steps of *Air Force One.* Together they accompanied the body to Bethesda Naval Hospital, where the autopsy took place.

While the doctors carried out their grim task at Bethesda and Caroline and John slept fitfully at the White House, a lone light shone in one of the Presidential offices as Lyndon Johnson composed the first letter he would write as President of the United States:

> *Dear John,*
>
> *It will be many years before you understand fully what a great man your father was. His loss is a deep personal tragedy for all of us, but I wanted you particularly to know that I share your grief. You can always be proud of him.*
>
> > *Affectionately,*
> > *Lyndon Johnson*

Twenty-four hours earlier, Jacqueline Kennedy had been First Lady. Now, at thirty-four, she had become the most famous widow in the world. She returned to the White House from Bethesda Naval Hospital in the early hours of November 23, walking into the East Room with the Marine Honor Guard (from the Third Infantry Regiment—the President's own) who bore the flag-draped coffin.

As always aware that the eyes of America were on her, Jackie pushed away her mind-numbing grief and turned for solace not so much to religion as to ritual. Determined that Jack would not be forgotten by "bitter old men" who would diminish his role in history, she had summoned the White House staff and ordered them to the

Library of Congress to search the history books for every detail of Abraham Lincoln's state funeral.

Jackie resolved that John F. Kennedy would be buried in a manner befitting one of America's greatest heroes.

Thus, according to historical precedent, the coffin containing his body was placed in the center of the East Room on the same catafalque that had borne the coffin of President Lincoln nearly a hundred years earlier. Two candelabra and large urns filled with magnolia leaves stood next to it. The catafalque was dimly lit by chandeliers draped in the same dark webbing that covered the East Room's windows.

All through the night of November 23, an army of men worked feverishly to prepare for the state funeral. The service was to be executed by the Military District of Washington under Major General Philip Wheel. Seven thousand men from all services would march in the procession or stand at intervals along the street. At that moment, drumheads were being loosened and, by old military custom, shrouded in black to muffle them in recognition of the tragedy.

Just two and a half hours after Jackie returned to the White House with her husband's body, exactly at seven o'clock on the morning of November 23, Janet Auchincloss, who was sleeping that night in the White House in the late President's room at her daughter's request, was awakened by Caroline, carrying a large toy giraffe her father had given her, followed by John, pulling a toy.

"Who is that?" Caroline asked, seeing a newspaper with the dead President's face blazoned across the front page.

"Oh, Caroline," Janet said. "You know that's your daddy."

"He's dead, isn't he?" Caroline said. "A man shot him, didn't he?"

Janet found it impossible to reply.

A low Mass for the President was due to be conducted for the family by Father John Cavanaugh in the East Room at 10 A.M. Before it began, Jackie gently approached White House usher J. B. West and asked him to take her to the Oval Office. By the time they arrived, the movers had already started dismantling the office, packing up Jack Kennedy's model ships, his books, his rocking chair.

Jacqueline Kennedy looked around the Oval Office as if committing it to memory: the walls, the pieces of scrimshaw, the desk she had so painstakingly restored, which John so loved to play in. Then, after one final glance, she walked out of John F. Kennedy's office for the last time.

Motioning for West to follow her, she went into the Cabinet Room and sat down at the massive mahogany conference table.

"My children. They're good children, aren't they, Mr. West?" she asked.

"They certainly are."

The Cabinet Room offered a view of the playground, and for a long moment both looked down at the sand pile, the trampoline, the tree house, and the garden where John Jr. had lost his tooth and been so proud. Then Jackie averted her eyes and was quiet for another moment.

"They're not spoiled?"

"No, indeed," West said.

Before Mass began, Jackie visited John and Caroline in the nursery.

"I would like you to write a letter to your father, telling him how much you loved him," she said.

John marked an X on a piece of paper while Caroline, who would be six the following week, wrote:

Dear Daddy,
We're all going to miss you. Daddy, I love you very much. Caroline.

Holding their hands, Jackie led them downstairs to the East Room, where she knelt with them in front of the casket and prayed.

When the Mass began for the family, staff, and close friends, John and Caroline watched through the open doors of the adjoining Green Room but did not take part.

Jamie Auchincloss and his sister, Janet, took John and Caroline to Manassas Battlefield. The day was gray and rainy, and Jamie attempted to brighten the atmosphere by bringing along Baron, the German shepherd, and a French poodle.

When they arrived at the field, the children walked the dogs, then let them off their leashes for a run. The dogs raced into the Visitors' Center. Seeing them, a National Park Service ranger yelled, "No dogs allowed!" Then he glanced at the offending children, who had failed to control their pets. "At that moment, he realized that he was talking to the children of the slain President," Jamie Auchincloss remembered. "His jaw flew open and he had a hard time controlling his emotions."

When they got back to the White House, just in time for tea, Jackie and her mother came to see them in the nursery. With tears streaming down her face, Jackie hugged John and Caroline as if her heart was breaking. She had shed the pink Chanel suit so lightheartedly donned in Dallas, now caked in her husband's blood.

The dress she wore now was black.

On the next day, November 24, 1963, the caisson—which had once borne the body of Franklin D. Roosevelt—took exactly forty-eight minutes to transport the casket containing the body of President Kennedy from the White House to the Rotunda of the Capitol, where it would lie in state on the Lincoln catafalque.

John Jr. and Caroline rode in the procession in a limousine with Maud Shaw; Secret Service agent Bob Foster walked next to the car. The Secret Service agents had been more than John and Caroline's watchdogs—they had also been their friends. As the car pulled through the White House gates, Caroline stretched her hand out of the limousine window and clutched Bob Foster's in a gesture of trust and need. The tough Secret Service agent fought to keep back his tears.

At the steps of the Capitol, as the band played "Hail to the Chief," Jacqueline Kennedy gripped her children's hands, then bowed her head and cried. With Bobby by her side, she struggled to regain her composure before leading the children up the steps.

While she and Caroline entered the Rotunda and knelt beside the casket, Miss Shaw took John (considered too young to participate) into another Capitol office. He was instantly riveted by a large collection of miniature flags decorating a notice board. Noticing his interest, a kindly official offered him a flag.

"Yes, please," said John, adding, "and one for my sister, please."

Smiling, the official proffered two flags.

John took them.

"Please, may I have one for Daddy?"

Silently the official handed him one. John took that flag home to his mother, who, on hearing about the incident from Maud Shaw, placed the little flag in the President's coffin, a memento from his son.

On the morning of November 25, instead of celebrating his third birthday, John attended his father's funeral. Before the cortege departed the White House for the procession to St. Matthew's Cathedral, Jackie escorted John and Caroline to a limousine, which drove them to the site of the service ahead of the procession. Then, her face hidden by a heavy black lace veil, she took her place behind the caisson at the head of the cortege and began the walk to the cathedral.

Holding Caroline's and John's hands, she walked slowly up the steps to a dais halfway between the pavement and the cathedral door. There Cardinal Cushing of Boston waited for her. He had married her and Jack, had baptized Caroline, and only a short few months ago had presided at Patrick's funeral. His hand faltered as Jackie knelt to kiss his ring.

Inside the cathedral, John grew restless and was given the only book in sight, *The Church Today: Growth or Decline?* by Emmanuel Shuard. He was still clutching it when he came out into the sunlight after the ceremonies were over. Jackie, kneeling close to her husband's coffin, cried during the Pontifical Requiem Mass, as did Caroline.

John, in the same blue coat he had recently worn at a White House ceremony when he had sat on his father's knee and enchanted him with his laughter, did not really understand the import of what he was witnessing and did not cry. As he stood outside St. Matthew's Cathedral, his slain father's casket was carried past him to the strains of "Hail to the Chief."

John F. Kennedy, Jr., raised his tiny hand, saluted, and America wept.

John F. Kennedy was interred at Arlington National Cemetery, the quiet, wooded burial ground on the Virginia side of the Potomac where, just thirteen days before, he had been worried that his son might be lonely when John ventured away from his side during the Veterans Day ceremony. Jacqueline had chosen the burial site, high on a hill overlooking Washington, where John F. Kennedy had once ruled with such grace and vigor. After lighting the eternal flame, she placed a bouquet of lily of the valley on the grave.

Even as her world disintegrated by the second, Jackie, demonstrating her capacity to plan on a grand scale, had arranged to greet the 220 representatives from 102 nations in the State Dining Room of the White House. Over high tea in the Oval Office, she gave a private reception for President De Gaulle, Emperor Haile Selassie, Prince Philip, and President De Valera. But she hadn't forgotten that this was also her son's third birthday. Upstairs in the family quarters, John's party proceeded as planned.

Everyone who observed her that day in the White House could not help being dazzled by her poise, her ability to throw herself into life again, just hours after her husband had been buried.

Greeting each head of state personally, she spent added moments with General De Gaulle, inexplicably presenting him with a fresh daisy. To her cousin John Davis, she seemed lively, but Toni Bradlee noticed that as she smiled graciously, thanking the assembled dignitaries for their condolences, her normally clear eyes were red.

Upstairs, despite the somber mood, John's closest family and friends had assembled to celebrate his birthday, just as his father would have wished. Patricia Kennedy Lawford and Peter Lawford, Bobby Kennedy, Lee and Stash Radziwill, John's godfather, his grandmothers Rose and Janet, and his father's friend Dave Powers were all there, holding back their tears, joining to wish him a happy birthday.

Still in a marching mood, John, with Dave Powers clapping his hands in military rhythm, spent the first part of his birthday party stepping smartly around the room, his rifle held tightly by his side. Silently the family watched.

While Jackie was receiving condolences downstairs, the birthday congratulations continued upstairs. As he unwrapped each present—an electric car, a toy fire engine—the family managed to marvel at his gifts and to wish him "Long life, John."

Caroline watched solemnly, waiting for the cake with three candles to be lit, watching her brother, his paper hat secured on his thick hair, blowing his party horn.

Finally the dignitaries departed. Teddy and Jackie joined the party, and Jackie lit the candles on John's cake. Bobby entered just as the group began singing "Happy Birthday, John Fitzgerald Kennedy, Jr." John delighted in being called by his name in all its entirety. Bobby turned and raced down the hall, convulsed by tears. After he composed himself and returned, they sang traditional Irish songs whose lyrics flowed in the blood of the Kennedy family, as much part of their heritage as Ireland itself. Then Dave Powers joined Bobby and Teddy Kennedy in singing "Heart of My Heart," the popular hit that had been one of Jack's favorites, containing the line "when we were kids at the corner of the street." Singing this song his brother had so loved and would never hear again, Bobby Kennedy was again overcome, and the singing had to stop. Part celebration, part tribute to the dead, and part invocation of hope for the living, John's third birthday party, a fitting wake for his father, had now ended.

Jackie, Jack, and the children had planned to travel to Hyannis to celebrate Thanksgiving with the family as always. Rose had expected Jackie to go into seclusion, to cancel their trip. But on the Wednesday evening before Thanksgiving, just two days after Jack's funeral, Jackie, Caroline, and John arrived at Hyannis Port.

Intensely aware that for her life would never be the same, Jackie nonetheless resolved that life should go on for the children as if the world remained normal. At the compound she spent hours with Joe, telling him how his son had died, not caring whether her words meant anything to him.

The past was now all-important to her, and she determined to use all her power to influence the way it would be projected in the future. Summoning *Life* journalist Theodore H. White to Hyannis Port, she spent four hours impressing on him the importance of Jack Kennedy's being remembered as a hero.

"Jack's life had more to do with myth, legend, saga, and story," she explained, "than with political theory or political science."

She had always been an artist, ever aware of Jack's place in history and her own in his life. A dramatist and a romantic, she bypassed Shakespeare and great thinkers of the past in searching out a symbol that would capture the essence of the Kennedy years. She seized on a far more commercial image, that of the hit Broadway musical *Camelot.*

"When Jack quoted anything, it was usually classical, but I'm so ashamed of myself—all I keep thinking of is this line from a musical comedy," she said, then quoted the appropriate passage from the Lerner and Loewe musical: " 'Don't let it be forgot/That once there was a spot/For one brief shining moment/That was known as Camelot.' There'll be great Presidents again—and the Johnsons are wonderful, they've been wonderful to me—but there'll never be another Camelot."

On their last day in the White House, Jackie threw a joint birthday party for Caroline and John. Sixteen young friends (eight invited by Caroline and eight for John) sat at two separate tables, each with its own birthday cake, sang "Happy Birthday," gorged themselves on ice cream, and played games, oblivious to the fact that this was the Kennedy family's last day in the White House.

Looking pale and drawn, Jackie joined the party. She smiled for the first time in weeks at the sight of the sixteen happy guests. She wore no jewelry and was dressed in a simple black cocktail dress. She talked to each child while serving the birthday cake.

Their family quarters in the White House looked barren now, bereft of their personal belongings. In anticipation of a second term in the White House, the First Couple had sold their Georgetown house; Jackie and the children were now homeless. Averell Harriman, John Kennedy's assistant secretary of state for Far Eastern affairs, and his wife volunteered their eleven-room, three-story residence at 3038 N Street, and Jackie accepted, knowing that this would be merely a temporary home for her and her children.

Evidence of the sympathy of strangers flooded into the White House. A group of 180 Japanese girls attending a knitting school in Wakayama designed a cream-colored cardigan, jacket, and cap for Caroline and a brown, cream and black sweater and cap for John. With the gifts came a letter to Jackie.

We wish our humble Christmas present will help console the hearts of your two little children.

When he saw his beloved toys packed away into boxes John panicked, convinced that he would never see them again. He was slightly pacified when Maud Shaw allowed him to wear the Marine uniform he had been given on his birthday. He helped her set aside a selection of guns, mechanical toys, and swords, which were then packed in a separate suitcase that John carried to his new home himself.

The White House staff had gathered early that morning in an upstairs sitting room to say good-bye to the family. Emotions ran high as Jackie presented each of them with a copy of a painting of the Green Room. It was the gift President Kennedy had selected for them all for Christmas of 1963. Telling them that the painting would be "a continual reminder of the President," she moved on to bid farewell to the White House telephone operators.

"Jacqueline Bouvier Kennedy leaves a shining gift of beauty in this historic house," said Lady Bird Johnson earlier that day. "At every turn, we are freshly conscious of our heritage.

"The most knowledgeable expert, as well as the busloads of schoolchildren who visit, will always know that a young and radiant First Lady lived here. We know her better than ever before and hold her close to our hearts with inexpressible pride."

Later, in the State Dining Room, President Johnson posthumously awarded the Presidential Medal of Freedom, the nation's highest civilian award, to Jack "on behalf of the great republic for which he lived and died."

Bobby accepted the medal for Jackie, who, as she was still in mourning, would not make an official appearance at the ceremony.

She sat behind an Oriental screen just outside the room, where she had once presided over gala evenings.

After the ceremony, Bobby handed the medal to her and, with Lee Radziwill, Secret Service agent Clint Hill, Dave Powers, and the children, she moved slowly toward the ground-floor oval reception room. Dave Powers had given John a small flag which, for no particular reason, he began waving. Pausing in the middle of the reception room, Jackie looked at her son, then impulsively handed him the black case containing the Medal of Freedom.

"John, here's something else you can carry out of the White House," she said. "Keep it, and be proud of it always."

And so, waving the American flag and clasping his father's Medal of Freedom next to his heart, John F. Kennedy, Jr., walked out of the White House. The assassin's bullet had not only killed his father but was also tearing him away from the only home he'd ever known.

During those first few days in Georgetown, Jackie remained in seclusion, guarded by police and Secret Service men, who kept the traffic moving in front of the Harriman house, ensuring that sightseers did not harass the former First Lady and her children.

Jackie spent most of the day hidden away in her second-floor bedroom, lonely and depressed. As a child, she had dreamed of being the daughter of the Emperor Charlemagne. As an adult, she had ascended to heights more spectacular than any child's daydream. Now death had ripped away her exalted status and left her alone, her life relegated to mundane details, her grief that of any woman who has lost her husband.

When her personal secretary, Mary Gallagher, came to visit her, Jackie, who normally exhibited iron self-control and rarely displayed emotion in front of other people, dissolved into tears.

"Why did Jack have to die so young?" Her voice was bitter.

"Even when you're sixty, you like to know your husband is there. It's so hard for the children."

On the first floor of the house, staff members scurried around, intent on creating a semblance of order. A Navy cook, on loan from the White House staff mess, prepared meals. Secret Service agents were on hand to monitor an endless stream of telephone calls from sympathizers and to search through the massive bouquets that arrived at the house every day. Jackie dispatched Maud Shaw and the children to a local park, where John climbed on the jungle gym, as if life were once again normal.

Caroline, however, had registered the truth. She was listless, often staring into the distance as if searching for answers. As Caroline left her favorite desserts untouched, her French teacher from the White House school, Jacqueline Hirsh, watched carefully.

"She just looked ghastly. She was so pale and her concentration broken," said Hirsh. "She comprehended the assassination fully, absolutely. You could see it was on her mind, that it was rough on her. But she never did complain, never. Mrs. Kennedy, I could see sometimes that her eyes were red, or the child's eyes were red. But never one complaint."

Hirsh took Caroline out for a drive with her cousin Sydney Lawford. Looking out the window, Caroline was spotted by several members of the press.

"Hi, Caroline!" one shouted.

She had been America's child and had become the child of tragedy; some reporters seemed to believe they owned her. Stricken, Caroline slid down in her car seat.

"Please tell me when nobody's looking."

She had always been the object of an enamored public's elated curiosity, but young as she was, Caroline sensed that the tenor of that curiosity had changed. And she was afraid.

John, too, knew instinctively in those early days that his life had been suddenly made bereft. Jackie enlisted Dave Powers to pay daily lunchtime visits to John, during which they spent an hour or so marching through the rooms of the Georgetown house together. There were many afternoons at Bobby's home in Virginia, and John's face brightened whenever Mary Gallagher came for a visit.

One day, just as Gallagher was about to leave, John looked at her quizzically.

"Where's Mrs. Lincoln?"

By now, the President's former secretary had a large office in Room 300 of the Executive Office Building, where, surrounded by photos of the President and models of his PT boat and his rocking chair, she was working diligently to decipher his often illegible notes and jottings. Not willing to try and explain that Lincoln no longer worked in the White House, Mary Gallagher hesitated.

"She's in the office."

"Who's with her?"

Gallagher did not answer.

His questions continued, and finally it was decided that it would be better if John called Evelyn Lincoln instead of visiting her new office. Maud Shaw taught him how to dial Lincoln's new telephone number.

"Mrs. Lincoln, this is John."

"Why, John, what a wonderful surprise."

Touched, Lincoln fell into the pattern of chatting to him almost daily. One day he called to inform her he would be visiting her in the office the following Thursday.

"That would be lovely, John. I'm looking forward to seeing you."

"Me, too," John said. "Mrs. Lincoln?"

"Yes, John?"

"Is Daddy there?"

Mrs. Lincoln was unable to reply.

Sometimes John would point out photographs of the White House to Maud Shaw.

"That's where we live, isn't it, Miss Shaw?"

"No, John, we don't live there anymore, do we? Don't you remember we moved into another house with Caroline and Mummy?"

Miss Shaw's reminder eventually made an impact, and some time afterward she saw John and Caroline looking at a picture of the White House and heard John explain, "That's where we used to live, Caroline."

His attitude to the legions of tourists who gathered outside the house armed with cameras, eager to catch a glimpse of him or Caroline and Jackie, had changed from gleeful acceptance to irritation. "What are those silly people taking my picture for?" he would ask querulously.

On December 11, 1963, Congress voted Jackie office space for one year, providing her with a staff. Other measures designed to pay tribute to the late President were taken in quick succession. President Johnson, at Jackie's request, renamed Cape Canaveral Cape Kennedy; Washington's National Culture Center was renamed the John F. Kennedy Center for the Performing Arts; and Jackie was also awarded the usual yearly pension of $10,000 set aside for the widows of Presidents, lifetime mailing privileges, and the protection of two Secret Service agents for herself and the children over the next year.

During the debate regarding Jackie and the children, Democratic representative James H. Morrison of Louisiana said it was "the unanimous judgment" of security agents that "there remains an element of danger to his widow and children." Two weeks after the assassination, 293,000 condolence letters and 26,000 telegrams had already been received at the White House, as well as 250,000 other letters and messages sent to Hyannis Port. While the correspondence was sympathetic, it was acknowledged that the possibility existed of the former First Family's being threatened in some way.

Jackie remained afraid. To her cousin Michel Bouvier, who visited her at the Harriman house, she seemed overwrought to the point that he "feared for the stability of her emotions and wondered whether her sanity would hold up under the terrible strain of the adjustments she was having to make."

Living with all the pressures and none of the perquisites she had experienced as First Lady, Jackie still suffered the continual scrutiny of the media, who charted her every move. At one point, while sifting through wallpaper samples and selecting paint shades for her next house, she cried out to decorator Billy Baldwin, "Can anyone understand how it is to have lived in the White House and then, suddenly, to be living alone as the President's widow? There's something so final about it. And the children. The world is pouring terrible adoration at the feet of my children and I fear for them, for this awful exposure. How can I bring them up normally? We would never ever have named John after his father if we had known."

President Kennedy's will, which had been drawn up on June 18, 1954, was filed for probate on December 23, 1963, and left to Jackie $25,000, together with all of his personal effects, furniture, silverware, dishes, china, glassware, and linens, as well as half of his property, the net income of which was to be paid to her by the Joseph P. Kennedy, Jr., Foundation. To John and Caroline, his surviving children, the President left the other fifty percent of his estate, estimated at several million dollars.

Holding fast to family tradition, Jackie and the children spent Christmas in Palm Beach, traveling there on December 18 with Maud Shaw and Lee Radziwill's children, Tony and Tina.

Wearing white, as befitted temperatures in the mid-sixties, Jackie was nevertheless a sad figure. Although she did her best to preserve the spirit of Christmas, her thoughts inevitably returned to the previous year in the White House.

Caroline and John helped trim the Christmas tree, with John raucously throwing tinsel all around the room before performing a Nativity play for the family. But as they re-created the Christmas story, both John and Caroline thought of their father.

"Will Patrick be looking after him up in heaven?" Caroline asked.

After a pause which no one in the family seemed able to break, John chimed in with, "Do they have fish chowder in heaven?"

To any other group, the question would have been silly. But to the mourning family, his question was easier to answer in the affirmative than Caroline's. Fish chowder had been one of the President's favorite dishes, and no God worth His salt would be without it.

They returned to Georgetown on January 6, with Teddy, to find four hundred spectators outside the Harriman house, desperate to glimpse them just for a moment. Their time at the Harriman residence was to be brief. Jackie had just paid $175,000 for a three-story, fourteen-room Colonial-style mansion at 3017 N Street, just across from the Harrimans' and only three blocks away from the house where she and Jack had lived during the first years of their marriage.

Designing the decor for 3017 N Street took up Jackie's attention, and now and again Maud Shaw and Mary Gallagher thought they detected a hint of the old sparkle in her eyes as she debated the shade of gold for a chair's upholstery (she had co-opted the upholsterer from the White House) or supervised the painting of the children's rooms (which, like their old rooms in the White House, were to be blue and pink).

Despite Jackie's attempt to re-create the White House atmosphere for the sake of the children, she still could not bear to look at pictures of the past. She simply didn't have the emotional strength to unpack the cases. Finally, tackling the task with Mary Gallagher during the day, Jackie began opening the envelopes stuffed with pictures of Jack.

"It's so much easier doing it while you're here than at night," she said in a whisper. "When I'm alone, I just drown my sorrows in vodka."

The children, however, were ecstatic on opening up the packing cases containing all their toys, which had been in storage since they had first left the White House. Amid squeals of delight, John unpacked his machine gun, gleefully firing it all over the house. At the end of January 1964, when he was confined to bed with chicken pox—which he passed on to Caroline—he had to be forcefully restrained from jumping up and making an inventory of all his newly discovered treasures.

Dave Powers still visited him, but Jackie was beginning to rely heavily on Bobby, depending on him for support and to become the father figure that John now lacked. She saw her brother-in-law nearly every day. Bobby parked his car a few streets away so as not to alert the media.

Excursions to Hickory Hill, the 140-year-old white brick house in Virginia that Jackie and Jack had owned in the early years of their marriage—now owned by Ethel and Bobby—soon became a regular event for Jackie and the children. Caroline had lost her front teeth, but she couldn't contain her smiles at the sight of her cousin David making faces while plunging head first into one or the other of Hickory Hill's two swimming pools. Bobby did his utmost to make Caroline and John feel part of his family.

In the aftermath of the assassination, Bobby quickly perceived the marked difference between the two children. He sensed that John was relatively untouched and dubbed him "a rogue," but acknowledged sadly that now that her father was dead, "Caroline doesn't let people get close to her." Bobby was particularly gentle and affectionate with his niece while roughhousing with John very much as his father had.

John delighted in playing hide-and-seek with his uncle, crouching in the play shelter while Bobby made a big show of looking for him and muttering, "Where's John? John's disappeared! Hey, John! John! Where's John?"

Finally Bobby would give up and John would crawl out of his hiding place, smiling with pleasure at having eluded his uncle. Bobby wanted very much to be a substitute father to John, and Jackie was grateful. Maud Shaw, however, aware of the less than cordial relationship between Jackie and Ethel, wondered out loud whether or not Jackie might be overstaying her welcome at Hickory Hill.

Bobby disregarded any tensions. By the spring of 1964, he had developed a pattern of picking John up each morning and taking him to the Justice Department, where he would play with his cousins Kerry and Michael. When French Ambassador Herve Alphand presented Bobby with a check for $100,000 on behalf of the French government for the projected Kennedy Memorial Library, John was observed dressed in navy-blue overalls and a blue and white T-shirt, standing in the corner of his uncle's office.

Jackie found herself becoming a national monument, a tragic figure whom the public never tired of watching. She had made a crucial error in selecting the house at 3017 N Street; it was easily accessible to the myriad passersby determined to catch a glimpse of the former First Lady and her children at home. The house soon became a major tourist attraction, with sightseeing buses crammed full of people driving up and down the street day after day, night after night, desperate to see Jackie or the children.

Close friends knew that Jackie and her family were living like prisoners, unable to keep the drapes open, protected by police lines.

In February, Jackie fled to New York with the children, staying with them at the Carlyle Hotel. She enjoyed her time there, rediscovering old friends like Truman Capote amid the bustle of Manhattan. She and the children also paid a visit to Bill Haddad, Sargent Shriver's Peace Corps deputy, in his apartment in the East Sixties, so that John and Caroline could play with Haddad's daughter, Laura, and her cousins in their top-floor playroom.

Bill Haddad, his sister-in-law, and Jackie watched the children playing, making sure everything went smoothly. Gradually, John edged toward Bill, obviously remembering him from White House days. In no time, he and Bill were playing with a set of toy cars. Noticing that John was arranging them in a particular formation, Haddad immediately understood the scene he was re-creating.

"That was what he knew best," said Haddad. "It was what he had grown up with—a Secret Service convoy."

All the adults watched John's unself-conscious play.

"Daddy?" said Haddad's daughter, trying to catch his attention from across the room.

"Yes?" Haddad said.

Suddenly John looked up. "Are you a daddy?"

"Yes, I am."

"Then throw me up into the air."

Without a word, Haddad picked him up and threw him in the air—then burst into tears.

"At that moment," Haddad said, "I realized that the assassination hadn't just meant the loss of a leader, or a President, or a friend, but that someone had taken the life of this child's father."

John took to calling Bob Foster, the Secret Service agent he had known all his life, "Daddy." For a time, Jackie stood by helplessly as Foster tried gently to discourage the boy. But John stubbornly refused to be deterred and carried on until Jackie asked that the agent be reassigned.

Their life in Washington was becoming unendurable. Caroline

was still attending the White House school, which President Johnson was retaining until late May, but was scheduled to start at the Convent of the Sacred Heart in Bethesda at the end of the year. John was due to begin his schooling in a small cooperative Jackie was setting up for him with the help of former teachers from the White House. Yet since her visit to New York, Jackie had begun to hunger for life in Manhattan, far removed from Washington and its tragic memories.

Her resolve to leave Washington increased after May 29, which would have been President Kennedy's forty-seventh birthday, when she attended a requiem Mass at St. Matthew's Cathedral and broke down in tears.

After Mass, still tearful and shaken, she took Caroline and John to their father's grave in Arlington. A crowd of more than a thousand people waited on the hillside across the Potomac near the grave. Her face hidden by a black lace mantilla, Jackie held fast to John and Caroline's hands. Both children wore matching white linen coats, and a gold tie clasp in the shape of his father's boat, *PT 109*, was pinned to John's lapel. When he and Caroline knelt at their father's grave, John removed the clasp and placed it on the pine boughs covering the grave. Next, Bobby, Ethel, and seven of their children laid long-stemmed roses near the eternal flame.

After the ceremony, Jackie flew to Hyannis Port. There, with Teddy by her side in the sitting room of the compound, she made a worldwide memorial broadcast. In a voice soft with emotion, she talked of the President's ideals, and of the John Fitzgerald Kennedy Library to be built on the banks of the Charles River in Boston. Then she and Teddy talked by satellite to Mayor Willy Brandt of Berlin, Prime Minister Harold Macmillan of England, and Prime Minister Sean Lemass of Ireland.

Jackie's satellite broadcast was partly a plea for world peace, but her personal life remained far from peaceful. At times she was racked with guilt at not having done something to avert the tragedy; at other times she was bitter with anguish that the Secret Service hadn't saved her husband's life. President Johnson, too, served as a continual reminder of her powerless position. She took to calling him and Lady Bird "Colonel Cornpone and his Little Porkchop."

Johnson, with an eye to the political advantages of maintaining close ties to Jackie, invited her to the White House constantly, but Jackie, unable even to drive past her former home, categorically refused.

By the middle of 1964, she had made a firm decision to move to New York and put both the N Street house and "Wexford" in Atoka up for sale. Later that year she bought a fifteen-room cooperative apartment at 1040 Fifth Avenue for $200,000 and then invested $125,000 to furnish and redecorate it.

She would now be close to her stepbrother, Yusha Auchincloss, and to Stephen and Jean Smith, Peter and Pat Lawford, and Bobby, who was making a bid for the Senate—running in New York, where he now had an apartment.

Bobby's campaign seemed to her to represent renewed hope and the possibility that a Kennedy would once more reign over Washington.

"He must win," she said. "He will win. He must win. Or maybe it's just because one wants it so much that one thinks that he will win."

They moved to New York in the middle of September 1964 and stayed at the Carlyle while renovations were being carried out at the new apartment. Jackie had always stayed there with the President, as had the children. Remembering the past, she found herself incapable of visiting the Carlyle suite she and Jack had shared together—where, she would later learn, he had also had the occasional rendezvous with Marilyn Monroe.

The anniversary of the assassination was looming, and Jackie was going through radical mood changes. She felt disorganized and had disjointed conversations with visitors. Inexplicably, she decided to arrange for John to be shown around her former suite.

Carlyle housekeeper Nancy Marr took John through the suite. He was accompanied by a Secret Service agent and by the ubiquitous Miss Shaw, both of whom followed him around the room. Looking at the bed, John paused.

"Did my daddy sleep here?"

"Yes," said Miss Shaw.

Then he saw the rocking chair. "Did my daddy sit here?"

"Yes."

Satisfied, John bowed courteously and thanked Nancy Marr so effusively that she afterward declared, "He was a polite little gentleman in the image of his father."

Determined that the children wouldn't be what she called "just two kids living on Fifth Avenue going to nice schools," Jackie aimed to re-create the rustic peace of Atoka by renting a ten-room summer house in Glen Cove, Long Island, for a weekend retreat.

Central Park, too, became their playground. Jackie took them to ride on the carousel without arousing the notice they had attracted in Washington. A lone policeman, riding through the park on his red motor scooter, did pluck up the courage to ask for her autograph. Seeing John eyeing the motorcycle enviously, Jackie—who despised autograph seekers—sized up the situation and made the policeman an offer.

"I'll give you an autograph if you take John for a ride on your motor scooter."

The policeman had to decline; regulations forbade him to take on any passengers.

John was now living in a different world, one that had not been exclusively constructed especially to cater to him. But he still couldn't enjoy life like an average little boy. An outing to the World's Fair on September 21, 1964, required that he be guarded by two Pinkerton security officers, as well as by the usual pair of Secret Service agents.

Once at the fair, he demanded to be allowed to sign the guest book. Grasping the pen at the wrong end, he got ink all over his fingers before making four circles on the page. Undeterred by the stains, he happily answered questions from the crowd, who were captivated by the sight of a blissful John riding the Swiss Sky Ride on the back of a Secret Service agent.

"Where's Caroline?" someone called out.

"She's in school," he shouted back, "but I'm too young."

At Walt Disney Magic Skyway, he was presented with a toy car as a souvenir. Before settling down on the ground to play with it, he announced to all the onlookers, "Hi, everybody! I'm going to play car."

A huge audience was now watching the little boy in blue shorts and red shoes playing with his car. Later, when he was taken to see the tyrannosaurus exhibit at Sinclair Dino-Land, he emerged looking a trifle frightened, confiding to the army of strangers, "The lights and the dinosaurs ... I was a little bit scared."

The press, on hand to cover his outing, scribbled feverishly, captivated by the poignancy of the late President's son riding on a Secret Service agent's shoulder, sporting a button that read "I Have Seen the Future."

Aware of the public's fascination with the Kennedy children, Bobby had asked Jackie for permission to include them in certain events in his campaign. On October 18, 1964, he interrupted his street-corner campaigning in the Bronx to take John to pray at St. Margaret's Church on Riverdale Avenue, where his father had been confirmed.

Bobby and John's visit, reported in the New York press and perhaps prompted by genuine nostalgia, did nothing to harm Bobby's campaign for the Senate. He easily beat Republican Kenneth Keating by 700,000 votes.

On November 13, 1964, in an order signed by Surrogate S. Samuel Di Falco, Jackie was designated successor custodian of her two children. The order also gave her control of securities and money on deposit for the children in a Manhattan bank, which in John's case amounted to securities valued at $9,740, and $770 in cash.

Jackie spent the anniversary of the assassination alone with the children. For a time she walked by herself in Central Park, totally unrecognized by the crowds; she sat for a while on a bench, crying. Later that night, in her bedroom, her maid Provi heard her crying again.

In a *Look* article Jackie wrote movingly of her feelings:

> Soon the final day will come around again—as inexorably as it did last year. But expected this time. It will find some of us different people than we were a year ago. Learning to accept what was unthinkable when he was alive changes you.
>
> I don't think there is any consolation. What was lost cannot be replaced. Now I think I should have known that he was magic all along. I did know it—but I should have guessed it could not last. I should have known that it was asking too much to dream that I might grow old with him and see our children grow up together.
>
> So now he is a legend when he would have preferred to be a man.

John, Jackie, and Caroline celebrated John's fourth birthday at their Fifth Avenue apartment three weeks after they had moved in. Jackie served the ice cream, cake, and favors while John played games with some of his cousins and a few friends. Bobby joined the party, and for a moment they seemed like a family. Jackie hoped desperately that Caroline and John could, at last, begin to lead a normal life.

CHAPTER FIVE

Off
to
School

A life-sized tableau featuring Jackie, Caroline, and John, saluting his father, was displayed at the National Historical Wax Museum in Washington in February 1965. In many respects, the tableau was the perfect representation of the way in which the assassination had brought their lives to a standstill. Yet time, like the currents of the Potomac River, carried them along regardless.

John was to start school that month, and Jackie prayed he would be able to blend in with the other boys and be treated like anyone else. He would attend St. David's School at 12 East Sixty-ninth Street, an independent elementary Catholic school for boys founded in 1951 for "the scholastic and moral preparation of young men as Christian gentlemen."

Jackie walked John to school on his first day, accompanied by a Secret Service agent. John joined a class of twenty other children, attending from nine to twelve each day. As his mother handed him over to his first teacher, she worried that her son might feel lost in this new environment.

She needn't have been anxious. At the end of John's first morning, one hapless little boy ran home to his mother in tears.

"Why are you crying?" she asked.

"The new boy punched me in the nose!"

Surprised, his mother said, "Oh, I didn't know there was a new boy. Who is he?"

"I don't know," said her son. "He says his name is John Kennedy."

All through John's four years at St. David's, reports of his boisterousness and lack of concentration seeped through the curtain of secrecy around the school. "School life is difficult for virtually everyone," acknowledged his half uncle Jamie Auchincloss. In defense of John's raucousness, he added, "After all, John started life surrounded by the pageantry of the White House and hordes of people watching his every move, so it must have been particularly difficult for him to settle down and learn his ABCs."

A teacher at St. David's, Malachy Cleary, now principal of St. Theresa's in the Bronx, goes to great pains to stress that "John was always a first-rate young man." Another teacher, who requested anonymity, said John had been "bright, quick and had mixed well with the other children."

The other children were all too young to understand the significance of John's presence in their midst and were oblivious to the Secret Service agents, who spent most of their time out of sight in the basement.

With his fashionable Beatles haircut, John was now virtually indistinguishable from the other small boys of his age. Yet in 1963, John's hair had been the subject of considerable conflict between Jack and Jackie, leading to a heated national debate.

Jackie had always favored a more European Little Lord Fauntleroy haircut, but letters had poured in to the White House from irate Americans demanding that the First Son revert to a more nationalistic hairstyle. Some people had been so incensed by his un-American haircut that they wrote to the President, advancing money to pay for a trim. Mrs. Caroline Lowry and Miss Ann Moore dispatched one dollar in cash from Clarksville, Tennessee. Robert Daughtery of Lebanon, Pennsylvania, contributed a dollar via Western Union money order. A Mrs. John Duncan of Council Bluffs, Iowa, sent a check for $1.75, and a consortium composed of Eleanore C. Guay, Lauretta Rickel, Andrew F. Ecklund, and Daniel LeRoy, all of Peshtigo, Wisconsin, amassed four dollars, which they sent in cash.

Jackie's social secretary, Letitia Baldridge, had initially broached the subject to the First Lady, arguing that America was not ready for long hair, but Jackie stuck to her guns. Strong-minded and acutely aware of the avalanche of protest letters that continued to pour in to the White House, the resourceful Baldridge forwarded some of those letters to the President.

Taking up the battle with Maud Shaw (who was fully aware that Jackie wanted John's hair long in the European style), the President had asked, "Can't we cut John's hair a little?" Miss Shaw nodded mutely, caught between Jackie's strong objections and the President's charm. Jack, however, aware of Jackie's stance and conscious of Miss Shaw's discomfort in defying the First Lady, grinned.

"I know ... I know, but let's have some of that fringe off. If anyone asks you, it was an order from the President."

To the great relief of the American public, Miss Shaw trimmed John's hair the next day.

Since that time, American fashions had caught up with Jackie's

European tastes, and John blended in so well that when a photographer from *Women's Wear Daily* arrived at the school vowing to take the first photograph of John at St. David's, he found it impossible to determine which one of the children was John.

Afterward, when Jackie heard that John had been unrecognized, she later confided to a friend, "Oh, I'm just so glad. I just so hope that no one does!"

John's best pal at school was his cousin William Kennedy Smith. They spent hours playing together and forging a friendship that would endure throughout their lives. The other boys, who sat with John during morning prayers in the school's beautiful chapel and who eventually played soccer with him in Central Park, accepted him as one of their own. He was a friendly, outgoing boy, starved for male companionship, eager to have friends. He made them quickly, and when attendance was called on May 12, one of those new friends stood up and, in a matter-of-fact voice, announced, "John's not here. He's gone to London to see the Queen."

A memorial to President Kennedy at Runnymede, just outside London, was being dedicated; John had indeed gone to London to see the Queen. Caroline and Jackie, Maud Shaw and Dave Powers, Bobby and Teddy Kennedy, and Secretary of State Dean Rusk flew with him on *Air Force One.* Recognizing the same Air Force sergeant who had normally accompanied the First Family during their days in the White House, John couldn't stop chattering about being "back on Daddy's airplane."

During the journey, he also amused Dave Powers, who asked him to describe the biggest thing that had happened to him at his new school. John flatly answered, "The teacher said, 'John Kennedy,' and I stood up and said, 'Present.'"

There was another reason for the trip, involving Maud Shaw. She had been with them for seven years now, and had seen Caroline, who was a schoolgirl at the Convent of the Sacred Heart, mature into a young lady. John, too, was growing up, and Miss Shaw planned to retire. When the family returned to the United States, she would not be with them.

In the meantime, she and the children thoroughly enjoyed their fortnight in London. John had been told in advance that he would be presented to the Queen, and Miss Shaw spent many hours preparing him for the big event. Caroline grasped the finer details of protocol immediately, but some of the subtleties escaped John.

"When you greet her, you bow and say, 'Pleased to meet you, Your Majesty,'" Miss Shaw said. "Now, let's practice."

John bowed at the waist and said, "Pleased to meet you, My Majesty."

"Very good," said Miss Shaw, suppressing a grin. "Almost perfect, except you should address her as 'Your Majesty.'"

"No, she would be 'My Majesty.'"

The two went back and forth several times, with John adamant that he was correct, but Maud Shaw's patience eventually overcame his stubbornness, and she was able to convince him of the correct protocol. The audience with the Queen went according to the script.

This was the children's first trip to London, and Jackie wanted them to see all the sights. Unfortunately, the British press dogged their every move. They were staying with Lee and Stash Radziwill. On their second day in London, they attempted to evade the media by creeping out the back door of the Radziwill house. The ruse didn't work, and the reporters recorded a small incident in Regent's Park when John fell, skinned his knee, and started crying.

Caroline turned on him, taunting, "Crybaby."

Scowling, John doubled his tiny fist and started toward Caroline. Miss Shaw and the Secret Service agents quickly intervened.

Peace was restored, and John was distracted by a rowing expedition on Regent's Park lake with his cousins Tony and Tina Radziwill. From Regent's Park, they went on to watch the Changing of the Guard. Entranced, John not only saluted the Guardsmen but later on, in Whitehall, couldn't be torn away from the cavalrymen at Horse Guards Parade, whose shiny armor dazzled his eyes and rivaled the U.S. Marines in splendor.

By the fourth day, the press had intruded to such an extent that Jackie appealed for privacy.

"In view of the full coverage given to the children already," she said, "it is very much hoped that the remainder of the visit here can be kept private."

But she and the children were considered the closest thing to American royalty, and Jackie's pleas were in vain. The press continued to catalog every aspect of the Kennedy children's London trip.

Even the crush of reporters couldn't inhibit John's delight during their visit to the Tower of London on May 18. Ignoring the Crown Jewels, John charged toward the big cannons guarding the Tower and insisted on crawling onto one as his indulgent guide, a Beefeater, looked on. John cajoled Caroline to join him inside another cannon.

"Come on, Caroline. Let's crawl through here."

"It's a bit dirty," said Caroline, who was definitely no tomboy.

"Oh, come on!" John yelled.

This momentary impatience with Caroline was rare; normally John was very loving toward her. "You never had to urge him to be kind to his sister," said Maud Shaw, "since he shared his things with her and remembered her when he was given anything. And, if he happened to hurt anyone's feelings, he was quick to make up for it."

When it came time to leave for America, Miss Shaw gave them each a big hug.

"I'll see you in a few weeks," she said quietly.

Happily waving good-bye to her, they boarded the plane. Both

John and Caroline seemed exhausted, happy to be returning to their regular lives in New York.

By the time they were informed that Miss Shaw was not coming back from England, they were again established in their usual routine. Each day, Jackie walked Caroline to the Convent of the Sacred Heart at Ninety-first Street and Fifth Avenue. If anyone doubted that she was more mother than cosmopolitan jet-setter, the doubt was dispelled when one of her New York friends offered her a glass of champagne one evening in the middle of the week. She refused.

"She said it would give her a headache when she took Caroline to school in the morning," remembered the friend. "I urged her to skip the morning walk, but she'd have none of it; it's obviously important to her."

Jackie also walked John to and from school; he trotted beside her in his uniform. He especially enjoyed wearing a tie because it gave him the opportunity to wear his father's *PT 109* pin. After school, he played with friends in Central Park. He was becoming increasingly interested in baseball, football, and boxing. Friends came to play at the apartment after school and on special occasions; an invitation to one of Caroline's or John's parties was especially coveted.

Looking back at those parties, one of John's school friends reported, "Jackie had a big notice board in the apartment filled with family snapshots, just like any other mother would have. One or two of the children sneaked away with some of the snapshots to take home to their parents afterwards because they wanted souvenirs of their visit to the Kennedys'."

Other parents, far from craving Kennedy souvenirs, went to the opposite extreme for fear of looking like social climbers. They avoided asking John and Caroline to their parties altogether.

"I simply don't want to be thought of as using a child for social prestige," said a Park Avenue socialite whose daughter went to school with Caroline.

Finally Jackie intervened, writing carefully worded notes to the parents who had excluded Caroline and John from their parties, explaining that they were only children and wanted to be included.

Bobby continued to visit Jackie and the children as often as possible, as did Dave Powers, Lyndon Johnson, and Haile Selassie, among others from the White House years. Except for her illustrious visitors, Jackie and the children lived much the same way that any upper-crust Fifth Avenue family would. Caroline took ballet lessons (though Jackie confided to a friend that she wished she herself were taking part); Jackie attended a gym (Nicholas Kounovsky's on West Fifty-seventh); John played cowboys and Indians in Central Park and had his hair cut at the Carlyle Hotel.

The Secret Service still followed them everywhere. Although the public still treated the former First Family reverentially, Jackie was terrified of strangers. The Secret Service were instructed to vet everyone with whom she or the children might come into contact. She was aware that the Kennedy children were big news and was intent on protecting them from being exploited or harmed in any way.

On November I, All Saints' Day, she was taking Caroline to church when a crazed harridan came hurtling toward them. Caroline shrank toward her mother in horror. It appeared that Jackie's worst nightmare was about to come true.

"Your mother is a wicked woman who has killed three people and your father is still alive," shouted the woman.

The Secret Service agent sprang into action, putting himself between the woman and her targets. Trembling, Caroline and Jackie were taken home to safety.

Home was their sanctuary, and there both Caroline and John had started to build their own versions of altars to their dead father. Apart from framed photographs of John and Jackie, Caroline spent hours cutting pictures of her father out of magazines and sticking them to the walls. John amassed a collection of scrimshaw to go with the pictures of his father and records of his press conferences and speeches. He soon developed the habit of dragging visitors to his room, where he would show them his baseball cards. Then, sometimes completely out of the blue, he would ask, "Do you want to hear my father?" When the visitor inevitably acceded, John proudly turned on the record player, and the voice of John F. Kennedy echoed through the apartment.

A natural comic, John was also something of a show-off and loved entertaining his mother and sister with his imitation of the Beatles. Striking a saucy pose, he strummed an imaginary guitar and sang, "Yeah, yeah, yeah," until Jackie and Caroline collapsed in hysterical laughter.

His Kennedy cousins were still very much a part of John's life, and at St. David's he inevitably gravitated to Steve and Willie Smith. On August 25, 1965, John attended Richard, Cardinal Cushing's seventieth birthday party in Boston, along with fifteen of the other Kennedy grandchildren. The family traveled to the celebrations from Hyannis in a chartered bus, with a great deal of singing and merriment along the way.

In October, John and his cousins went trick-or-treating in Hyannis, with John dressed as a tramp and Caroline as a Dutch girl. No one would have realized who they were if it hadn't been for the out-of-costume Secret Service escorts shadowing them in their usual ghostly fashion.

On the second anniversary of the assassination, Jackie sent John and Caroline to school, not wanting to interrupt their routine. But as she and John walked home after school, she heard boys following them, laughing. After a minute or two, one of them began taunting, "Your father's dead, your father's dead," and the others took up the chant.

Turning around quickly, Jackie recognized some of them from John's class. Neither she nor John said a word; they just continued walking.

"Your father's dead, your father's dead," the boys shouted over and over.

Glancing at John, Jackie saw that he was composed. She never understood what had motivated the boys' cruelty, but she was heartened by John's reaction.

"He just came closer to me, took my hand, and squeezed it," she said. "As if he were trying to reassure me that things were all right. Sometimes it almost seems that he is trying to protect me instead of just the other way around."

Several days later, on his fifth birthday, John celebrated by going to the Rodgers High School–De La Salle Academy football game in Newport. Then he went to his grandmother's house for cake and ice cream.

Watching John blow out the candles on his birthday cake, Jackie felt intense relief at his exuberance and happiness. But she knew that the previous day's incident was just a foreshadowing of the treatment he would face from an intrusive public.

She was aware of the cruel taunts and of John's sensitivity, and while she desperately wanted to protect him, she knew he would do better if he could protect himself. She enlisted the help of the Secret Service agents to teach him boxing and wrestling. At St. David's, he practiced with Malachy Cleary's son, John, and fought bravely to win.

Wrestling with schoolmates was one thing; learning to wrestle with the social problems that plagued the country was another matter entirely. But even at his young age, John was developing a social conscience. On one of his many visits, Bobby sat down with John and Caroline and, in great detail, described the poverty in which the children of Harlem lived. John's eyes grew round and filled with tears as Bobby told of children living just a few miles away in conditions so terrible that their windowless apartments were infested by rats.

Silent for a moment, John suddenly announced, "I'm going to work and I'm going to take all the money I earn and buy windows for all those houses."

Despite their growing consciousness of the world outside their insular Fifth Avenue existence, Caroline and John lived undeniably privileged lives. There were skiing trips to Sun Valley, and weekend trips to their new ten-room farm in Bernardsville, New Jersey, which Jackie had bought in November 1965. The Murray McDonnells, who lived next door, had sixty-five grandchildren and six great-grandchildren, providing perfect camouflage whenever John and Caroline went out in public with them.

In December 1965, Jackie took the two children to Antigua, where they stayed with millionaire Paul Mellon and his wife, Bunny, at his luxurious Mill Reef Club estate. It seemed a perfect hideaway, overlooking the turquoise, coral-studded waters of the Caribbean. Yet despite the island's exclusivity, photographers still managed to find them. No matter how secluded the surroundings, the press inevitably managed to thwart Jackie's attempts to escape their prying eyes.

In the winter of 1965, Jackie discovered the joys of skiing and began a love affair with the sport that would play such a large part in John's and Caroline's childhood. Taking her first lesson in Aspen on December 27, during a holiday with Bobby and his family, she watched as Bobby taught John to ski on the gentle slopes of Ajax Mountain.

She was so enthralled with skiing that in January 1966 she took

Caroline and John to Gstaad for two weeks. They not only skied as much as possible, but also took private French lessons.

The European press was elated at having the Kennedys so close at hand, and day after day spun a multitude of tales involving America's former First Family: John and Caroline were leaving America and going into exile; they were moving to Switzerland forever; Jackie was afraid for her life ... and so on.

Enthusiastic photographers barged around the slopes, clicking away incessantly. At one point, as Jackie was trying to show her daughter how to hold her poles properly, two photographers began fighting each other for position and wound up bumping into Caroline, who fell into the snow. Jackie was incensed.

"My daughter gets knocked down by a charge of photographers when I take her out to try to teach her to ski," she said bitterly. "How do you explain that to a child?"

She was still consumed by memories of the assassination when her cousin John Davis saw her in New York in March 1966. They met at the New York apartment of his mother, Maud Bouvier Davis. Jackie's manner verged on paranoia. Wrapping herself protectively in her coat, she had the air of a hunted animal. Struck by her fear and vulnerability, Davis escorted her into the lobby, but even as she walked with him through the guarded vestibule Jackie seemed terrorized. Years later at the funeral of her Aunt Edith, she tried to explain the trauma of a bullet from nowhere killing your spouse, and the dread that another one may come for your children.

"There are some things you never get over," she said finally.

At Easter 1966, Jackie took John and Caroline to Córdoba, Argentina, where they were guests on the cattle ranch of Argentinean foreign minister Miguel A. Carcano. Jackie had been there with Jack and had enjoyed the rugged isolation. Still, reports of their vacation leaked out from the ranch. When John tried skinny-dipping in a small stream, headlines proclaimed, "JFK Jr. Takes Dip in the Nude."

Hyannis Port, however, remained a relative sanctuary from the press. No advance reports leaked out of a surprise Jackie and the Kennedy clan had spent months planning for John. He was only five and a half, but still absolutely in love with any machine that flew.

When they had lived in the White House, John's father had catered to his son's passion for aircraft. On the rare occasions when he couldn't take John with him on his flights to Andrews Air Force Base, he explained to the boy, "You can't go with me this time, John, but here's a play airplane for you until I get back." Then he would present John with a tiny plastic plane. He had purchased a large supply for just that purpose.

The ritual was repeated regularly in Hyannis Port, especially during the summer weekends when the children stayed and Jack went back to Washington.

One day as he prepared to leave, Jack bent over.

"You fly this one, son," he whispered. "And as soon as you grow up, Daddy's going to buy you a real one."

John looked at him solemnly, his eyes large and round. "Promise, Daddy, when I grow up. Promise?"

Jack squeezed him tight, and buried his face in his hair. "I promise. Someday I'll get you a real plane."

John would run toward Rita Dallas, Joe Kennedy's nurse.

"My Daddy's going to get me a real one when I grow up."

Then he ran to everyone with the news, tugging at each of them, waving his toy plane, and repeating his father's promise.

Jackie, who had vowed to keep Jack's promise, secretly arranged for John's very own plane to be delivered to the compound on May 27, 1966. Gordon Donald, Sr., president of Shore Air Services, Inc., was sworn to secrecy as he and his mechanics reconditioned a World War II Piper Cub observation plane.

"Not even the mechanics who worked on the plane were told of its destination," remembered Donald, twenty-seven years later. "The plane was completely rebuilt, recovered, and repainted. The entire process was extremely expensive, but we knew it didn't matter because it was a surprise for young John and that was all that counted."

Jackie was now thirty-six years old. When she went to Madrid in the early summer of 1966, rumors flared in the gossip columns about a love affair with Spain's ambassador to the Vatican, sixty-two-year-old widower Antonio Garrigues, but there was no evidence.

She knew that the public was watching avidly, hungry for a sign that the President's widow had found romance again. And she knew that the Kennedy clan, aware of her political value, were set on her remaining single and forever retaining her status as America's icon. Her relationships with Jack's sisters, Eunice, Jean, and Pat, remained cool and distant, unchanged from the early years when Jack had first brought her to Hyannis as a young bride and they had mocked her poise and she their coarseness.

Still, despite the enmity that simmered beneath the surface, Jackie hadn't clashed directly with the sisters, at least until June 1966.

Peter Lawford was having a party at his house in Santa Monica when he received a phone call from Jackie.

"Peter, the children and I are going to Hawaii from San Francisco, and I'd like you to come along."

"That sounds wonderful," Peter said without a moment's hesitation.

In quick succession, Peter gathered up his children, Christopher, Sydney, and Victoria, contacted his friend John Spierling, and called his personal pilot, Hal Connors, to arrange the travel plans. Connors arrived in short order, landing his helicopter on Peter's lawn, and the group was off to the airport for the rendezvous in San Francisco.

Once in Hawaii, Jackie and the children stayed at a $3,000-a-month, three-bedroom Japanese-style beachfront house in

Kahala owned by Republican senator Peter Dominick of Colorado. Peter Lawford stayed at the Hideaway Cottage in the Kahala Hilton.

They spent part of every day together, and for the first time in years Jackie seemed to soften and relax. They even managed to slip away from the children one afternoon to have a picnic on the beach. They made a handsome couple. Peter could throw on a simple sweater and look dashing, and Jackie had the same eye for style.

Jackie had always been attracted to Peter, and he thought the world of her. Each in their own way was a rebel, doing exactly as they pleased, especially when it came to the Kennedys. Peter's first language was French, which he and Jackie loved to speak when together. Of course, this infuriated the rest of the clan, who could barely speak at a high school level. Jackie loved to write, and Peter composed wonderful poetry.

But best of all, Peter could always make Jackie laugh with his imitations of other Hollywood stars as the two sat on the beach watching the children play together. To anyone casually passing by, they must have appeared to be a pair of fond parents, happy to spend time together with the kids.

He threw a party in her honor at the Kahala Hilton for having suggested the vacation, and she returned the compliment by spending the entire evening dancing with him.

"Jackie, you are very fey and you live in a tree," Peter said. "But it's your own tree."

The idyll was splintered by Patricia Lawford's explosion when she discovered the truth and called Peter at the Hideaway.

"I won't put up with this!" she screamed. "How dare you go away with that woman!"

"Pat, we've got the children with us," Peter said calmly.

"That's supposed to make it all right?"

"Pat—"

"How could you go to Hawaii with her? That's where we went on *our* honeymoon!"

Her vitriolic outburst, whether or not justified, was not unforeseen. Peter and Patricia Kennedy Lawford had just divorced after twelve years of marriage, and Pat was bitter and depressed. She had always been Daddy's girl, adored by Joe Kennedy, who once sent her a letter that read in part, "My Darling, I don't know how you manage to stay so beautiful staying up so late, drinking so much Scotch and smoking so many cigarettes. But whatever you are doing, keep on doing it!"

Her marriage to Peter in 1954 hadn't pleased Joe one iota; he had grumbled, "I don't like the British. I don't like actors. And I don't like men who wear red socks."

Peter loved to say in later years, "The only thing I gave up was the red socks."

But although his wedding to Patricia at the Church of St. Thomas More in New York was gilded by the presence of such luminaries as Greer Garson and Marion Davies, their wedding song—"No Other Love"—proved less than prophetic.

Goaded by his great friend Frank Sinatra, whom Peter characterized as "the lovable land mine—something no sturdy American household should be without," Peter was shamelessly unfaithful to Patricia during their marriage. He developed a strong friendship with his brother-in-law Jack Kennedy ("the brother I never had," as Peter described him) and introduced him to Marilyn Monroe.

"She knew all about his involvement in the Marilyn affair," said Patricia Seaton Lawford. Peter's last wife, who lived with him for ten years, knew his secrets and had access to clandestine notes he made about his life. "But Peter told me that Jackie never mentioned the subject to him. As a womanizer himself, he admired Jackie for the way in which she handled Jack's indiscretions."

Now, because of this vacation, the idea of turning the tables on the rapacious Kennedys tickled them immensely. Patricia Seaton Lawford elaborated, "I only know that Patricia Kennedy was livid that they were there together. And I do think that they had a flirtation. Jackie definitely was sexually attracted to Peter."

Regardless, the hysterical telephone calls from Pat continued, until an incident involving John brought them all back to earth.

During a visit to Laurence Rockefeller's Mauna Koa Beach Hotel Resort on Hawaii Island, John tripped and fell into the smoldering coals of a fire that had been built for a wiener roast. Secret Service agent John Walsh grabbed the screaming child and pulled him out of danger.

Distraught, Jackie rushed him to the nearest doctor, Keith Nesting, in Hilo. After examining the crying child, Nesting confirmed that he had suffered first- and second-degree burns on his right arm and hand. John was quickly flown from Hilo to the home of multimillionaire industrialist Henry J. Kaiser, where plastic surgeon Eldon R. Dykes got ready to operate.

"He doesn't appear to be seriously hurt," Dykes told Jackie. "He was burned on his lower right arm and his backside, but these burns were mild."

The news of John's accident spread through the island, and a group of reporters gathered outside the Kaiser home. Some of them, caught up in the drama, swore they could hear John's screams as Dykes sedated and then operated on him.

After the accident, Jackie praised Walsh for his quick thinking and rescue of John, recommending him for a government citation. The family's Secret Service protection had been extended once already and was now due to end. But after noting that the family were still being pestered every day and might be in some danger, the House Judiciary Committee approved a bill continuing Secret Service protection for the Kennedy family until 1969; the protection was extended again until John's sixteenth birthday in 1976.

John's accident, coupled with Pat's continuing harassment, cast a pall over the vacation, and Peter cut short his stay. On his return, he discovered the price of their dalliance. When Peter's pilot flew back to Santa Monica, he was arrested for landing his helicopter on the Lawford lawn. Up to that point, he had always done so.

"But why am I being arrested?" Hal Connors asked.

"Because," said the officer. "Lawford isn't a Kennedy anymore."

Long after the Hawaiian vacation, Patricia Kennedy continued to be violently jealous of Jackie, exhibiting an obsession that Jackie did nothing to alleviate. During the 1983 wedding reception of Peter's daughter Sydney Lawford at Hyannis Port, Jackie switched place cards so that she would be sitting next to Peter.

"Pat was furious," says Patricia Seaton Lawford, who witnessed the event. "But Jackie stuck by Peter's side the entire evening, having a great time with him. They were the outcasts of the family and they both loved it."

Patricia Kennedy's jealousy never subsided. An acquaintance during the 1980s, journalist Richard Zoerink, confirmed the rift. "There are two things I was told never to mention around Pat," he said. "The assassination and Jacqueline Kennedy Onassis."

Jackie, John, and Caroline flew back to New York on July 26, 1966, and, although John still felt sore, the only evidence of his injuries was his right hand, which was encased in a white glove.

His high spirits had not been dampened by his Hawaiian escapade. Just four days later, at the wedding of his aunt, Jackie's half sister, Janet Jennings Auchincloss, to Lewis P. Rutherfurd, John was more boisterous and unruly than ever. The wedding was held at St. Mary's Roman Catholic Church in Newport. Jackie, who had been married there herself, found the occasion laced with poignant memories.

Two thousand spectators jostled one another outside the church, fighting for the chance to see Jackie, John, and Caroline. Hundreds of spectators climbed trees and telephone poles and clambered onto rooftops, hoping to see the former First Family, some waiting five hours for the opportunity.

Jackie arrived first, dressed in a yellow coat, and five hundred frenzied fans surged forward, trying to touch her. Smiling stiffly, she stood back while Secret Service men cleared a path for her into the church. John and Caroline were both in the thirty-one-member bridal party; Caroline as a flower girl and John, outfitted in full Little Lord Fauntleroy regalia, as a page.

He was uncomfortable enough wearing a white silk shirt with a ruffled front, a blue satin cummerbund, and white silk shorts, so when a spiteful onlooker yelled, "Sissy!" in his direction, it was obviously the last straw. Scowling, John stopped dead in his tracks and shook his fist at the offender. At that moment, a resourceful Secret Service agent whisked him into the church and out of harm's way, though the insult rankled John all afternoon.

Finally, at the wedding reception at Hammersmith Farm, he let off steam by pulling out his silk shirt and fighting with another page who had irritated him, rolling around in the mud until his wedding outfit was covered with dark stains.

"John was not being bratty," said his half uncle, Jamie Auchincloss. "It was just that he didn't like wearing pale blue silk and satin and having his hair combed all the time. He liked to clown around in a nice way."

Another relative pointedly disagreed and, surveying John's wild behavior at the reception, sniffed disapprovingly, "That boy travels ninety miles an hour, at right angles to everyone else."

One of John's favorite expressions had become "Watch me!" as he dashed off in a thousand directions. The day after the wedding, he made himself known even to the patrons of the exclusive Bailey's Beach club, where he yelled, "Watch out!" before throwing handfuls of sand

at bathers, crowing "Wham!" when his missiles hit their intended targets.

"The poor boy badly needs a father," commented an onlooker.
Few realized how soon his mother would supply one.

CHAPTER SIX

The Extravagant Greek

On December 28, 1966, a Gallup poll reported that Jackie Kennedy had been named by the American people for the fifth straight year as the most admired woman in the world. All through 1967, the press breathlessly cataloged her travels, as if recording the procession of some celestial princess and her angelic offspring.

During a March 1967 stay in Lee's Acapulco villa, Jackie attempted to elude the press. John proved to be a staunch ally in her battle for privacy by firing a water pistol straight into the face of an intrusive photographer. But journalists following Jackie believed she had finally come to terms with her high profile and was even beginning to enjoy it.

"Jackie really loved publicity," said *Women's Wear Daily* reporter

Agnes Ash, who covered one of Jackie's other trips to Mexico. "She thrives on publicity and really loves to play peek-a-boo. She knows how to pretend graciously that she doesn't enjoy all the attention, but in Mexico it was clear to me that she did. If she had wanted to sneak away from us, it wouldn't have been too difficult. Instead, we kept getting mysterious tips about where she was going to be each day. And I had the feeling that Jackie somehow had engineered those tips."

Despite his mock attack on the photographer, John basked in the attention, chatting freely and easily with anyone who crossed his path. Ruefully, Jackie admitted, "John makes friends with everybody. Immediately."

He enchanted his Irish Kennedy relatives when, in June 1967, he visited them in Duganstown, County Wexford. The visit was the first Jackie and the children had ever made to Ireland. On their arrival at Shannon Airport Jackie was filled with emotion.

"I am so happy to be here in this land my husband loved so much," she said. "For myself and the children it is a little bit like coming home, and we are looking forward to it dearly."

They stayed in Ireland for a month, residing at Woodstown House, a fifty-three-room mansion their New Jersey neighbors the McDonnells had rented for them. But although eight of the McDonnell children accompanied them on the trip, partly in the hope that John and Caroline would be lost among them, their presence did nothing to discourage the press.

They had a short spell of privacy during a bus ride to Waterford, during which John entertained the passengers by bursting into a medley of Irish ditties, including "Sweet Rosie O'Grady" and "When Irish Eyes Are Smiling."

"He has a grand voice and he knew all the names," said the driver, who uncannily bore the name John F. Kennedy.

When they finally arrived at their destination, the delighted Mr. Kennedy taught John how to write his name in Gaelic. John skipped off contentedly reciting "Sean O Cinneide," his Gaelic name, over and over.

The bus interlude was a rare private episode. More than fifty reporters and photographers followed the children when they went swimming in Waterford. The balconies of Dublin were packed with spectators waving at them frenetically, and passersby applauded when they encountered Jackie and the children riding on Woodstown beach.

The Kennedys made the front pages in Ireland every day during their stay. Every detail of their trip was deemed newsworthy to the avid Irish public, including one of John's bouts of stubbornness, much to Jackie's chagrin. He had refused to swim with Caroline at Waterford and had instead insisted on going into a candy store.

"What did you want, dear?" the shopkeeper asked.

"I want everything."

"Now John," she said, "you know you can't have everything."

"I can too!" John shouted, before Jackie pulled him out of the store.

Back in America, rumors were rampant that John was about to have a new stepfather. Lady Harlech, wife of the British ambassador to Washington, the former David Ormsby-Gore, had died in a tragic car accident in May 1967. Jackie and the former ambassador were seen together often. Lord Harlech seemed the perfect candidate to marry the former First Lady.

She visited him briefly soon after his wife's death, and he returned the courtesy in Hyannis Port during the fall of 1967. John took quickly to the tall British aristocrat, calling him David. He dragged Harlech to see his collection of scrimshaw and begged the august peer to take him to the beach.

Jackie and Harlech traveled to Cambodia in November, but their trip was primarily political—conceived by Secretary of Defense Robert McNamara, who believed Jackie's presence could help reverse Cambodian anti-Americanism; the trip was sponsored by the State Department. It was clear by now that Lord Harlech would never become John's stepfather. But he and Jackie remained friends, and when he died on January 26, 1985, she went to Wales for his funeral.

Jackie was young and beautiful and America wished her well, waiting breathlessly for her to find love and happiness. Rumors continued to swirl: she was in love with Roswell Gilpatric, who had been deputy secretary of defense during Jack's presidency; she was besotted with her financial adviser, André Meyer; she was enthralled by Adlai Stevenson, and so on. Privately, Jackie was most distraught about the gossip linking her with her brother-in-law Bobby Kennedy. Ethel had always despised Jackie, and this just added fuel to the fire.

"To this day, Ethel avoids talking to Jackie or going near her at any public events," said Patricia Seaton Lawford. "Instead, Ethel and the sisters sit in a group and clack away. Peter used to say that—for the sisters—when Jack married Jackie it was as if Audrey Hepburn had married into the family and they were forced to compete with her. Next to Jackie, Ethel and the other sisters looked like klutzes."

Bobby was in the race for President now, and Jackie supported his bid completely. On April 11, 1968, for the first time since December 1963, she brought the children down to Palm Beach, where they all stayed with her friends Jayne and Charles Wrightsman.

After church on Sunday, April 14, 1968, she took the children to visit Joe Kennedy, and then the children joined in an Easter-egg hunt with their cousins.

Later that day, there was a large family gathering during which Bobby read aloud the latest polls charting his chances in the upcoming presidential race. When he had finished, his face broke into a large grin and the family cheered and began shouting, "We are going to make it!" The atmosphere was infectiously optimistic and, for a moment, brought back the Camelot days.

"Won't it be wonderful when we get back into the White House?" Jackie called out jubilantly.

"What do you mean 'we'?" said Ethel Kennedy.

The remark lashed Jackie like a bullwhip, and she immediately withdrew into herself.

"Jacqueline Kennedy looked as if she'd been struck," said Joe Kennedy's nurse, Rita Dallas. "She flinched as though a blow had actually stung her cheek. I'll always remember the look of pain in Jackie's eyes."

Aristotle Onassis was waiting in the wings to assuage Jackie's pain. They had known each other since 1957, when Onassis had invited the young senator from Massachusetts and his stylish wife to a cocktail party in honor of Sir Winston Churchill on his yacht *Christina*. Intrigued by Jackie, Onassis had later observed, "She's got a carnal soul," and made a mental note of her simmering sexuality, charm, and self-confidence in the ostentatious setting in which he received her.

Jackie had always been drawn by money and by powerful older men. From the beginning, Onassis won all prizes as the wealthiest and the most powerful man in her orbit—indeed, in the world. Twenty-nine years Jackie's senior, born in Smyrna, the son of a Greek tobacco merchant, Ari fled to Greece after the Turks captured Smyrna. From there he went to Argentina at the age of sixteen with $100. His checkered career took him from extreme poverty to the ownership of a merchant fleet larger than those of most countries and an accumulated fortune of $500 million.

He was a ruthless deal maker, a relentless social climber (he numbered Greta Garbo, Eva Perón, Elizabeth Taylor, and Richard Burton among his close friends), and a womanizer who had married Tina Livanos, the daughter of his archrival Stavros Livanos. He then discarded her for a passionate affair with legendary opera star Maria

Callas. He was a pirate and a gangster, a man who feared no other man and who lived life by his own rules.

"He was a peasant," remembered Zsa Zsa Gabor after observing Ari with Maria at Maxim's.

Undoubtedly the chic-est restaurant in the world, Maxim's has an unspoken dress code. The women usually wear dazzling jewels and the men behave like princes—no doubt because many of them *are* princes.

Ari and Maria entered the restaurant and followed the maître d' to their table, unaware that everyone in the room had stopped to watch their progress. True, they were both famous, though for different reasons. But the whispers that accompanied their arrival had nothing to do with their celebrity.

Maria, an internationally renowned diva, on the arm of one of the wealthiest men in the world, was wearing a babushka.

Acting as if there were no one around, they sat without speaking a word. The more appropriately dressed patrons went back to their caviar and Cristal champagne, but glanced over again when Ari ordered a large tureen of chicken soup. When the waiter brought it to their table, Ari and Maria reached in and began greedily pulling pieces of chicken out of the soup. The stock dripped off their hands as they devoured piece after piece with perfect picnic manners.

Shocked by their unconscious display, the other patrons returned quickly to their more genteel fare, while Zsa Zsa applauded.

"I loved Maria for that and I loved Onassis," she said. "He was a peasant and he ate like a pig, but I loved him for it."

"He could be the cheapest man in the world," said Iranian-born oil heiress Lilly Fallah Lawrence, whose father was one of Ari's oldest friends. "Instead of ordering a bottle of wine, he would order a glass. Yet while everyone thought of Ari as a peasant, he was multifaceted. He could discuss literature, history, arts and, of course, his great passion for the sea. People thought his relationship with Churchill was about his power, when it really wasn't. He cared about Churchill because Winston was Sea Lord of the Admiralty and Ari just loved the sea."

Jackie, too, loved the drama of the sea, the privacy and the adventure. So did her sister, Lee. At twenty-nine, Lee possessed a sexual charisma that was uniquely different from Jackie's more elegant appeal. She was more earthy, less ethereal. Their mother often told the story of trying to teach Lee to tell the truth as a child. She illustrated her point by telling the story of George Washington and the cherry tree. Lee thought for a moment and then ingenuously piped up, "Couldn't he have waited until the morning and told his father then when he wasn't so mad?"

Lee was an aspiring actress, but try as she might she succeeded neither in her fledgling theatrical career nor in her attempt to become Mrs. Aristotle Onassis. Her failure in acting could be attributed to her lack of talent, her failure in capturing Ari to a fatal lack of judgment. After the 1963 death of baby Patrick Kennedy, as a way of distracting Jackie from her grief and perhaps also as a means of ingratiating herself further with Ari, she convinced Jackie to accompany her and other guests on a cruise on the *Christina* around the Mediterranean.

Before Jackie left, Bobby expressed his concerns over Ari's sometimes shady business dealings. "This business with Lee and Onassis, just tell her to cool it, will you?"

Bobby needn't have worried. As soon as the *Christina* set sail from Piraeus, Onassis himself seemed anxious to cool things with Lee. Meanwhile, he did all in his considerable power to beguile Jackie, charming her with tales of his deprived youth and, on the last night of the cruise, presenting her with a magnificent diamond and ruby necklace.

The irony was inescapable, and Lee was acutely aware of the degree to which she had been supplanted in Ari's affections by her sister.

"All I've got is three dinky little bracelets that Caroline wouldn't even wear to her own birthday party," Lee said.

Yet when Jack was assassinated, it was to Ari that Lee turned to accompany her and her husband to America for the funeral. There Onassis had been one of the few dignitaries invited to stay in the White House. That evening, over dinner with Secretary of Defense Robert McNamara, Bobby Kennedy, Dave Powers, and William Manchester, Ari had boasted of his grandeur, his yacht, his wealth, his famous friends, expounding his simple philosophy: "I have never made the mistake of thinking it is a sin to make money."

Once the glare of publicity after the death of the President had faded slightly, Jackie and Ari had begun a clandestine relationship. She had visited him at his Avenue Foch apartment in Paris; he called on her at 1040 Fifth Avenue. Their meetings had remained a secret, although now and again they risked dinners with friends like Rudolf Nureyev in the more fashionable New York restaurants, such as 21.

The public never guessed that the regal former First Lady and the Greek tycoon had developed a strange understanding with one another. In May 1968, after the visit to Hyannis Port when Ethel had lashed out at her, Jackie—conscious of how much her actions would incense the Kennedy clan—defiantly cruised the Caribbean with Ari on *Christina*, visiting St. Thomas in the Virgin Islands. It was eminently clear to all around them that marriage was imminent.

She told Bobby of her plans to marry Onassis, and he reacted sharply.

"If you do," he said, "you'll ruin my future and tarnish Jack's image forever. Onassis is a lout."

Jackie didn't say a word for a moment; then she said, "I promise that I will wait until after the election."

Her agreement to wait to marry Aristotle Onassis became moot on June 6, 1968, the day Bobby Kennedy was killed in the Ambassador Hotel in Los Angeles by Sirhan Sirhan.

"I hate this country," Jackie cried. "I despise America and I don't want my children to live here anymore. If they're killing Kennedys, my kids are number one targets."

Persistent myths have it that Jackie only decided to marry Aristotle Onassis and to sever her ties with the Kennedy family after Bobby's death, at that moment making her decision to leave America forever. But she had merely been biding her time before wedding her destiny to that of Onassis.

While the country mourned the loss of the Knight of Camelot, Jackie mourned, too, mourned the brother-in-law she had loved and lost. Simultaneously, she found herself free to marry Aristotle Onassis.

The decision did not simply involve Ari's wealth. With the death of Bobby, John had lost another father figure. The man who would become his stepfather and the primary male influence over his life during the next seven years was as different from Bobby Kennedy as the Aegean Sea from the Potomac.

When his mother married Onassis, John wouldn't merely gain a stepfather; he would also gain a stepbrother and stepsister. Alexander, twenty-one, and Christina, nineteen, were Ari's children by his first wife. The Onassis children were alternately spoiled and neglected.

"Ari was typically Greek," observed his personal secretary, Lynn Alpha Smith. "He was an old-fashioned seaman who believed that the raising of children should be left to the woman."

Onassis's world, into which John Kennedy, Jr., was about to be transported, was an exotic universe consisting of a villa in Monte Carlo, a penthouse in Paris, a hacienda in Montevideo, Uruguay, and a mansion outside Athens. But the crowning glory of his empire was the yacht *Christina*, a floating poem to the exotic, which the flamboyant King Farouk of Egypt had once dubbed "the last word in opulence."

Ari had lavished $4 million on the 322-foot Canadian frigate, which he had bought for only $50,000. It was outfitted with nine luxury suites, faucets of Sienna marble and gold in the bathrooms, and a swimming pool that could with the flick of a switch be dramatically transformed into a dance floor. The crew of sixty included two hairdressers, three chefs, a team of waiters (schooled in the fine art of serving caviar correctly), a small orchestra (able to switch from the Greek tunes Onassis favored to the Broadway shows his guests loved), and a Swedish masseuse ready and willing to dispense all manner of pleasures.

The White House had once been John's personal playground, but its splendor was surpassed by the decadence of the Onassis universe. Onassis not only owned the *Christina,* but also a private Greek island called Skorpios, and the Greek national airline, Olympic Airways.

In the summer of 1968, Ari spent as much time as possible with Jackie and the children in Hyannis Port and at Hammersmith Farm. He was still involved with Maria Callas, but he devoted many hours to Caroline and John, walking on the beach and swimming with them and telling them that although their mother needed someone to take care of her and he was going to marry her, he would never try to replace their father.

Ari's touch with John was sure. "He filled a great void in his life," said Jackie's cousin John Davis. "He liked to play with children, to take John to baseball games and to go fishing with him, and I think John enjoyed the male companionship."

"Ari wanted to gain points with Jackie by paying attention to her children," said Lynn Alpha Smith. "Ari didn't love Jackie, but he was determined to have her. To him, marrying Jackie was like buying the largest ship in existence. He always had to have the biggest and the best. He paid three million to Jackie so that he could marry her."

When Onassis was working out the prenuptial agreement with Jackie, according to Lynn Alpha Smith, he commented, "If I paid any more this would cease to be a marriage and become an acquisition."

But it was an acquisition from the start. Ari primarily married Jackie because he wanted to thumb his nose at the U.S. officials who used to call him "The Little Turk."

"He clinched the deal because, although he wasn't in the least bit handsome, he could be extremely charming," said Lynn Alpha Smith. "As for his interactions with the children, Ari was a consummate actor."

He could simulate emotions at will. Once, Ari was in the midst of negotiating a deal with Boeing for six new planes. Suddenly he discovered that someone was getting a secret commission on the deal behind his back. He started screaming and jumping up and down. His face turned livid with rage. Then, right in the middle of the rampage, he stopped and walked out of the room and into his secretary's office. The purple drained out of his face and his complexion went back to normal.

"Lynn, I'm very thirsty; would you get me a drink of water, please?"

She did.

"Thank you," he said calmly, then drank the water. As he strode back into the meeting room, his color rose and his voice hit the identical note as before. In the midst of the second screaming bout, he turned around and winked at Smith.

Before Ari's visit to Hyannis Port, Jackie dispatched him to see Rose Kennedy, who was then in New York. If anyone could match the golden Greek, it was this New England dowager.

"Rose thought Onassis was charming, but badly dressed," said Rose's secretary, Barbara Gibson. "He presented her with a gold bracelet studded in red and white stones. Rose thanked him politely and assumed the bracelet was a trinket, just a piece of costume jewelry. Later she discovered that the diamonds and rubies were real!"

Whatever her true motives for marrying him, Jackie and Ari gave the impression of being very much in love. During their time in Hyannis, neighbor Larry Newman saw them together walking arm in arm up the hill near the compound.

"I think she was very much in love with him. You could really watch their romance developing," said Newman. "He had women at his feet and was very charming. And she really seemed in love with him."

The rest of the world, however, did not agree with Newman's assessment. On marrying Onassis, Jackie, once America's most pitied and adored widow, would quickly become as reviled as she had previously been admired. To some extent, she married Ari because Bobby's death had unhinged her and he provided a refuge and safety for her and the children. She was terrified at the thought of her children being kidnapped. Ari, with his private island and army of employees, could supply them with an undreamed-of degree of security.

"She once told me that she felt she could count on Onassis," said Roswell Kilpatric. "It was an attribute she looked for in all her friends. One of the things she is seeking for herself and her children is a private life—not being in the public eye all the time—and he can afford to give her that privacy and protection."

Even Lynn Alpha Smith, who observed at close hand the ravages that marriage to Jackie wrought on her beloved employer, made allowances for her.

"I used to dislike Jackie intensely, but over the years I have realized many things about her," said Smith. "Her personal assistant and friend Nancy Tuckerman told me, 'Jackie was almost half crazy when Jack was killed. But which woman wouldn't be after having had her husband's brains blown into her lap.' After that, everything which followed was understandable."

The Extravagant Greek

At 6 P.M. on October 17, 1968, Jackie, Caroline, and John, with the aid of Secret Service men, fought their way through a gauntlet of more than two hundred people gathered outside 1040 Fifth Avenue. The crowd was buzzing with rumors of the impending wedding, and when the family climbed into a limousine bound for Kennedy Airport, a chorus of disapproving shouts followed them. Jackie believed her marriage to Ari would bring her privacy, but now that the goddess had become mortal, the worshippers were angry and vengeful.

She became the target of jokes and vilification and so, by proxy, did John and Caroline. One joke that immediately went the rounds had John calling Ari "a frog"; when Ari asked him why, John replied, "Because my mother says when you croak we'll be really rich." Aside from the jokes, countless public figures felt compelled to make statements on the upcoming marriage. Gore Vidal, Jackie's relative, dubbed the match "highly suitable," and Maria Callas, emotionally shattered by the news, managed to rally and say, "Jackie did well to give a grandfather to her children."

Jackie's sister, Lee, who had been involved with Onassis and had once hoped for marriage to him herself, was more diplomatic. "Mr. Onassis is a man who will know how to give my sister the kind of life she needs."

In a prewedding display of power, Ari had ninety people bounced from an Olympic Airways flight so that Jackie, the children, and the wedding party—consisting of Janet and Hugh Auchincloss, Patricia Kennedy, and Jean Smith—could fly to Andravida Airport, a military airfield some three hundred kilometers from Athens. From there, the group flew by helicopter to Skorpios, Ari's five-hundred-acre private island off the west coast of Greece.

Proud to receive his new bride and her family in his private realm, Ari demonstrated his power to protect Jackie by banning all chartering of small planes in the area. To top that, he had security guards and sixty employees on hand to combat the press. But all his efforts were in vain. Just before 11 A.M. on October 19, John, who had slept on board the *Christina* with Caroline, Jackie, and Ari, left the yacht for a ride along the shore in a white golf cart driven by one of the *Christina's* crew. Spying him, an army of thirty-six screaming photographers and reporters charged toward him. Terrified, John burst into tears, and the crewman took him back to the yacht and to safety.

He had been happy until then, playing on board the *Christina*, waving to photographers, and in general enjoying the adventure.

"They have to earn a living, too," Jackie explained as she dried his tears. She then went out on deck and, wearing her trademark dark glasses, white trousers, and a black sweater, reluctantly posed for the photographers. Despite her cooperation, some of them still attempted to board the *Christina*, and a scuffle broke out between a security guard and a photographer.

The madness continued for the next few days, as Skorpios was besieged by armies of photographers and reporters, all attempting to invade the island and immortalize the wedding.

The 5:15 P.M. candlelit ceremony in the tiny seventy-five-year-old Chapel of the Little Virgins was punctuated by rain. While most were enchanted as the jasmine rustled and bougainvillea trees trailed over the trellises at the gate, others were struck by the dark stares of Alexander and Christina Onassis, neither of whom favored the marriage.

Hugh Auchincloss, Jackie's stepfather, was uncomfortable, nervously lighting a cigarette outside the chapel just before the service began. His wife, Janet, looking at her grandchildren, later sadly observed, "It's been hard on them. Hard and confusing."

Caroline and John were familiar with the solemnity of the Catholic Church, but this Greek Orthodox ceremony had a pagan quality to it. Their mother, beautiful in ethereal beige chiffon designed for her by Valentino, and Ari looking more earthy in a blue suit and red tie, were crowned with a white beribboned wreath, like some Druid high priest and priestess. Instead of the majestic ceremonies they had witnessed at the White House, this Greek spectacle had taken on the aura of a circus. The sideshow included several reporters who tumbled off rooftops into the water and were fished out of the sea.

As reporters strained for a glimpse of the newlywed Jacqueline Kennedy Onassis and her diminutive husband leaving the chapel, Caroline looked distinctly glum, while John's eyes were downcast. He refused to be cheered up, even when Onassis presented him with his very own Accutron watch. John expressed his disdain and discomfort by trying to feed the watch to one of the cats that roamed the island.

Yet however disturbing their mother's marriage may have been to John and Caroline, any secret fears about radical changes in their everyday life would prove groundless. Jackie had made an agreement with Ari that she and the children would continue to live in New York for part of the year, so that their lives had every chance of continuing undisturbed.

CHAPTER SEVEN

Collegiate

As if to symbolize that they were still Kennedys even though their mother was now an Onassis, Caroline and John flew back to America on October 23 with their aunts Patricia Kennedy and Jean Kennedy Smith.

John, dressed in a tan topcoat, short pants, gray kneesocks, and brown shoes, skipped down the steps of the TWA plane, patently glad to be back in America and away from the wedding-related limelight.

His high spirits vanished with the prospect of starting at his new school. Before the wedding, Jackie had broken with tradition and passed up the more fashionable Buckley and St. Bernard's for Collegiate, a school with a high percentage of scholarship students recruited from the Boys Club of New York and the East Harlem Protestant Parish. The oldest school in Manhattan, Collegiate had been founded in 1628 by the Dutch West India Company and the Classis of Amsterdam, the parent ecclesiastical body of the Dutch Reformed Church for the colonists of New Amsterdam. The school's racial mix was conducive to instilling in its students the tolerance John's Uncle Bobby and his father would have wanted.

Of course, the sons of such notables as Leonard Bernstein, Edgar Bronfman, and Jason Robards also attended Collegiate. They, however, were not heirs to Camelot and thus did not attract the cadre of photographers and gawkers gathered around the schoolyard when Jackie Kennedy Onassis and the Secret Service agent Mugsy O'Leary escorted John up the steps.

One probing journalist approached a brown-eyed sixth-grader. "How would you like to help me get the story of John's first day at school?"

The student shook his head. "We're supposed to give him privacy. The teachers told us the Kennedys deserve a lot of privacy and not to ask John about his family. And to treat him like any other boy at Collegiate."

John, who had overheard the exchange, walked smiling through the doors with his mother. The halls were filled with white boys, black boys, Oriental boys. John was accustomed to meeting people and children from all over the world, and this new school was very cosmopolitan.

He soon joined eighteen other students in his homeroom. They sat at sturdy wooden desks while the teacher outlined the studies for the day: English, French, reading, spelling, and geography. Two boys began whispering behind him, and John heard one of them say, "John-John wears short shorts."

John waited until the break and approached one of his tormentors, who had a slight advantage in height.

"Do you know how to box?" John asked politely.

"Good enough to whip you, John-John."

Dropping his British-style manners, John drove his fist into his opponent's nose, hard enough to knock him backward. Stunned, the boy looked up from his prone position and decided not to continue the fight.

His Irish still up, John whirled as someone tapped him on the shoulder. He relaxed his fists when he saw the smile on the other boy's face.

"Nice punch," said Hans Hageman, a ten-year-old full scholarship student from Harlem. "Who taught you how to hit like that?"

"The Secret Service."

Hageman smiled. "Well, if you can learn to box, maybe you can learn to wrestle, too."

"I'd like that," John said. Several of the other boys had referred to Hageman as a promising wrestler and runner, and John had wanted to meet him.

John soon became fast friends with Hageman and with another black scholarship student, Geoffrey Worrell. He was regularly seen huddling with them during breaks.

After lunch in the gymnasium (roast beef, broccoli, mashed potatoes, and strawberry ice cream), the boys were taken to Central Park to play football, soccer, or baseball. Then John was whisked away home.

"I don't know why they are making such a fuss over that new boy," a student named Peter said when he greeted his mother. "He's only in the third grade!"

Soon John shed the short pants and demonstrated his athletic prowess. Sports were fast becoming an obsession for him. He idolized Babe Ruth (although he once said, "He's fat and he's dead") and made no bones about the fact that he liked football better than studying.

Where there are school sports, there are also mothers cheering their children on, and Jackie was no exception. After Field Day, when the parents chip in to help, Carol Rosenwald remembers seeing Jackie emerge with a run in the back of her sweater, her hair in a mess, and her fingernails filthy.

"She was involved in everything John did," Rosenwald says. "She was a wonderful parent."

John Mosler, Sr., whose son John was in the same class, points out that "Jackie attended every single Collegiate event and if Aristotle Onassis was in town, he came, too."

It was not uncommon for parents to approach Jackie after school events and say, "You know, my son is a good friend of John's, and we want to have him over to the house. Why don't you bring him and stay to tea?"

"Thank you very much," Jackie would reply graciously. "If I can, I certainly will."

Once accepted in the group on their terms, John became one of their own. They could be as protective of him as the Secret Service agents, sometimes helping him evade the official coverage that had started to irk him.

John would have loved to ride the big yellow Collegiate bus, which made various stops along Fifth Avenue every morning to pick up the school's Upper East Side residents. Instead he was ferried to school in a cream and tan Oldsmobile, after running the gauntlet of Kennedy watchers clustered outside the house.

"There he is, there's John-John!" They screamed, they waved, they shoved. John held fast to his dark brown leather briefcase (emblazoned with stickers from Gstaad and Athens) and kept his head down until he reached the car.

At first the two Secret Service men were unobtrusive, disappearing into the school's basement, where they played gin rummy, read the paper, or just fell asleep until four in the afternoon, when they escorted John home. They had always been his friends, stand-in fathers who trailed his every move. But at Collegiate, they began to interfere with his growing sense of self and independence.

Evading the men soon became a game for John, whose friends enjoyed helping trick the agents. Once, however, when the children all went off to the Museum of Natural History, the message to alert the agents of their departure quite innocently went undelivered. The bored agents, who had fallen asleep in the basement, awoke to find the school empty.

They raced to the museum and hurried through the exhibits looking for their charge. The other children, who by now knew the agents as well as John, would signal him in time to hide while the agents went past. When the game reached the point where the agents were boiling, John popped out from behind a pillar and smiled.

"Hi, guys. Have you seen the caveman exhibit?"

David Dobkin was a classmate of John's, and Marjorie Dobkin remembers her son's description of their bus rides. "The Secret Service agents followed behind them in a car," she says. "John and all the other kids would start rooting for the driver to lose the agents. They'd joke around, 'Come on, bus, get going there, let them get caught behind the next bus.'"

Jim Bailinson, a student in the class ahead of John, remembers, "It was always a game for us, trying to lose the Secret Service guys. But to John it was more serious. He just didn't like all the attention."

Whether he liked it or not, the presence of the Secret Service in John's life was still imperative. Five years after the assassination, the FBI was still investigating death threats against the former First Lady and her family. And during John's time at Collegiate, the school received numerous bomb threats, while his mother lived in constant fear of John's or Caroline's being kidnapped or harmed in some way.

Yet despite the hidden clouds that menaced his mother's new life, John remained a happy boy with an open, fun-loving nature.

"He had a good sense of humor," Marjorie Dobkin says. "He

and David enjoyed themselves at the expense of the Kennedy watchers—old ladies in hair curlers who often hung around the lobby waiting the whole day in the hope of seeing John.

"Funnily enough, they didn't really know what he looked like, and one of them crept up to my son—who looked a bit like John but is two years younger—and asked him if he was John F. Kennedy, Jr., David said, 'Sure I am.'"

Another time, one of the Kennedy watchers came up to John Jr. and asked if John Kennedy was around.

John said, "I don't see him anywhere at the moment."

"Well, then, what's he really like?" she asked.

John took a minute to think, then said, "He's a nice kid and really, really smart."

Growing up surrounded by servants, Secret Service men, and extended family meant that John's daily life was insulated from the intricacies of his mother's relationship with her new husband.

Jackie arrived in America from Greece on November 18 and, gathering the children up, spent the fifth anniversary of the assassination with them in New Jersey. She had passed the first month of her marriage to Ari redecorating as much of Skorpios and the *Christina* as the imagination of her cherished decorator Billy Baldwin could engineer.

Ari divorced himself from the entire proceedings and traveled to Athens, where he threw himself into business dealings that excited him more than did the former First Lady. Now that the deal was done, now that Jackie was his at last, the acquisition had begun to lose its luster.

"There was a basic conflict in that marriage from the very beginning," Lynn Alpha Smith says. "Ari suffered from insomnia, and he and I used to walk through the streets of Manhattan for hours together, while he just talked and talked. He never understood Jackie and she never understood him. He was a Greek—that says it all, really—a Greek seaman who'd be home for a short while, then go away all over the world, then expect his wife and children to be waiting for him at home whenever he got back. There was no way Jackie could give him that kind of continuity. Nor did she understand his world. She was Catholic, Anglo-Saxon. He was an Eastern Orthodox, Mediterranean, and Jackie just didn't understand. Maria Callas, though—she understood him completely. They were both survivors. Jackie is a survivor, too; like a cat, anywhere you throw her, she survives. But Maria was far earthier and that was what Ari craved."

He had never denied himself anything, yachts or tankers or women. As soon as Jackie left for New York and the children, Ari flew to Paris and Maria. At first she tortured him by refusing his phone calls and ignoring his flowers. Her resistance only fueled his passion, and although he failed to see her before he left Paris, bound for New York and Jackie, it was apparent that his formidable will was fixed on winning Maria back.

He arrived at JFK on an Olympic Airways flight at 6 P.M. on the evening of November 22. Having chosen to arrive on the anniversary of the assassination, he was not met at the airport by his wife. Instead, accompanied by somberly clad business associates, Onassis went straight to his suite at the Pierre Hotel at Fifth Avenue and Sixty-first Street, then dined with Christina and his sister at 21. He and Jackie had been married just one month.

It was patently clear that Jackie was not pining for the company of her new husband. But Ari did travel to see her and the children so that he could celebrate John's eighth birthday with them at the estate Jackie had rented in Peapack, New Jersey.

Set in the Somerset Hills amid 15,000 acres of fox-hunting country, hidden away in a village of only 1,950 residents, Jackie's gray clapboard house, named Windwood, was an ideal refuge for her and the children.

They spent most of their time in Peapack riding, walking in the woods, reading, or having dinner with their neighbors the McDonnells. It was clear from the start that Aristotle Onassis did not belong in Peapack. He was an inveterate walker, whether in Paris, London, Athens, or New York. As soon as he arrived in Peapack he went out for his evening stroll, only to be stopped by a patrolling policeman, suspicious of the sinister-looking elderly gentleman walking so late at night.

"May I see your identification?" the officer said.

"I am just taking a walk." Onassis, king of the sea, ruler of Skorpios, and owner of Olympic Airways, patted his jacket pocket, then smiled and spread his arms. "Besides, I do not normally carry identification."

"Why not?"

"I am Aristotle Onassis."

The policeman looked at Ari's plain slacks and sports jacket.

"Come along with me," he said, bundling the indignant billionaire into his police car. At the police station Ari telephoned Jackie, who dispatched a Secret Service agent to identify him.

Ari loved nightlife, from the sophistication of El Morocco to the lusty atmosphere of a Greek taverna, complete with plate smashing and frenzied bouzouki music. Tramping along muddy lanes, watching horses deposit their dung over green fields, and living the life of a country gentleman had no appeal whatsoever for him.

John, too, seemed ill at ease in fox-hunting country. Jackie persisted in ignoring his allergy to horses. Set on transforming him into the masterly rider his sister promised to be, she kept entering him in riding events. Earlier in the year he had injured himself in one such event, and at Peapack during the annual Essex Fox Hunt he narrowly escaped another spill when his horse stumbled and threw him forward in his saddle.

John called his stepfather "Mr. Onassis," not "Ari." There was never any expectation that John would call him "Daddy." No matter how valiantly the displaced Greek braved mud puddles to watch John and Caroline ride in horse shows, no matter how lavish his gifts to both of them, Ari remained an occasional interloper in their Manhattan existence with Jackie.

The patchwork family spent Christmas of 1968 on the *Christina*. Jackie's gift to Ari was a pen-and-ink sketch of the yacht (the kind of present Jack would have understood and appreciated); Ari gave Jackie a $300,000 pair of diamond earrings (which Jackie appreciated and understood).

Yet despite such largesse, he could be cheap, in the petty fashion at which only the truly wealthy excel.

"Ari made a point of always asking Jackie to write thank-you notes to friends or business acquaintances on special occasions," Lilly Fallah Lawrence remembers. "He knew what value other people placed on Jackie's notes, so he figured they would substitute as gifts and he wouldn't have to spend any money. And at airports, if he gave someone a tip, he used to fold two dollars in half so it would seem to onlookers that he was dispensing a great deal of money."

In the beginning, though, he enjoyed showering Jackie with gifts, playing Big Daddy to an adored daughter, gilding her with a $1-million 40.42-carat Cartier ring; a pair of sapphire, emerald, and ruby earrings; a silver filigree bracelet engraved with the letters J.I.L.Y. ("Jackie, I love you"); and an allowance of $1.5 million during the first twelve months of their marriage.

Occasionally he gave her compliments or showed tenderness—in a way that cost much less but was just as meaningful. She often flew to the island of Corfu to attend Mass at the Church of Saint Francis. As she knelt to receive the host, the priest reached for a special wafer. She opened her mouth to receive it, and saw that it had been engraved with her initials.

He was wildly generous to John and Caroline, over the years

buying John a speedboat, a jukebox, a space-age watch, and a Jeep so that he could speed around the streets of Skorpios under his own steam; Caroline received a sailboat and a horse. The saga of Caroline and the horse epitomizes Onassis's attitude to both children and the gifts he so readily bestowed upon them: Jackie complained to him that Caroline had fallen in love with a particular horse and longed to own it. Ari cut her off in midsentence.

"Buy the horse's mother and sisters and brothers. Don't worry about the expense—I'll pay the bill."

Jackie had always adhered strictly to her policy of not spoiling the children, but she abandoned her principles and allowed Ari to indulge them shamelessly. Perhaps this reflected the transactional nature of their relationship. He made it easy for her to relax her hitherto inflexible standards, simply because he wanted to spoil her children and would brook no resistance. His pride and his masculinity were somehow enmeshed in his desire to give Caroline and John everything; this was his way of relating to those close to him.

Lynn Alpha Smith was once the beneficiary of Ari's unstoppable generosity, albeit on a small scale. During her days as his secretary, he sent her out to buy him an expensive camera; on returning to the office, she handed him the change, $200 in cash. Looking up from the papers he was intently studying, he motioned her to put the money away.

"I want you to keep the change."

Shocked, Smith staunchly refused. He listened to her protestations for a minute or two. Then, his eyes flashing fire, he interrupted and, firmly but gently, said, "Lynn, don't deprive me of giving you a gift. You forget, two hundred dollars to me is like one dollar to you."

During school terms, John lived the life of the average upper-class Manhattan schoolboy. Vacations were an entirely different matter. He not only flew to Greece for Easter 1969, but also got to take his pet rabbit with him. As it turned out, the rabbit led indirectly to a rude awakening for Jackie. She had assumed that since her husband owned Olympic Airways, his wife's word would be law among his employees.

She knew very well that airline regulations dictated keeping animals in the baggage compartment, not inside the plane's cabin.

"The rabbit flies first-class," she declared. "John will not be parted from the rabbit."

The captain of the plane categorically refused to let the rabbit share John's seat, which stunned Jackie as much as it made her angry. Finally a compromise was achieved: the offending animal was permitted to travel to Athens seated in the cockpit with one of the crew members.

Rose joined them later. In theory, at least, she was pleased that Ari had invited her.

It was the measure of Ari's desire to make his new marriage work that he endured a visit from his wife's ex–mother-in-law. Rose was suitably grateful, later saying, "It's wonderful to me to have this pleasant relationship with Ari so I can visit my grandchildren quite comfortably without intruding."

The elements, however, conspired to make life aboard the *Christina* anything but comfortable. No sooner had the yacht set sail than the sea became horribly rough. Rose, shaky and nauseated, retired to her stateroom. When she emerged four days later, Ari solicitously inquired about her health. Then, as an afterthought, he added that he had checked on her during her sickness and had been glad to find her sleeping.

"Did you or did you not enter my stateroom without my knowledge?" she demanded.

"I ... I did," he confessed.

Without another word, Rose returned to her stateroom and locked the door.

Despite the presence of the rabbit, his grandmother, and the many other blandishments Ari supplied in his attempts to amuse his young stepson, John was not completely content on the high seas. Eleanor Lambert, legendary publicist and doyenne of the American fashion industry, remembers very well a weeklong cruise on the *Christina* with Ari, Jackie, John, and the Guinnesses. As John, who was around ten at the time, was the only child on board, every night after dinner Jackie asked the guests to play a game in the saloon he could participate in.

"John was very well-mannered," Lambert recalls. "And he never sulked. But he must have been bored stiff. He spent most of his time with the sailors, who played with him when they could. The after-dinner game was the highlight of his day, so Jackie made sure we never missed playing with him."

On this particular night the guests opted to play Spot. Ari, who never joined in the game, took a deck chair out by the rail, leaned back, and studied the stars, taking little interest in the proceedings inside the saloon. After a while his reverie was interrupted by John.

"Mommy won! Mommy won!"

"She did?"

"Ari never expected Jackie to win," Lambert says, "even though we were just playing a child's game. He just didn't understand how bright she is."

Sometimes Jackie's maternal instincts clashed with Ari's basic indifference to his stepchildren, and his explosive temper didn't help matters. John's perfect manners sometimes masked the reality that he was still a little boy with a little boy's passions and love of games.

One night Ari threw an elegant cocktail party on board the *Christina*. John wore his best suit and was expected to be on his best behavior as usual, impressing the adults. But on this particular evening he had a new toy gun and began firing rounds into the air, startling the assembled socialites, who laughed when Ari asked him to stop. John, full of high spirits, kept firing.

"Stop shooting—right now," Ari shouted.

John fired off another round.

Ari tore the gun from John's hand and flung it into the dark Mediterranean.

"Steward!" Ari called out. "Take the boy away and lock him in his cabin."

Before the steward could take a step toward her son, Jackie snatched up a valuable camera from Ari and sent it overboard after the gun. Then, white with rage, she turned on her heel and motioned for John to follow her. Together, mother and son walked out on the cocktail party.

Onassis, who allowed himself histrionic displays of emotion but had trouble reconciling such displays with his image of Jackie, swallowed his considerable pride and followed her, only to discover that Jackie had locked herself inside the stateroom with John. Deaf to her husband's threats and entreaties, she stayed there for the rest of the evening, eating chocolate, playing games, and reading books out loud.

Ari was volatile, but easily distracted by his many business interests. On his return from Athens, he showed renewed goodwill toward his unruly stepson. Neither Christina nor Alexander relished vacations in Skorpios and avoided the island as much as possible. Feeling rejected by his own children, Ari was sometimes momentarily diverted by John. He would sit with the boy at twilight, gaze out over the ocean that he appeared to command, and spin fantastic sagas of his whale hunting expeditions, while John listened in rapt attention.

Their love of the sea united stepfather and stepson to some degree. Onassis bought John a little red fishing boat, diplomatically naming it *Caroline*. Too busy to go fishing with the boy himself, he employed a local fisherman, Nikos Kominates, to take him out every day.

John wasn't the most accomplished of fishermen, but with Ari's tacit consent, Kominates hid some of his own catch on the boat.

Then, when they returned to Skorpios, he handed John the fish and the boy dashed up to Jackie and Ari waving his catch with pride.

Amused by his enthusiasm, Onassis joined in the fun, asking, "Well, what have you caught today, Poseidon?"

"All these fish!" replied John, brimming over with a sense of accomplishment. "When I grow up, can I be admiral of your fleet?"

John spent the summer of 1969 in Skorpios—relatively happy, to judge by photographs of him running along the island's dock. Ari had taken John water-skiing and, in an expansive mood, told him that they were now *filaracos*, the Greek equivalent of "buddies." Later that year, in October, he took John, Jackie, and Caroline to Shea Stadium to see the Mets play the Orioles in the third World Series game.

They arrived by limousine and took their place in the stands among 56,335 screaming fans. Ari understood soccer, the national game of Greece, but the intricacies and somewhat geometric nature of the American pastime were beyond him.

"What's the infield fly rule?" John asked.

"I don't know," Ari said.

"Why didn't the runner go to second?" John wanted to know in the next inning.

"I don't know," Ari said.

Having started out patiently trying to deflect John's questions, he quickly tired of playing this stepfather role.

"He made an attempt," an Onassis intimate said, "but in the end, Ari just didn't care enough."

Long before the game ended, Aristotle Onassis, one of the world's richest men, slipped quietly out of the stadium to drive back to Manhattan alone.

On November 18, 1969, Joseph Kennedy died at the age of eighty-one in Hyannis Port, the family seat where he had lived a virtual prisoner since his stroke eight years earlier. He was buried on November 20,

1969, in a grave marked simply "Kennedy" in Holyrood Cemetery, Brookline, not far from the house where his son John F. Kennedy had been born. He was buried on what would have been the forty-fourth birthday of Bobby Kennedy.

The simple funeral Mass was celebrated in the Church of St. Francis Xavier, just a few miles from the compound where Joe had lived for the past forty-one years. The white Mass (the family asked the participating clergy to wear white vestments) made a sharp contrast to the grandiose life he had lived and the once omnipotent family he had dominated. Only seventy mourners attended the service, including eighteen grandchildren, his surviving children and their spouses, and the widows of two of his dead sons, Ethel Kennedy and Jacqueline Kennedy Onassis, who attended without her husband.

Many of the grandchildren participated in the service as altar boys or honorary pallbearers, but it was John who stood by the altar and in a clear voice recited the Twenty-third Psalm in memory of the grandfather he had hardly known.

Most of the women, like Jackie, wore black lace mantillas. Only Rose, married to Joe Kennedy for fifty-five years, was fully veiled, also in black lace. And then there was Teddy, the last hope for family greatness, newly disgraced by the accident at Chappaquiddick, his voice faltering as he stood at the altar and read the words his brother Bobby had once written in tribute to the father who had sired them all:

"He has called on the best that was in us. There was no such thing as half-trying. Whether it was running a race or catching a football, competing in school—we were to try. And we were to try harder than anyone else. We might not be the best, and none of us were, but we were to make the effort to be the best. 'After you have done the best you can,' he used to say, 'the hell with it.'"

Two days later, on November 22, 1969, John was back at St. Francis Xavier, wearing a black cassock and a white surplice as he assisted the priest at Mass during the memorial services for his father. Jackie and Caroline watched proudly as he took the wine and the water to the altar and helped Monsignor Thomson light the candles. Two hundred fifty people attended the service, including Rose, Teddy, and Joan. Again, Aristotle Onassis was not present.

On December 7, 1969, John was back on Skorpios, with his mother, Caroline, and his eleven-year-old friend, Martin Luther King III. The young minister's son must have marveled as he boarded the *Christina*, with its pink marble bathrooms, exotic murals, and art collection that included paintings by Impressionists (who, according to Ari, "gave themselves that name because they wanted to make a big impression"), as well as a questionable El Greco and a series of other paintings that photographer Peter Beard, a guest on the yacht, described as "sort of what you'd see in a Greek restaurant."

The ambiance on board the *Christina* was not exactly conducive to the education of young children. The ultra rich invariably need artists to entertain them and pranksters to act the court jester, and so it was with Onassis. On one voyage, Ari amused himself by betting Peter Beard $2,000 that he couldn't stay under water for four minutes. Beard won the bet but in the process broke his ankle on Ari's trampoline.

Although Jackie had abandoned her strictest child-rearing standards, some of the lessons available on the *Christina* were not to her liking. She kept their December 1969 stay as brief as possible, whisking John and Caroline away from Skorpios to England's serene Berkshire hills, where they (minus Ari) spent Christmas with Lee and Stash in their Queen Anne mansion. Instead of spending their vacation amid bored glitterati celebrating on the high seas, John and Caroline walked in the English woods with their mother and aunt, searching for fir cones and holly.

Ari was expected, but his arrival was by no means guaranteed. Married to Jackie for only fourteen months, he showed little interest or involvement in her life. More and more he seemed to treat his wife like a tanker he had bought that had gone aground and would eventually be scrapped.

Instead of flying back to Skorpios with the children for the rest of the Christmas vacation, Jackie arranged for John and Caroline to spend the weekend of January 7, 1970, in her beloved Paris. Accompanied by two Secret Service agents and two bodyguards, they were met at the airport by Ari's chauffeur, who ferried them to the Onassis apartment on Avenue Foch in his navy blue Ford.

A nurse, whose name Jackie kept a closely guarded secret, accompanied the children all over Paris. John, as usual, was in high spirits.

"I'm going to the top of the Eiffel Tower," he announced. Only the first two levels were open, but John consoled himself by buying a toy model. Later he ate a pastry at a local patisserie and went to Mass at Notre Dame, where he and Caroline took Communion and fell in love with a canary at the Paris bird and flower market.

"Please, can I buy it?" John pleaded.

"No!" the nurse said.

"Oh, please?"

Finally she agreed and began asking the seller what the bird ate and how it could be brought into America.

"But won't he be bored all alone?" said John, who was soon the proud owner of not one but *two* canaries.

In the summer of 1970 they were back on Skorpios again, this time with their cousins Timothy and Maria Shriver. Jackie had flown there first, and when Caroline and John arrived on June 24, Ari met them in Athens, radiating energy as he bounded up the stairs of their Olympic jet to greet them before flying with them to Skorpios by seaplane.

The four children spent a happy summer on the island, sleeping on the *Christina* at night and during the day swimming, snorkeling, and fishing before joining the adults for dinner at Ari's house. His business dealings often made it seem as if he were merely a weekend guest at his own house, spending weekdays in Athens and flying to Skorpios on Fridays, much as JFK had commuted in the summer from the White House to Hyannis Port.

That summer on Skorpios was slavishly recorded by photographer Ron Galella, the New York paparazzo who was fast evolving into Jackie's nemesis.

Back in America, Ari made another attempt at family togetherness, joining the entire Kennedy clan at Hyannis Port for a three-day celebration of John's and Caroline's birthdays.

"I took Aristotle Onassis out on the *Marlin* with John and he was very, very charming," remembers a Kennedy family friend, Dick Gallagher. "When he bought John a small fishing boat, we went to the marina to buy some equipment. He and John seemed to enjoy each other."

A few weeks before her thirteenth birthday, Caroline was interviewed for an Associated Press article that ran in the Sunday edition of the *New York Times.* "I don't think of myself as famous," she said. "I'm not really bothered by too many reporters or photographers. It seems they're only around when I'm with my mother."

Asked about her life in general, she said, "Greece is very beautiful, I can't say which place I like better, Hyannis or Greece." Her face lit up when she talked of her pets, but a reporter gleaned most of his information from several of Caroline's friends, who described her as very reserved, often sad.

"I feel sorry for her," one friend said.

"I don't think I would like her life," said another. "Did you know she once brought her nurse along to a slumber party?"

Manhattan, Hyannis, and Skorpios were far removed from Washington, by many more factors than geography. But in February 1971, Jackie accepted an invitation from President Nixon to fly with

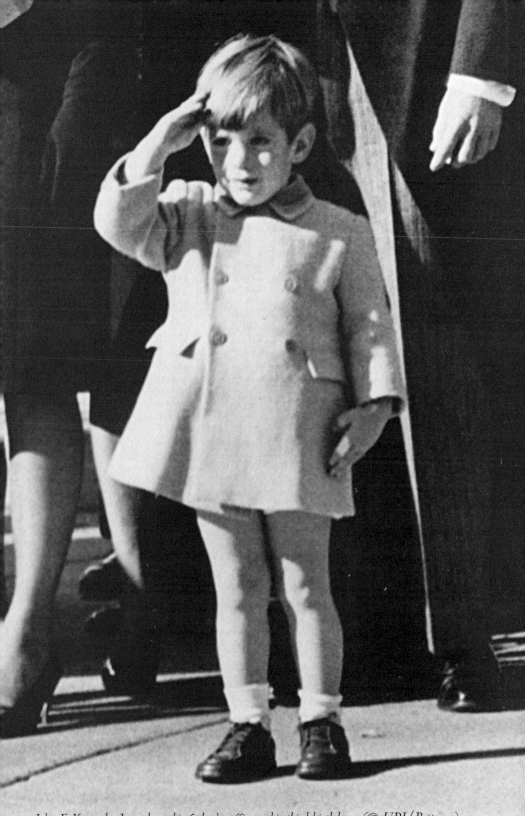

John F. Kennedy, Jr., salutes his father's coffin on his third birthday. (© UPI/Bettman)

ABOVE: Jacqueline Kennedy with her only son. (Courtesy of the John F. Kennedy Memorial Library) LEFT: The Kennedys return home with new baby, John. (Courtesy of the John F. Kennedy Memorial Library)

One of John Jr.'s favorite places to play in the White House was under his father's desk. (Courtesy of the John F. Kennedy Memorial Library)

ABOVE: *The Kennedy family at Palm Beach in April 1963. (Courtesy of the John F. Kennedy Memorial Library)* BELOW: *John and Caroline on the White House lawn with their nanny, Maud Shaw. (Courtesy of the John F. Kennedy Memorial Library)*

ABOVE: Young John takes the wheel of a speedboat over Labor Day, 1963. (Courtesy of the John F. Kennedy Memorial Library) BELOW: John as young engineer. (Courtesy of the John F. Kennedy Memorial Library)

ABOVE: The paparazzi pursue John, Jackie, and Caroline. (© Photofest) LEFT: Jackie takes John and Caroline on a skiing vacation at Baldy Mountain in Sun Valley, Idaho, in 1966. John is holding his new Samoyed puppy. (© Photofest)

ABOVE: Peter Lawford and Jackie arriving in Hawaii with their respective children. (Courtesy of Patricia Lawford Stewart, Peter Lawford Collection, Special Collections, Arizona State University Library) RIGHT: Shortly after marrying Aristotle Onassis, Jackie took part in the annual St. Bernard's Horse Show in Gladstone. She and John took second place in the family event. (© Photofest)

ABOVE: Jackie and Aristotle Onassis leaving the Plaza after lunch with John, in February 1969. (© Photofest) LEFT: John's photo in the Andover yearbook shows his comic side. OPPOSITE: John's 1983 graduation from Brown University. (© Russell C. Turiak)

ABOVE: Peter Lawford with Jackie and John, at Sydney Lawford's 1983 wedding in Hyannisport. (© Brian Quigley) LEFT: With former girlfriend, Sally Munro. (© Brian Quigley)

RIGHT: At a fund-raiser at the Kennedy Library. (© Brian Quigley) BELOW: With uncle, Senator Ted Kennedy, Caroline, and Jackie, announcing the Profile in Courage Award. (© Albert Ferreira/DMI)

ABOVE AND LEFT: "The Hunk" displays his athletic prowess. (© *Angie Coqueran*) *OPPOSITE: John at the beach.* (© *Brian Quigley*)

LEFT: Rollerblading throug *Manhattan. (© Angie Coqueran* *OPPOSITE: Commuting to wor* *as an Assistant District Attorney i* *Manhattan. (© Paul E. Adao)*

ABOVE: Arriving at Clinton's inauguration with Daryl Hannah. LEFT: Daryl and John in private moments. (© Angie Coqueran)

the children to Washington and visit the White House. Artist Aaron Shikler had spent nearly three years sketching Jackie and the children in the New York apartment. The result, the official White House portrait of Jackie, the President, and his children, was to be unveiled at a February 3 White House ceremony.

Jackie had a clear vision of the way the President should be portrayed in Shikler's work. "I don't want him done the way everybody does him," she said, "with that puffiness under the eyes and every shadow and crease magnified."

Shikler obliged, noting that Jackie had "a childlike, magical quality and at the same time an aspect of great force." He described John, who brought his pet guinea pig to a sitting, as "all boy—restless, impatient, all elbows and knees." He was, Shikler recalls, "monumentally bored with the whole business. The sooner he could get out of the room, the better. He hates to pose."

First Lady Patricia Nixon had originally invited Jackie and the children to the White House for the official viewing, but Jackie demurred. "As you know, the thought of returning to the White House is difficult for me. I really do not have the courage to go through an official ceremony and bring the children back to the only home they both knew with their father under such traumatic conditions. With the press and everything—things I try to avoid in their little lives—I know the experience would be hard on them and would not leave them with the memories of the White House I would like them to have."

Jackie finally agreed to make a low-profile visit to the White House, after first requesting that Mrs. Nixon not reveal to the staff that she and the children would be coming.

Once the arrangements had been made to her satisfaction, Jackie, John, and Caroline flew from La Guardia to Washington on *Air Force One*, courtesy of President Nixon. They returned to the White House on February 3, 1971, driving through the gates they had left seven years and two months earlier.

Julie Nixon, the President's daughter, who with her sister, Tricia, had been co-opted to take care of the children, had been nervous about John and Caroline's reaction to the portrait. Her fears proved groundless. "Caroline and John stood briefly in front of the portrait, told their mother they liked it, then turned expectantly to us, their eyes full of excitement, as if to ask what was next on the tour."

They viewed the portraits, then had an elaborate lunch with the four Nixons.

For all the grandeur of the meal and the warmth of the Nixons' welcome, the visit was a somber experience for John and Caroline. Apart from the more obvious ghosts, there was the familiarity of such White House features as the dining room with wallpaper that depicted historic moments in American history, including scenes of the Revolutionary War. During his White House years, John had spent hours studying the soldiers, resplendent in their brightly colored uniforms, asking, "What is he doing?" "Why is he like that?"

But the fond memories of the dining room wallpaper were eclipsed by those of "Daddy's office." Back then, to John and Caroline, the President's domain had represented paradise. Now it belonged to their host, President Nixon.

John's memories came alive as Julie and Tricia showed them around the White House, taking them to the third-floor solarium, which had once been Caroline's school, to their old bedrooms, and to the Oval Office. Tricia and Julie, judging the moment to be a private and emotional one, stayed outside the Oval Office while their father showed John the desk where he had once played. John had been just three years old when he had last set foot in the Oval Office. Now he remained silent.

Traveling home from Washington that night, a still emotional Jackie felt a strange peace and happiness as she listened to the children chattering away about their former home. Later that night, before she tucked John into bed and read his nightly story to him, Jackie turned to some of the pictures of his father arranged around the room. He listened quietly as she explained, "There you are with Daddy right where the President was describing the Great Seal there, on the path where the President accompanied us to our car."

John nodded off to sleep, happy. His visit to the White House had rendered the shadowiest memories of his earliest years more real, more alive than they had ever been, and he was content.

The next day he wrote a letter of thanks to President and Mrs. Nixon.

In August 1971, John and his cousin Anthony Radziwill spent two weeks at the Drake's Island Adventure Center, off the southwest coast of England, in Plymouth Sound. Taking a risk, Jackie wrote to the island's general secretary, Philip Kemp, requesting accommodations near Plymouth Hoe (on the mainland) for the men who would accompany John to England. There the ever-present Secret Service agents could be sequestered out of sight but could still watch the island through binoculars.

John embarked on an exhilarating adventure. The center was housed in a former fortress, and he and Tony loved being billeted with four other boys in a dormitory that had been a gun emplacement.

In the daytime John, along with sixty-four other boys of his age, took courses in sailing, went rock climbing and camping amid the wilds of Devon's Dartmoor country, and lived out every adventure fantasy ever dreamed of by a boy. John returned to America talking about Drake's Island in such glowing terms that Jackie immediately resolved to arrange similar adventures for him every summer.

Although John had survived his fortnight in the rugged Devon countryside without the close surveillance of the Secret Service to which he was accustomed, back in America another battle was looming.

On October 14, 1971, the federal government obtained a temporary restraining order to keep Ron Galella from interfering with the Secret Service's protection of the children of President Kennedy.

Galella was the personification of the paparazzo, which literally means a constantly buzzing mosquito; the word was coined by Fellini in his 1959 film *La Dolce Vita.*

Galella was relentless in his pursuit of his prey. Richard Burton once told him, "If you follow me to the South of France, I shall have to be constrained to keep from killing you." Marlon Brando was so exasperated by Galella that he punched him, knocking his teeth out. The next day Galella was back on the job, wearing a football helmet.

But Jackie was his true obsession, from the moment he was first assigned to photograph her in 1967. He began positioning himself outside the Fifth Avenue apartment every morning at 8:30, waiting for Jackie to take John to school. He dogged her footsteps until she returned home at night.

He made Jackie and the children into his professional Holy Grail, even following them to Greece, where Ari confronted him.

"Why do you do this?" Onassis asked.

"You have your job, I have mine," said Galella.

"Just stop."

"Okay, give me a job with Olympic Airways."

"Yes," said Ari. "And for that I will pay you one dollar."

Galella continued his pursuit of Jackie undeterred, but when he nearly caused John to fall off his bike, and embarrassed Caroline by following her to school, Jackie ordered the Secret Service to arrest him. She went to court to seek a permanent injunction barring Galella from coming within 100 yards of her or the children.

He countersued, charging that he had been falsely arrested.

A deposition from John that was among the government papers

read in part, "Mr. Galella has dashed at me, jumped in my path, discharged flash bulbs in my face, trailed me at close distances—generally imposed himself on me. . . . I feel threatened when he is present."

In subsequent actions, Jackie would allege that Galella's unstoppable pursuit of her and the children had turned life into a "nightmare"; finally Galella would be prohibited from coming within thirty feet of Jackie or the children.

The injunction was a declaration of war for Galella, who was half in love with her and had practically become her shadow. He followed her to Greece, Capri, Naples, and Peapack, and all over Manhattan.

He used every conceivable telephoto lens, dated Jackie's maid to try and get information about her movements, and wore countless disguises so that Jackie wouldn't spot him. For his invasion of Skorpios, he disguised himself as a sailor.

Today Galella's tactics seem relatively harmless. But to Jackie, he was the embodiment of the ruthless, disgusting media that hounded her family.

John, in the meantime, appeared in *Oliver!*, the musical version of Dickens's *Oliver Twist*, which was being produced by the Collegiate drama department for Christmas 1971.

John was cast as one of Fagin's gang and spent many happy hours rehearsing at home, driving Caroline crazy with his enthusiastic and constant singing. During this period, she sent a poem titled "John" to her Grandmother Rose which not only crystallized her deep affection for her brother but also demonstrated Caroline's own sense of humor and intelligence.

John's stage debut attracted a number of photographers but on the whole was extremely low-key.

"The usual Secret Service agents in gray suits were on guard, along with a few photographers, but none of the boys in *Oliver!* made a big deal of being in the play with John, or of John himself," recalls Peter Cohan, who also played one of Fagin's boys. "To us, John was just another kid from a rich family, like a lot of the other kids at Collegiate. We didn't feel sorry for him or anything like that. He just blended in."

Peter's mother added, "I saw John and Peter in *Oliver!* two or three times and you wouldn't have picked John out as the most handsome boy. He was just one of the boys. But I do remember that his mother and Caroline came to see *Oliver!* and that Aristotle Onassis and several bodyguards came with them."

Ari and Jackie were now married in name only, though Ari sporadically made a stab at winning points in the stepfather stakes. He was generous with his property, allowing John and Caroline to invite as many of their friends and relatives as they wanted to cruise on the *Christina* and stay on Skorpios.

An invitation to join John on the yacht was regarded as an invaluable prize by his schoolmates, some of whom made bets with each other as to who would be invited. One of John's friends, Bob Cramer, remembers his two weeks in Skorpios clearly.

"We were playing softball one spring afternoon by the Hudson," Cramer explains. "John asked me if I wanted to go to Greece for the summer. I always went to summer camp at Androscoggin in southwestern Maine, but I went to Greece for two weeks, flying first-class in the front section of Olympic."

Willie Smith and John were already at Skorpios, and the three eleven-year-old boys had the run of the island in the Jeep Onassis had bought John.

They started each morning by drinking coffee with the crew. After a while, the boys were given the job of polishing the brass on the railing.

"We got paid a tiny wage," says Bob. "But later we went on strike because we weren't getting enough money."

When the work became boring, the boys would dive into the water, jump on the trampoline, go water-skiing, or coax seafaring stories from the crew members. At night they would have dinner together, then sit with Ari and Jackie.

"I always remember how warm Ari was and how he hugged each of us good-night," says Bob. "John liked Ari a lot. He was more like a grandfather figure."

While most adults dream of spending a summer in Greece, Bob Cramer's reaction on his return underscores the impressions of other visitors to Skorpios and the *Christina*. Far from envying John's access to the Onassis realm, Cramer pitied him for having to be there. Bob declared that his Greek vacation had been "mostly a big bore" and that even a cruise on the legendary *Christina* had been "pretty boring, too."

Years later, when the two bumped into each other, John introduced Bob as "the person who taught me how to dive."

Bob and John got on so well that Jackie decided at John's request to check out Camp Androscoggin. Jackie telephoned Mrs. Cramer, who, after registering shock at the name and voice of her caller, described the camp and then added, "I do think you should know it is primarily a camp for Jewish boys." Jackie said that as long as John could go to Mass every Sunday, she would be delighted for him to go to Androscoggin with Bob.

Unfortunately, the directors refused to let the Secret Service park a trailer near the camp. Other precautions were allowed, though: John's name was blocked out on the mailing list and his name tags were kept in the director's care. Bob was enlisted to protect John from the press.

Reservations were made, but at the last minute the FBI received word of a plot to kidnap John. They deemed that his trip to Androscoggin would be a security risk, and it was canceled.

It turned out that the FBI's caution had been justified. On July 15, 1972, Greek authorities announced the arrest of two gangs who had been plotting to kidnap John. A twenty-two-page statement issued by the police revealed that the first gang consisted of four West German members of the terrorist 20th October Movement. The second group consisted of eight Greek leftists who hoped to carry out a series of kidnappings, robberies, and bombings.

The Greek gang, claiming to be modeled on the Uruguayan Tupamaros, had been more serious in its plan to kidnap John; one of the suspects, forty-five-year-old Panayotis Kabanis, confessed that they had had every intention of kidnapping John because "We could have blackmailed her [Jacqueline Kennedy Onassis] for as much money as we wanted."

The leftists had suffered under the right-wing military reign of Greek president Papadapoulos. Onassis represented the capitalist establishment, and snagging John F. Kennedy, Jr., in addition to garnering a huge ransom, would have been a major statement for the leftists, who considered the United States supportive of the repressive regime.

On the night of October 22, 1972, Jackie and Ari threw a party at El Morocco to celebrate their fourth wedding anniversary. But although the stellar assembly of guests (including Doris Duke, Mike Nichols, Oleg Cassini, Pierre Salinger, William F. Buckley, Jr., and Oscar de la Renta) feasted on bead-sized pearl-gray caviar flown in for the occasion, there was no anniversary cake, and Ari spent part of the evening dancing with a mysterious and beautiful young blonde who was rumored to be Jackie's eventual replacement.

There was no hope for the marriage and never had been. Never slow to express her disdain for her husband, Jackie made it nearly impossible for him to stay at the Fifth Avenue apartment, serving up excuse after excuse as to why there was no room for him. Ari, who was generally in the habit of treating women like chattels once he had conquered them, had likewise taken to treating Jackie with contempt, making it clear that he was interested in younger women and arguing publicly with her at every turn. Privately he was incensed at her vast extravagance and insatiable passion for shopping.

"Ari would weep like a child about the way in which Jackie was exploiting him financially," said Lilly Lawrence, the daughter of his close friend. "I knew he had every reason to cry. My father invited Ari and Jackie to Iran and paid for their nine-day trip. Jackie spent the whole time charging everything to my father's account and the hotel bill for her and her entourage (which included gifts she had charged to her room) came to a total of six hundred fifty thousand dollars for the nine-day stay.

"Jackie did her best to isolate him from his friends, like Prince Rainier and Princess Grace, who really didn't like her because they loved Maria so much. In the end, he was like a beaten person and used to cry to my father, or to Maria.

"Ari also had tremendous guilt over how he had treated Maria, that he had abandoned her for Jackie. He loved Maria. But he really did try to make things work with Jackie and the children. I remember that Caroline wrote him a poem and he had it framed and put up in his stateroom because he liked her so much."

Even as he was celebrating his fourth wedding anniversary, Aristotle Onassis was contemplating divorce from the most famous woman in the world, whom he had once craved to marry. It seemed to Lynn Alpha Smith, his secretary, that Jackie knew the truth and was taking steps to protect herself.

"She sent her assistant, Nancy Tuckerman, to the office, fishing for information about Ari's assets. She came over so often that in the end I started joking, 'What is she doing, working for the feds?' Ari knew what Jackie was doing to him financially and he despised her for it."

By the end of 1972, the couple were hardly on speaking terms. In the interests of keeping up appearances, they sailed to Palm Beach on the

Christina so that John and Caroline could see their grandmother. Jackie's nerves were on edge and she clashed with Rose's personal security guard, Jim Connors.

"Mrs. Onassis asked me to drive her to the *Christina,* but I told her I couldn't, as Mrs. Kennedy had asked me to wait for her," said Connors. "Jackie was livid and she turned on me and said I was fired. Mrs. Kennedy heard the argument from upstairs and stormed into the room and told Jackie point-blank, 'You can't fire him. He works for me.' Jackie flounced off in a huff."

Divorce seemed inevitable until, on January 22, 1973, Ari's only son, Alexander, died in a plane crash. Just as Patrick's death had brought Jack and Jackie closer together, Alexander's death brought a truce and new understanding to Jackie's relationship with Onassis.

A photographer who followed them during an Easter cruise to Antigua after Alexander's death remembered, "Onassis was devastated, and I knew from the crew of the *Christina* that he was drinking two bottles of vodka a day. Whenever he got off the boat, he looked strained and old.

"John did his best to amuse himself and spent most of the time playing with the crew, who took him fishing. Jackie was very close to him, very careful in how she handled him. I never saw her kiss him in public or embarrass him in any way. And Ari did his best to treat John as if he were family. But no one could replace Alexander for Ari—just as no one could replace the President for John."

On the tenth anniversary of President Kennedy's death, Jackie and the children attended a morning Mass at St. Bridget Roman Catholic Church in Peapack. They each sent a simple bouquet of baby's breath, heather, and blue cornflowers to Arlington National Cemetery to be placed at his grave.

Although John had known his father only for the first three

years of his life, uncanny similarities between father and son were already apparent. John was bad at spelling; Jackie would console him after he had failed tests by telling him about Jack's notoriously atrocious spelling. The President's sense of humor had been celebrated, and it appeared that John, at thirteen, had inherited it.

"He tells these long, involved old Irish jokes, in an accent. He's one of the funniest guys I've ever known," said his cousin Chris Lawford.

It had also once been said of Jack that he would rather have become a great football player than President. John loved the game, gleefully evading the Secret Service to play in Central Park after school.

"To Jack the cardinal sin was boredom; it was his biggest enemy, and he didn't know how to handle it," remembered television reporter Nancy Dickerson. "When he was bored, a hood would come down over his eyes and his nervous system would start churning. You could do anything to him—steal his wallet, insult him, argue with him—but to bore him was unpardonable."

John, too, had a low threshold for boredom, was hyperactive, and couldn't tolerate stillness. His hyperactivity was such that for a time Jackie sent him to a psychiatrist, Ted Becker, who specialized in treating adolescent problems. Restless and recalcitrant, John had much against which to rebel. The Secret Service were ever present and would be until he reached his sixteenth birthday. They dogged him wherever he went, and though he sometimes mischievously dispatched them to buy pizza for him and his friends, he generally felt he was their prisoner.

He and a few Collegiate friends went to a dance at a girls' school but, still totally uninterested in girls, John suggested they leave and persuaded a dozen friends to follow him home. At the apartment, he grabbed a couple of Frisbees, and the group ended up playing on the steps of the Metropolitan Museum of Art until after midnight. The Secret Service hovered in the background, trying hard not to intervene. Finally the game grew so rowdy that an irate passerby complained to the police, and John and his friends were asked to move on.

He struggled relentlessly to live his life as an average, active teenager; he took drum lessons, had tennis lessons from coach Hank Fenton (who taught him on the public courts in Central Park), bought his T-shirts from Serendipity (a much-loved ice cream parlor and boutique), and gorged himself on candy from Ellen's Pastry Shop on the Upper East Side.

In the spring of 1974, he managed to escape the Secret Service agents and, with two friends, decided to see the R-rated Mel Brooks film *Blazing Saddles,* then playing at the Trans Lux movie theater in Manhattan. John boldly approached the ticket window and asked for three tickets.

When cashier Marie Schiefelbein asked if he and his friends were seventeen, he looked her straight in the eye.

"Yes."

She sold them the tickets, and John and his friends sidled into the movie theater to enjoy the ribald comedy. Emerging at the end of the show, they were confronted by two Secret Service agents shaking with fear at having lost John.

John's propensity for evading the Secret Service was a terrible embarrassment to them. "John always used to boast to me about the Secret Service that 'they will never follow me into Central Park,' and he liked that fact," said one of his Collegiate friends.

On the afternoon of May 15, 1974, John and a friend slipped away from a Secret Service agent, asking him to meet them at the Central Park courts. John, riding his $145 ten-speed Italian-made Bianci bike, pedaled along Central Park's East Drive with the friend, relishing his freedom from surveillance. Suddenly a man jumped out of the bushes, waving a stick at him and screaming, "Get the hell off the bike! Get the hell off!"

His father had been assassinated; he had been the intended target of kidnapping plots; and he had grown up with the continuous threat of violence, but John was totally stunned at being the victim of a plain and simple mugging. In a daze, he dismounted from his bike and watched speechless as the mugger grabbed his tennis racket, got on the bike, and pedaled off into the park.

The mugging made headlines around the world and caused an uproar about the efficiency of the Secret Service. A few months later, a twenty-year-old heroin addict named Robert Lopez was arrested after a holdup and confessed to stealing John's bicycle. Jackie, abhorring publicity as she did, refused to prosecute, and the case was dropped.

As he entered his teenage years, John began learning the practical lessons of manhood, including the art of relating to women. Whatever positive images he had absorbed earlier from Onassis were now tempered by his awareness of and disdain for his stepfather's adulterous relationship with Maria Callas.

"John had ups and downs with Onassis," said Jackie's cousin John Davis. "The relationship got a bit sour when John, in his early teens, began to realize that Onassis was driving his mother crazy with his affair with Maria."

There was no way to discern the effect this had on John's adolescent psyche. In later years John would say, "There has always just been the three of us, my mother, Caroline, and me." He saw himself as his mother's guardian, her knight in shining armor, ready and willing to do battle with the fiercest foe to protect her from harm.

It was inevitable that John would learn the truth about Jackie's extremely visible humiliation at the hands of Aristotle Onassis. Callas had been blatant about her affair with Ari, declaring her love for him to Barbara Walters on *The Today Show* in front of millions.

Ari's treatment of Jackie wasn't the only unpleasant revelation with which John was compelled to grapple.

During President Kennedy's lifetime and for ten years after his assassination, the media had maintained a respectful silence about his infidelity and his sensational affair with Marilyn Monroe. But by December 1975 that silence was broken when Kennedy's inamorata Judith Campbell Exner revealed intimate details of her liaison with the President at a press conference; around the same time, books by White House dog keeper Traphes Bryant, columnist Earl Wilson, and Norman Mailer all revealed glimpses of the President's womanizing.

The American public had long revered the memory of the great romantic marriage of the king and queen of Camelot; but by the mid-seventies it appeared that the romance had been a sham. As the myth of Camelot unraveled and its participants shrank to mere mortals, John, too, heard whispers of the truth. Devastated, Jackie swore to close friends that she would have paid a king's ransom to keep the truth from her children.

As a wife she had always known the truth about her husband, but as a mother she had fought long and hard to sanctify him for the benefit of the two children he had left behind. Now the revelations of his many infidelities threatened to unravel the tapestry of untruths she had so skillfully woven.

Whenever a book or an article appeared about one of Jack's mistresses, Jackie felt compelled to reassure Caroline and John that their father had loved her and them and that they must all love his memory. The family believed instinctively that they must consistently deny all stories of Jack's womanizing both to the public and to his children.

"Jackie did not want her children to remember that side of him," said her half brother, Jamie Auchincloss. She felt that Jack's sexuality had nothing to do with his role as John and Caroline's father. "I don't think Caroline and John believe anything they have ever read about Kennedy's other women."

Although Jamie Auchincloss's assessment may have been correct when John was in his early teens, in later years it became impossible for John to lie to himself about his father's philandering. Still, his only tacit admission of the truth was to switch channels whenever the sultry image of Marilyn Monroe appeared on the television screen.

Jackie and Ari traveled the world apart, taking great care not to be in the same city at the same time. Jackie hid her humiliation by spending her husband's money relentlessly, once sweeping through a shop and instantly charging two hundred pairs of shoes to Onassis's account for a total of $60,000.

Now suffering from the incurable disease myasthenia gravis, Ari was once again planning to divorce her. A proud man who never forgot a slight, he was devising the perfect scenario by which to revenge himself on Jackie for her extravagance and coldness. He would strike at her greatest fear: personal exposure. He would divorce her in the most public fashion possible, airing her excesses, foibles, and emotional eccentricities to the press she so despised.

He began his campaign by contacting crack investigative journalist Jack Anderson and not only revealing to him details of her vast extravagance, but also accusing her of virtually laundering his money by charging couture clothes to his account and then reselling them to a consignment store in New York.

Despite the fervor of his anticipated revenge on Jackie, he was old, ill, and almost destroyed by his son's death. Worst of all, he was lonely. At 10 P.M. on Christmas Eve, John Kessanis, the New York–based general manager of Olympic Airways, was working late in his seventeenth-floor office at 888 Seventh Avenue, the temporary headquarters of the Onassis empire. Onassis's chauffeur, George, knocked on the door and asked whether Kessanis had the morning editions of the Athens newspaper for Ari.

"I didn't," Kessanis remembered, "but I still wanted to say goodnight and wish Mr. Onassis Merry Christmas. When I got up to the office, the room was completely dark, except for one spotlight over his desk. Mr. Onassis was sitting facing the desk, in the visitor's chair (he never liked sitting behind his desk), reading the papers, all alone."

Seeing him, Kessanis, a family man with a wife and children eagerly waiting for him at home, turned and crept out of the room without disturbing him.

"I had tears in my eyes," said Kessanis. "Here was one of the richest men on earth, sitting alone on Christmas Eve, just reading the papers."

On March 15, 1975, Aristotle Onassis died in Paris of bronchial pneumonia. Jackie was in New York, but on hearing the news, she flew to Paris immediately. She was met at Charles De Gaulle Airport by Onassis's chauffeur, Jacinto Rosa. Arriving at 7 A.M. in the early light of the Paris morning, dressed in a black leather coat and her trademark dark glasses, Jackie seemed eerily aloof, yet almost smiled as photographers captured the newly widowed Mrs. Onassis.

She rested at the Avenue Foch apartment until late in the afternoon. Then, still wearing the same coat and shoes, she went to the American Hospital to view the body of Aristotle Onassis, now lying on a bier behind the bronze doors of the hospital chapel. After praying for less than ten minutes, she left. Her eyes, unveiled, were dry.

In New York, speculation was already at a fever pitch, with Onassis's friends alternately reviling Jackie as "the black widow" and "the merry widow." The press estimated that she would receive $120 million in his will, with John and Caroline each getting trust funds valued at $15 million.

On March 18, Onassis's body was flown by a Boeing 727 Olympic Airways plane from Paris to Greece for burial. Jackie and Christina Onassis accompanied the body on its journey to Skorpios. During the flight they hardly spoke. Christina blamed Jackie for her father's unhappiness and did little to disguise her hatred for her stepmother.

When Jackie finally arrived in Skorpios, John, Caroline, and

Janet Auchincloss were waiting for her. They had flown to the island the day before and had been besieged by reporters. John, clutching a comic book, stuck his tongue out in disgust. Then he and Caroline were ferried to the *Christina,* whose flag was now flying at half-mast.

Aristotle Onassis was buried in the chapel on Skorpios where he had married Jackie and where his son, Alexander, was interred. Among the wreaths lay a simple arrangement bearing the words "To Ari from Jackie." During the brief funeral service, Jackie knelt to kiss the coffin, but remained composed. In Paris, Maria Callas, hearing of his death, pronounced the words, "I am a widow"; two years later she went to his grave, knelt and, her eyes full of tears, spent hours praying for his soul.

On March 21, 1975, John, Caroline, and Jackie were back in Paris. French protocol forbade Jackie from accepting any formal invitations during the period of mourning, so John and Caroline represented her at a lunch at the Élysée Palace hosted by President Valéry Giscard d'Estaing. Eunice Shriver was being honored for her work on behalf of retarded children. John was introduced to the French president, who presented him with a 1962 picture of the two of them, taken in the White House when Giscard d'Estaing was finance minister.

"You have the look and smile of President John Kennedy and I am very pleased that his children are here," said Giscard d'Estaing. John looked surprised by the gift and did not react to the comment.

On April 12, 1975, the *New York Times* revealed intimate details of Aristotle Onassis's plans for divorcing Jackie, hinting for the first time that their union had not been happy. Whether by accident or by his mother's design, John was thousands of miles away in Russia, on a cultural tour of the country with his cousins Timothy, Maria, and Bobby Shriver and their parents, Eunice and Sargent Shriver. Before the trip, Jackie had bought books and encyclopedias about Russia and studied them with John.

"We went to plants and factories and learned an incredible amount, and everywhere we went John asked good questions," marveled his cousin Timothy.

"John's mother has a lot of influence on him, but he's not as intellectually or artistically inclined as she is. He likes more active things," said Timothy, who expressed surprise that John at one point exhibited a modicum of enthusiasm for the arts. "He enjoyed the Russian ballet, which is kind of freaky, because he usually doesn't like ballet."

While warming to the cultural aspects of the country, John also reveled in the rich Russian food. "He was a garbage can," said Timothy. "He ate everything—ice cream, caviar, anything."

John and Timothy became firm friends during the trip to Russia and a subsequent diving expedition to the Caroline Islands. There they dived as deep as 180 feet and explored the hulls of sunken Japanese warships.

Timothy Shriver and William Kennedy Smith would remain John's best friends among all the twenty-nine grandchildren of Rose and Joseph Kennedy.

"He had problems with some of his cousins because they were jealous of him," said a Kennedy family friend who first met John in 1975 and observed his relationship with his cousins over the years. "The major reason for the jealousy while they were kids was based on the idea that John and Caroline were wealthy and the rest of the grandchildren weren't."

But if the other grandchildren assumed that Onassis's will would make John a millionaire, they were proved wrong when the details were published on June 6, 1975. Onassis had left just $25,000 each to John and Caroline. Incensed, Jackie proceeded to renegotiate the terms with Christina Onassis. In the end, Jackie and the children received a total of $20 million. Yet the legend of the $15-million trust fund Aristotle Onassis had purportedly left for John persisted, adding fuel to the already blazing jealousy of some of his cousins.

Money may not have been the only source of conflict within the extended family. Jackie had always stood apart from the other Kennedy wives; she had been more aloof, more aristocratic, more radiant. As the years passed, she had become a star who basked in the limelight that Ethel, in particular, craved. Ethel had always been star-struck.

Once, during Camelot's halcyon days, Eunice threw a party. Various Hollywood stars, including Carol Channing, were among the guests. Surveying the crowd, Ethel, a trifle disgruntled by the stellar group her sister-in-law had managed to snag, turned to reporter Nancy Dickerson and asked, "Does Eunice really know these people?" Dickerson informed her that she did, whereupon Ethel gazed at the stars, transfixed.

Jackie had now achieved greater celebrity status than Carol Channing or any other Hollywood creation. Inevitably Ethel's jealousy of her sister-in-law reverberated among her children, and there were moments through the years when John felt the sting of his cousins' envy.

"When John-John would not come out to play football or join the other games, they called him 'Mama's boy' and said he wasn't a real Kennedy," said David Horowitz, coauthor of *The Kennedys: An American Drama.*

The hostility certain of the cousins felt toward John resurfaced at the 1990 wedding of Mario Cuomo's son, Andrew, to Kerry Kennedy.

"There was a little sporting event arranged where Bobby's kids set up a slide rope so the kids could slide down into a pond," said a guest at the wedding. "A low branch, hidden from view, was hanging over part of the pond, which was quite dangerous, as it would have been easy to hit your head on it if you didn't duck.

"John must have joined the game after it started, because when it was his turn to slide down the rope, his cousins hadn't warned him about the branch and he hit his head and was injured. Some of us felt that the cousins hadn't told him because they were baiting him. Bobby's children, in particular, feel that John is the most exalted cousin, the crown prince, and they don't like it. But he isn't a snob. He's a friendly guy who loves sport like the rest of the family, but it has been bred in him to keep a distance from the others."

The competitiveness that Joseph Kennedy inculcated in his children simmered deep beneath the surface of the cousins' seemingly innocuous teenage pranks. John's cousin David Kennedy described one such exchange to the authors of *The Kennedys: An American Drama.* Once, when some of the cousins were discussing their ambitions for the future, John said, "I think whatever I do will probably involve working with blacks."

Bobby Jr. heard him out, smiled thinly, and said, "My father was more concerned about blacks than yours was."

Whatever undercurrents churned the relationship between the two cousins while they were teenagers, Bobby Kennedy, Jr., today has warm feelings toward his cousin.

"John is a good guy. He's his own man," said Bobby Jr. "The most striking thing about him is that he has tremendous self-confidence but it is combined with tremendous humility. That's a rare combination in people. He's a good guy. He has a tremendous sense of duty and responsibility—a very, very strong sense of responsibility, but he's not overwhelmed by it. He doesn't love the spotlight, but he's not uncomfortable there. Whenever any of the cousins need help on one of their projects, John is there."

A family friend who has known John and his cousins well since the 1970s said, "Teddy's children like John very much; Teddy Jr. is even a little like him, Patrick looks up to him, and Kara adores John. Tim and Maria Shriver like him, but Bobby Shriver has a nasty streak that I've seen come out when he's with John. John has always attracted so much attention, and Bobby very much wants to be the center of attention. Once in New York, after an event, he was waiting for his limo and I heard him screaming down the phone at the driver, 'I want that limo and I want it now. Don't you know who I am? I'm Bobby Shriver. Get that limo here!'

"He is very full of himself and he resents John. I was working out at Dunphy's Health Club [now called the Tara] on Cape Cod and John and Bobby Shriver were working out at the same time. As we were working out, a woman approached John and said something flattering to him. Bobby heard and walked right over to John and the girl and said, 'Well, la-de-da, what makes you think *he's* so great?' It was nasty."

More than anyone, Jackie had always been aware of the darkness overshadowing the genius for life that flowed in the blood of the Kennedy men. Their charisma, their ability to seduce, to beguile and win the world, was streaked with a ruthlessness and an amorality that sometimes bordered on evil, eclipsing all within them that was capable of goodness and truth.

From the first, it was clear that Jackie meant for John to be different.

"After Bobby died, Jackie deliberately kept John away from his cousins as much as she could," said Barbara Gibson, Rose's secretary during the seventies. "Ethel's children were raised wildly, with no system, no schedule, and Jackie didn't want her children to be brought up like that.

"She kept John, in particular, away from Rose, who hated her. Jackie didn't want the children to be too Kennedy. I noticed that she felt most strongly about John not being close to his grandmother. She seemed to want to keep him really close to her. In the end, it worked, because although Caroline and Rose were close—writing to each other regularly—Rose hardly had much to do with John at all."

Jackie had always valued good manners, and from the time when John was a small child, she and Maud Shaw had drilled him in politeness, instructing him to call the Secret Service agents "Mister" and to treat servants with consideration. That consideration was not always displayed by some of the other Kennedy children.

"Ethel Kennedy's children don't seem to care how rude they are to people who work for them," said Rebecca Michael of the London firm Compliments Caterers, which catered an Aspen New Year's Eve party for Ethel Kennedy. "I had spent hours making a pyramid composed of chocolate profiteroles and had just arranged it on the buffet table when one of Ethel's sons just marched in and pulled the top off.

"Very politely, I asked him not to do that and explained, 'I've spent ages making this, so please don't spoil it.' He mumbled something to the effect that he wouldn't and I walked out of the dining room toward the kitchen. Just as I was closing the dining room door, an instinct made me turn around. There he was, eating the profiteroles from the pyramid. He just didn't care how hard I'd worked making it and that it was for everyone at the party. He did exactly what he wanted."

Jim Connors, a former Palm Beach police officer, had the opportunity to observe John through the years and to contrast his behavior with that of his cousins.

"Jackie brought out the culture in John and Caroline," Connors said. "They are not like run-of-the-mill Kennedys. Everything is low-profile and they think before they leap. John isn't aggressive or forceful; he is a nice, quiet kid, smooth and easygoing. The other kids have a more 'go get 'em' attitude, while John is sophisticated and extremely polite."

Barbara Gibson said, "He was always more like Jackie's family than the Kennedys. In his teens he was awkward and gawky and I felt he was a mother's boy. It was always Mommy this and Mommy that. He was all boy, though, and had some mischief in him."

Once Gibson found a diver's watch in the yard and asked John if it belonged to him.

"Well, tell me what it looks like and what brand it is, then I'll tell you if it's mine," he said.

Gibson laughed. "But he isn't a greedy boy. I just don't think he realized what money was all about. All the family was very careless about money, they never had much, never carried any, and never had to worry about it."

Another time Gibson heard a noise outside her office in the compound. Her office was right across from what the family called the Golf Room, which had an adjoining bathroom. Realizing the sound had come from the garden, she looked out. There was John, in broad daylight, urinating under the window.

"All he had to do was go around the corner and go to the bathroom," she said. "But he was a nice kid, a real loner like his cousin Willie, who would usually be sitting up a tree or skimming stones at the end of a pier, a real loner."

Recognizing the pitfalls and obstacles in the way of her son's development, Jackie dedicated herself to building John's character and strictly supervised his schoolwork.

"She always made sure that John studied during the summer," said Dick Gallagher, a Hyannis Port family friend whose father, Ed, was close to Joe Kennedy for many years. Gallagher spent a number of summers with John, teaching him to fish and sail.

"Jackie brought him up superbly and he was always so polite and treated other people extremely well. When John was young, he was shy and his mother was very close to him, taught him water-skiing, and they had a great relationship."

While insisting on control over the influences around him, Jackie understood his teenage impatience to grow up and clearly allowed him a certain leeway. In the summer of 1975, she and John were in the general store just around the corner from the compound in Hyannis. She was comfortable in the store; she had been going there since she and Jack first met. When the children were born and the family visited the compound, Jack would delight in loading the assorted cousins onto a golf cart for a ride down to the store to buy candy.

On this particular summer day, the two were leafing through magazines. Jackie was wearing a bikini covered by a white T-shirt, and John was dressed in white shorts and white shirt. Jackie had just bought an emerald-green Audi and John, who was only fourteen, clamored to be allowed to drive it. Though she knew they were being observed, Jackie relented and let John drive the two blocks back to the compound.

A year later, when he was only fifteen, a Hyannis Port policeman named Cliggot caught John driving without a license.

"I saw John Kennedy, Jr., driving his mother Jackie and grandmother Rose home from church," he said. "I knew he didn't have a driver's license because he's only fifteen."

Later Cliggot saw John walking in the compound and asked, "John, do you have a driver's license?"

"No," John replied. "Talk to the Secret Service about it."

Cliggot never saw him driving again without a license.

On Skorpios, unsupervised by Jackie, John could blow off teenage steam. Jackie went back with him in the summer of 1975 but allowed him the freedom to play with some of his island friends. His close friend in the nearby village of Nidri was a Greek boy named Christos Kartanos, who was impressed by John's daredevilry, especially the way he tended to drive speedboats from the *Christina* with the throttle wide open, as fast and as far as he could.

"We spent a lot of time together, smoking and drinking wine, and I noticed he developed a taste for Scotch," said Kartanos. Afraid that his mother would see him buying Scotch, John cleverly circumvented the problem by giving Kartanos money to buy a bottle for them both and asking him to hide it.

"Whenever I went to see him, I carried the Scotch in a cloth shoulder bag," said Kartanos. "We used to swig it straight from the bottle. John said it made him feel good. But we never got drunk. I think all of the things John did—like drinking wine and whiskey and smoking Greek cigarettes—were his ways of showing off. It's as if he were saying, 'Look, I'm not a kid anymore.'"

To the public, John F. Kennedy, Jr., was the Prince of Camelot, but John just wanted to be fourteen and average. At Collegiate, he had found a perfect companion for his quest. The son of a Manhattan surgeon, Wilson McCray was (and still is) a self-confessed rebel. He was the perfect friend to accompany John when he walked on the wild side.

"John and I were in the same class and were really good friends. We were bad little boys," said McCray. "When we were at Collegiate together, John and I used to run away from the Secret Service together and hang out in Central Park and play Frisbee. It was easy to run away from the Secret Service; they were just there for protocol, unnecessary.

"When we were about twelve, we went to Madison Square Garden and there was some general article about bad little boys drinking there. The reporter never realized that John was one of them so it was left out of the article."

At fourteen, the two stole a Volkswagen van while vacationing in Switzerland. "We went out and spun it around on the ice, drove it around, then drove it back," said McCray.

Stealing the vehicle wasn't John's only illegal teenage escapade. At first, Caroline was his ally. "Caroline grew marijuana in Jackie's vegetable garden in Hyannis Port," said Barbara Gibson. "A patrolman discovered it and went to Jackie and told her. She said that she would deal with Caroline and John and that she wanted us to let her know immediately if anyone discovered them smoking pot or taking any other drugs."

Jackie was a committed mother who fought to keep John untainted by the other Kennedy children's propensity for wildness and drugs. Yet although John's politeness, gentleness, and kindness to other people invariably surpassed that of his cousins, during his midteens he demonstrated conclusively that, despite his public persona, in private he was no angel. The public to this day fervently believes that, unlike his cousins, John remained pristine. That is not the truth.

The drug excesses of John's cousins, both on the Kennedy and the Lawford side, have been well documented. But according to Wilson McCray, John, too, smoked marijuana during his teen years.

"At school we were always getting caught for getting stoned," McCray said.

There were no repercussions, and John grew more daring and took drugs in his mother's 1040 Fifth Avenue apartment.

"We used to go up on John's roof and get stoned," Wilson said. "John would smoke grass in the bathroom."

McCray spent a great deal of time with John and Jackie, occasionally vacationing with them. From his point of view, despite John's wildness, his relationship with his mother remained good. "Like everybody, John had to lie to his mother and bend to her will," McCray said. "She is wild, eccentric and removed; yet very sweet, very fun and loving. She wasn't strict but she kept tabs on him.

"His great-aunt on Jackie's side, Edie Beale, loved helping us get into trouble. We got caught smoking cigarettes and Edie was great— she taught us how to smoke cigarettes so no one would see."

No matter how often John flirted with danger and fought to be treated as a teenager instead of a prince, his heritage hovered in the background. At Collegiate he took a course on the U.S. presidency, and each time the teacher mentioned the early 1960s, he looked straight at John and spoke of "your father" instead of President Kennedy.

John remained silent; this was his response to any outsider's mention of his father. But the silence did not mean John was indifferent to the memory of his father. At the end of 1975, he and his cousins went on a skiing holiday to the Berkshires with Teddy and Joan. Leaving their hotel one morning, John stopped to gaze at a picture of his father.

"What's it say?" asked one of the smaller cousins, pointing to a plaque hung next to the photograph.

" 'Ask not what your country can do for you; ask what you can do for your country.' " John read the words slowly; his voice filled with pride. "That's his most famous quote."

CHAPTER EIGHT

Andover

The bicentennial year brought a new kind of revolution to John, his mother, and his sister. In 1976 John was registered to begin eleventh grade at Phillips Academy, Andover (Massachusetts), one of the country's most prestigious prep schools. Caroline was now in London, ostensibly spending a year studying art at Sotheby's auction house but actually spending much of her time cutting a glamorous swath through London society. Her favorite escort was art dealer Mark Shand, the brother of Camilla Shand, who would eventually become Camilla Parker-Bowles and Prince Charles's mistress.

For John, going to prep school would bring a new sense of freedom—which is not to say that he would be exempt from official Kennedy-related functions. Teddy, who was making a bid for reelection to the Senate in 1976, asked Jackie to allow John and Caroline to lend their luster to his campaign by making themselves available for a few photo opportunities. Jackie not surprisingly hated the idea, but found it hard to deny Teddy anything.

"Jackie and Teddy have a warm, emotionally intimate, loving, caring relationship," said a friend who has observed them at the Kennedy compound on many occasions. "Teddy adores Jackie. He's like a little kid with a crush on her. She talks to him in that breathy, little-girl voice, very charming, very seductive. I've seen him put his arm around her and look down at her, just adoring her. And she looks up at him the same way. It's not sexual intimacy, it's a genuine affection."

Teddy had always played an important role in the children's lives, especially after Bobby's assassination.

"Ted was definitely a father figure to them," family friend Dick Gallagher said. "He's always been there for John and Caroline, making sure they were brought into his own family's activities, playing touch football with them, going water-skiing and sailing with them.

"He used to talk to John about his father, about the wonderful things, educate him about his father's values. Teddy has always mattered a great deal to John."

After Chappaquiddick and the widespread media attention to Teddy's drinking and womanizing, most of the cousins began to deride him as a buffoon. But in the summer of 1974, Caroline had worked as an intern for Teddy at 431, Old Senate Building, his five-room office suite. In between sorting mail, filing documents, and running errands, she took the measure of Teddy's true abilities, discovering the intelligence and the passion for justice behind his red-faced persona. She conveyed her new respect for Teddy to John, who also began to see Teddy in a different light.

"Caroline found out how hard Teddy worked and I could see that changed her entire attitude," said Rick Burke, Teddy's assistant during the 1976 campaign and author of *The Senator.* "Caroline and

John made two appearances to help Teddy, and everyone loved them. John was obviously shy but handled everything very well. Jackie called all the shots and made sure they didn't do more than was necessary."

Jackie didn't want John and Caroline to be exploited by the family, but she did encourage John to do public service.

"I think she really wanted to steer him on the right track," said Jackie's cousin John Davis. "Of course, she was terribly worried—since he grew up in mansions and traveling on yachts—that he would become soft. She admired physical toughness in men and wanted to imbue this in John."

On June 30, 1976, John and Timothy Shriver traveled to Rabinal, a Guatemalan town of twenty thousand that had been struck by an earthquake in February. John and Timothy slept on a rain-soaked tent floor, ate only tortillas and black beans, and washed in a stream. During the day John hauled sand, built outhouses, and dug trenches. At night he helped distribute food.

"They ate what the people of Rabinal ate and dressed in Guatemalan clothes and slept in tents like most of the earthquake victims," said the Reverend Antonio Gomez y Gomez, a Catholic priest who directed the Family Integration Corps. "They did more for their country's image than a roomful of ambassadors."

In Guatemala, John adhered religiously to his desire for anonymity.

"He got along with everyone and tried hard to speak Spanish," said a fellow volunteer named Tom Doyle. "John wanted to be treated like the rest of us." Of course there were Secret Service men in tow.

Once back in America, John went up to Andover for registration. Founded in 1778, the nation's oldest incorporated boarding school was as famous for its celebrated alumni as for its high academic standards. Humphrey Bogart failed to make the grade, but Oliver Wendell Holmes, Edgar Rice Burroughs, Jack Lemmon, and George Bush were all graduates of the Ivy League prep school.

John's friend Wilson McCray had already started at Andover; John knew that Wilson would be able to help him sidestep the pitfalls of being away at school and enjoy the considerable freedom. After his admissions interview, John had a few hours to kill. He gave the Secret Service the slip and went in search of McCray, who took him up to the third-floor room of his friend Skip Owen. They proceeded to give John the inside story on Andover.

"The place was split up into groups," Wilson said. "The rich shits, the preppy kids, the jocks, and the very social set—which John doesn't give a shit about. (He doesn't give a shit about anything.) I told him about different girls, what set of people were taking which drugs. I was more involved in the very cool drug scene.

"John shared a room in Day Hall South with Tony Dodge, an all-American boy, who was also very attractive. John and Tony's room was just like anyone else's except that he kept a small picture of his father on his desk and his father was JFK. None of us ever asked him about his father, though; we didn't want to tread on his toes," said Andrew Gibbon Nyhart, who lived in the same hall.

Like his father, John was not one to give academic pursuits top priority. During his time at Andover, he devoted most of his energy to acting, sports, and a five-foot-seven-inch honey-blond student named Jenny Christian.

They met during his first few months at Andover. The daughter of a New York surgeon, Jenny Christian was sixteen and easily the most glamorous girl on campus. It was only natural that she should attract the attention of the most glamorous young man.

Jenny's poise and natural affection for John made their relationship easy for both of them. She liked him for who he was, not for whose son he was.

"If he had fallen out of a pickup truck he still would have been irresistible to me," she said. "He was extremely handsome, nice, and sweet. It was a great romance."

Though most of the female students knew he was attached to Jenny, John still had to fend off other admirers. He didn't help his own cause when his emerging hedonism found him barely clad and out in public.

"John used to skateboard around the campus in sexy, skimpy outfits," said Heather Trim, another student at Andover.

But except for the occasional exhibitionistic display, he was less conspicuous at Andover than at any other period in his life.

"Some people at Andover who didn't know John were really interested in him because of who he was," said fellow student Elizabeth Melaragno. "One person I know stole John's log sheet—we had to sign our names on lists outside the dorm if ever we went out—because he thought it would be fun to have the signature. Another girl's mother promised her a whole new wardrobe if she invited John home for Thanksgiving and he came. In the end, though, she didn't ask him, because he seemed so nice and cool and she didn't want to approach him."

"People were sucking up to him all the time," said Holly Owen, one of his teachers. "But he was cool and didn't pay attention to them."

People outside John's circle, of course, saw only his name and missed the real person.

John's three years at Andover would be the most normal he had ever known—especially once the Secret Service left, which they did when he turned sixteen. Of course, that also meant he could no longer send them out for pizzas.

"They used to wear dark glasses and stay at the Andover Inn," said George Dix, John's language teacher. "He was very embarrassed by all the attention."

His friends understood John's craving for an ordinary existence. "He's a great guy," said Wilson McCray. "He's the prince by virtue of his heritage, but when you are with him he is normal. He can't be normal in the public sense, but in private he is. He is very unpretentious. As long as I've known him, he's been very frustrated by any kind of come-on because of his name."

John's discovery of acting at Andover should have surprised no one. He had been a talented mimic since childhood, and drama provided a perfect outlet for him. It was also a perfect paradox. His involvement with theater could not fail to attract the media attention he abhorred, but it was also his salvation. Through acting—and only through acting—he could speak other people's lines, live out other people's lives and thus escape the role of John F. Kennedy, Jr.

Like any teenager seeking to establish his own identity, John was changing, and his new interest took him away from old friends.

"Once he got involved in theater we weren't really in the same group anymore," said Wilson McCray.

John was hooked on the smell of the greasepaint, if not the roar of the crowd. John's appearance in the Collegiate production of *Petticoats and Union Suits* had already drawn the attention of the *New York Times*: "One can't help be aware of 15-year-old John Kennedy in his role, although like others in his celebrated family, he seems to be trying painfully to avoid special attention."

His mother was less than enthusiastic about his attraction to acting, reluctantly going along with his decision and attending some plays he appeared in. She wore her dark glasses, and one of John's classmates said, "It looked like she was pretending to be somewhere else."

"He really got into theater," said Wilson McCray. "John loved acting and if he hadn't been born a prince I think he'd love to have gone further with it."

"His performances were wonderful," said Andover secretary Dickie Thieras. "He was just terrific and he loved acting so much that he threw himself into every performance."

"If he had worked hard at it, he could have been a good professional actor," said Holly Owen, who was John's soccer coach for one season and, as head of drama, also evaluated his acting.

"John's acting was superb," said Diz Bensley, his photography teacher. When asked whether his photography rivaled his acting, Bensley smiled and said, "I'm glad he went into drama." Considering the lifelong harassment John suffered at the hands of photographers, it isn't surprising that the subject didn't appeal to him.

In Andover's 1977 production of *Comings and Goings*, John starred with Jenny Christian. Their combined beauty, a student said, "really put a gloss on their fledgling skills."

"There was passion in his acting, but he had to be well directed for it to come out," Owen noted. "You might say the passion was latent. He had a facility for acting, a knack, a great deal of personal charisma, but he didn't have the inner drive for it."

The following year John appeared in *A Comedy of Errors*, but his performance elicited no special mention by the reviewers of the *Phillipian* (the campus newspaper). And in April 1979, he starred as McMurphy in *One Flew Over the Cuckoo's Nest*.

"Drama was a big part of John's life," said Douglas Creedon, who appeared in an Andover production with him. "He had a lot of dramatic flair, and I thought he was going to become an actor. I approached him with a kind of awe, thanks to his family history—I think the reality of his family affected other people more than him."

If there was one role that seemed appropriate to a young man who had grown up in confined if luxurious surroundings under the eye of Secret Service men, it was that of McMurphy. Who could better understand the crazy inner motivation of a character whose every move is watched closely, and who nurtures a desire to escape from constant judgment?

Besides theater, another kind of escape waited for John to discover it. Freed from parental scrutiny and the Secret Service, he could finally put in occasional time as one of the boys. Plunging into Andover's social scene with abandon, he became a regular at parties—which at Andover meant recreational drugs.

"He could really let go," said Wilson McCray. "John let go at parties and he never held back because of the Secret Service. They knew what he was about."

Most of the Andover students had well-off parents, spending money, and connections. Casual use of drugs had increased significantly across the country. In the students' minds, there was nothing wrong with smoking a little grass. But possession and use were still illegal.

At one party, John and a group of boys were smoking pot, deeply involved in a conversation about sports, and failed to notice one of the campus security officers sniffing the air.

"Oh, shit!" one of them said, trying to get rid of the evidence. He was too late; he and several other friends, including John, were caught.

That meant meetings with the administration and notification of the students' parents.

John didn't deny that he'd been smoking, but his straightforwardness didn't ease his mother's concern. He was a Kennedy, after all—what if he wound up like his cousins, whose drug use was all over the tabloids? His cousin Patrick later arrived at Andover with widely publicized drug problems; the teachers were constantly on guard.

Luckily for John, Andover gave students a second chance where casual usage was concerned. There was no way to eradicate drugs from the campus, but teachers and the administration watched the students carefully for signs of addiction.

"John smoked grass but it didn't appear to affect him," said Holly Owen. "I think that his drug escapade was part of the rite of passage, a light experimentation as part of a group. When John experimented with drugs it was only to be one of the boys, not because he was out of control."

The teachers seemed to understand John's desire to fit in with the others and his resistance to being held to expectations beyond his grasp. His passion for the theater also helped. There, he only had to be someone else, and he loved it.

In June 1977, John signed on for the twenty-six-day Outward Bound summer wilderness survival course on Hurricane Island, twelve miles off the coast of Maine. Jackie had pushed hard for the idea. She hoped to toughen John up, and the course included sailing, navigation, rock climbing, first aid, and three days at the island's boat rescue station. John and the 150 other participants paid $750 each to take the course, which, according to Penn Williamson, the survival school's development director, "is designed to instill confidence in people, to show them they can do things they thought they couldn't."

Although his Secret Service protection had ended in November, the government still seemed to be concerned with John's security. A surveillance boat was anchored off Rouge Island while he completed the last stage of the course. He was to survive alone for three days on a small, isolated island, with no food—just a gallon of water, two pots, one match for each meal, and a book on edible plants written by naturalist Euell Gibbons.

"It was good. I liked the course and I learned a lot more than I thought I would," John said at the end. But when his friend Linda Semans asked what the course had taught him about himself, he struck a Scarlett O'Hara pose.

"I learned I'll never allow myself to be that hungry again."

All of John's changes in this period weren't mental or existential. He was evolving into a rugged young man.

"John could have been a quarterback," said Dick Gallagher.

"He's got a great arm. He's very rugged, loves sports and does well at all of them. He's a water-skier, he plays a lot of touch football—even in the summer—and he's not the least bit afraid of the rough-and-tumble."

Away from Andover, John worked as an usher at the Robert F. Kennedy Tennis Tournament in Forest Hills on August 29, 1977. "I don't really know how to do this," he muttered after missing aisle and seat locations several times.

When not taking people to their seats, he slipped into a front-row seat with Meg Azozi, a bubbly brunette who watched excitedly as Teddy played in the pro-am finals.

John was beginning to generate a new kind of excitement himself. Having outgrown the part of a male Shirley Temple, he was evolving into a teen idol. On December 27, 1977, he attended the New York premiere of *Saturday Night Fever*. The movie's star, John Travolta, was waving to the crowd when John emerged from the limousine behind his. Suddenly most of the screams and squeals were directed at the student from Andover.

The shift was so abrupt that Travolta turned to see who had stolen his glory. John, who had hoped to slip in unnoticed behind the star, smiled apologetically and hurried into the theater.

There's an old saying that actors use math only to count the number of lines their character has in the script. Like another actor at Andover, Humphrey Bogart, John failed to make the scholastic grade. But unlike Bogart, who had to leave the school, John was held back to bring up his grade in math. When the news leaked out, some sources claimed that his dedication to drama and marijuana had taken its toll.

"I tried to help him," said Andrew Gibbon Nyhart. "I coached him a few times but I don't think I did enough."

Standards at Andover required students to take a stiff exam at the end of the eleventh grade in five subjects, including math. Normally, if any student failed the exam, he or she automatically flunked out of Andover. That rule was relaxed for John.

A Phillips alumnus, on hearing the news, said, "Young Kennedy appears to be getting special treatment. Phillips has incredibly high standards and seldom bends them to accommodate students who can't keep up."

John's academic stumble had created a flurry in the press. In an interview, he reluctantly confirmed that he had indeed flunked the eleventh grade and would be repeating his year as an "upper middler" at Andover. When asked if he was a good student, he said, "Well, I don't know. It depends on what you call a poor student."

The failure stung him—and gave his mother new ammunition in the fight against his acting. But his teachers, who watched his daily progress, understood the pressures and expectations surrounding him.

"John is not stupid," said Holly Owen. "He was a modest student, but there were some very bright kids at Andover and they blew him away academically."

There was also the problem of his having too much energy to sit for long periods. "John didn't show up at class a lot," classmate John Dabney remembers. "Although he was very bright, he was a restless student."

The failure did mark him in some of the other students' eyes. Asked to sum up John during his time at Andover, a fellow classmate simply pointed to the wooden figurehead of a topless maiden suspended from the ceiling of John's dormitory room and said, "That's John Kennedy. A fun fellow interested in parties and girls, not schoolwork."

Jackie, also stung by John's failure, decided he would spend the summer learning the virtue of hard work. As the spring semester of 1978 ended, he flew to Wyoming for a six-week stint working as a wrangler at the Bar Cross Ranch.

"I want him to be treated like any other ranch hand," she told the foreman, arranging the details of her son's so-called vacation. "No special treatment."

While his classmates backpacked through Europe or went sailing off the Atlantic Coast, John's mornings began with a 6:30 A.M. wakeup call and passed in grueling work. When he wasn't driving cattle, building dams, or digging ditches, he was hauling hay.

Ranch hand Melody Harding had expected a spoiled rich kid. To her surprise, she said, "He was fairly quiet, had a good sense of humor, and was willing to do anything."

The work was back-breaking, but John loved every minute of his time at the ranch and discouraged any special treatment. His behavior soon won the respect of those who worked with him.

Of course, they couldn't understand what a pleasure it was for him to peel off his shirt to help string a line of barbed wire and not have a battery of cameras record the event. He was proud of his body and his athletic prowess and enjoyed the opportunity to put them to the test.

The only bright lights he saw at night were the tips of the cowpunchers' cigarettes as they settled down after dinner to smoke and relax and swap stories.

"The ranch hands would tell you to go to hell as soon as say good morning," said Emory Anderson, a Bar Cross local. "So it's a compliment to John that they seemed to like him. He was friendly, he wasn't a snob. I think people expected a brat or a hell-bent kid. Instead, he showed he had true grit."

On November 26, 1978, Jackie threw a party for John and Caroline at Le Club on East Fifty-fifth Street in New York. She had chosen a sophisticated setting in which to celebrate John's eighteenth and Caroline's twenty-first birthdays; Le Club, with its French country ambiance and elegant tapestries, was one of Jackie's favorite private clubs and had been much favored by Aristotle Onassis as well.

The evening began on a sentimental note. In front of 140 of Camelot's most faithful—including Lem Billings, George Plimpton, Bunny Mellon, Ethel Kennedy, Pat Lawford, Jean Smith, and an assortment of cousins—Teddy stood with tears in his eyes to give the first toast.

"I shouldn't be doing this tonight," he said. "By rights, it should have been the father of these two children. Jack loved his children more than anything else. Young John and Caroline bring new life to the family."

Many eyes were misty as those who had loved and lost John F. Kennedy and now loved his children raised their champagne glasses in the birthday toast.

As always, Jackie had ordered a gourmet menu with an array of dishes from moussaka to lobster Newburg. Cheers rose as John's and Caroline's intricately iced birthday cakes, each decorated with sparklers, were wheeled into the room.

John had invited a large Andover contingent, many dressed in sneakers and trendily shabby clothes that contrasted with John's unusually neat attire of jacket, striped shirt, and tie.

"There was a lot of booze around," said Andrew Gibbon Nyhart. "A pitcher of beer and a pitcher of wine on every table. It was a really great party."

Once Jackie and the older generation (including Pete Hamill, her current escort) left the club at around one A.M., the overriding scent of French perfume that pervaded the club was replaced with *eau de* marijuana.

Jackie's departure signaled the Andover group to divide into two factions. The first faction fell asleep on the club's plush sofas or thickly carpeted floor; the second dropped all inhibitions and alternated between necking in dark corners of the club and dancing wildly on the club floor.

By the time the smoke thinned out it was four in the morning. The bleary-eyed Andover crowd straggled out of the club, where they were confronted by the blazing flashbulbs of an army of photographers who had lain in wait the entire evening.

The biggest and burliest of John's friends was a postgrad jock who wasn't close to John but liked playing his bodyguard. Unaccustomed to the subtleties of dealing with paparazzi, the outraged behemoth barged up to the photographers.

"I'm giving you fair warning," he shouted. "Stop taking pictures, right now."

Amused, the photographers perked up, anticipating an unusual photo opportunity.

John, wearing dark glasses, finally emerged from the club with a friend running interference. The would-be bodyguard pushed the photographer, who clicked away regardless. Tempers flared, fists flew, and a brawl ensued.

"It's okay, you'll just make things worse," John cried out, trying to restore calm. He waded into the middle of it all to separate the two combatants, lost his balance in the melee, and slipped.

The evening ended with the birthday boy lying flat on his backside in the New York gutter while a camera flashed away.

The brawl made headlines, but John had learned a valuable lesson. Not long after, he left Studio 54 with a young woman identified as Lynne Hutter at 3 A.M., only to be confronted by a swarm of photographers hoping for a reprise of the Le Club incident. This time John kept his cool.

Flashing cameras had always been a part of his life, but they had never been so intrusive as they were now. In the past, photographers had besieged him because of his heritage. Now that he was starting to emerge as a personality in his own right, pictures of JFK, Jr., were more salable.

"John had star quality," explained Howard Stein, whose club, Xenon, was New York's trendiest of the moment. Now, whenever John went to Xenon, it was inevitable that—brawl or no brawl—the photographers would fight for pictures.

The Andover friends who had been his guests at the eighteenth birthday party were also guests at a Christmas party at 1040 Fifth Avenue. Jackie invited a group of intellectuals and family, including Alexander Cockburn, John Warnecke (who designed President Kennedy's grave marker), Pete Hamill, Warren Beatty, Lee Radziwill, and Andy Warhol. Warhol, without asking Jackie in advance, brought *Interview* columnist Bob Colacello along.

"I'm so happy you're here, Bob," Jackie said. "What would you like to drink?"

"Perrier," he said.

"I'm afraid we're all out," she said. "In the meantime, share mine, it's ours." She handed him her glass of Perrier.

The next day, Warhol sent for Colacello.

"Jackie just called and told me off," he said. "She said, 'How dare you bring Bob Colacello to my house, Andy? He writes a column!'"

Andy told Colacello he had assured her that Colacello wasn't going to write about her Christmas party, but Jackie refused to be pacified. She was like a lioness protecting her young from harm—and to Jackie, publicity meant harm. Yet the Colacello incident was vintage Jackie; she had been appalled at Warhol's bringing him, yet she'd let him drink from her glass and treated him with perfect courtesy. Then she had complained to his boss.

It was a strategy she used often: disarm the enemy with charm, then strike.

Reaching the threshold of adulthood means being able to vote, to marry without parental permission, to be drafted. Significantly for John, being eighteen also meant being able to drink legally.

"Now John and I could hoist a few at the Campus Pub," said Andrew Nyhart. "He used to go often because he was amused at being able to drink at school."

Jenny Christian and John were still deeply involved. Christian was going to Harvard to major in psychology, and Jackie liked and approved of her. By now, Christian was so much a part of John's life that she was virtually one of the family. She accompanied him, Jackie, Lee, Tina, and Tony Radziwill on vacation to St. Martin, where they stayed at the luxurious La Samanna resort. At La Samanna John, Jenny Christian, and the family met an eighteen-year-old actress, Daryl Hannah, also on vacation.

"Daryl was eighteen but she was really strange and carried a teddy bear around with her wherever she went," reported an eyewitness. "John and Jenny seemed to think she was weird and laughed a bit about her, but not in a malicious way."

John continued trying to lead a low-profile life. In January 1979, with fifteen other Andover students, he began working as an unpaid intern with the Boston Juvenile Court. His cousin Joe Kennedy had completed an internship the year before, and the verdict on John was that he kept up with his cousin's record.

"Thus far he has shown a complete dedication to his work and is following the excellent example of his cousin, Joseph P. Kennedy," said Juvenile County Clerk Paul F. Heffernan, who also called John "a very competent and industrious young man."

Escaping from the limelight, John appeared willing to exert a certain amount of academic effort at the court; his internship included some practical work as well. But while photographers could still make money from his image, another medium beckoned.

On April 26, 1979, *Look* reported that producer Robert Stigwood had offered John the role of his father in a film of the President's life. Hollywood had long been aware of John's passion for the theater, and not only Columbia and Paramount but scores of other agents and producers had already offered John unlimited money and script control to sign with them.

Look Senior Editor Robert Vare said, "We hear he's very interested, much to his mother's chagrin. She feels that they're exploiting his famous name and face and that he's too young to handle it."

It was clear to all who knew him that John held his father's memory in quiet reverence. He had no intention of exploiting his father's life for the edification of the public and the enrichment of Hollywood.

Today, a spokesman for the Stigwood Organization denies that the offer was ever made. As for John's mother, one truth was incontrovertible: Jacqueline Kennedy Onassis would die before allowing her only son to become an actor or a Hollywood star.

On the morning of June 7, 1979, Jackie traveled to Massachusetts, where she hosted a champagne breakfast in John's honor at the Andover Inn. With Caroline, Secret Service agent John Walsh, who was considered part of the family, Teddy, and forty-three other friends and family members, Jackie toasted John's impending graduation with Great Western champagne. Those who weren't hungover from the party the night before ate scrambled eggs, Danish pastries, toast, and coffee.

"Andover was so tough, we were all ecstatic at having graduated at last," Andrew Nyhart recalled of the previous evening's festivities. "We deserved to celebrate!"

While the students were ecstatic, Jackie couldn't hide her emotions. She walked up to Teddy wearing her trademark smile, and began slowly rubbing his back. Then she leaned over close to his ear.

"Oh, Ted, can you believe it?" she whispered, looking lovingly at

John, whose tan double-breasted suit set off his bushy, fashionably long hair. "My baby, graduating!"

The late-morning ceremony took place on the lush, sun-drenched college lawn, where special seats had been reserved for Jackie, Ted, and Caroline. John looked hip and at ease among the 360 classmates who graduated with him.

"John F. Kennedy, Jr.," announced headmaster Theodore R. Sizer.

A loud cheer went up from the student body as John received his diploma. Jenny Christian, sitting with the family, exchanged proud glances with Jackie and gave John a hug when he arrived back at his seat.

After the ceremony John, Jackie, Caroline, Ted, and Jenny Christian tried to fight their way through the crowds toward the buffet lunch. Reporters and photographers intercepted them at every turn.

"Just a word, John," said reporter after reporter, hemming him in like a calf on the Colorado range.

At first he had seemed happy, running his hands through his long hair in embarrassment at all the attention, but as the legions of journalists swarmed over him, continuing to shout, "Just a word, John, just a word," he grew edgy.

Finally exasperated, but with as much politeness as he could muster, John stopped and said, "Look, I just want to spend some time with my mates and enjoy my graduation."

"I walked out of the ceremony next to John and his family," said Brian Crull, who also graduated that day. "To me, John had been a dashing figure at Andover. He always looked wonderful, had a kind of glow about him. But that day I got a completely different view of his life. Watching the photographers and reporters surge toward us, practically trampling people to get to John, was utterly and totally overwhelming.

"After experiencing about twenty minutes of what it meant to be

John, I really sympathized with his having to cope with all that attention every day of his life."

That attention affected others as well. Caroline Katz, an Andover resident, received the top academic award, which normally would have been big news. Instead of mentioning her honor, the local paper devoted the entire front page to John.

CHAPTER NINE

Brown

Before he registered at Brown University, Jackie spirited John away to Africa. She wanted him thousands of miles from pestering paparazzi, the bright lights of Studio 54, and his Andover classmates.

Her own life had settled into a fairly stable routine by now. In 1975 she had become a part-time editor at Viking in Manhattan, but in 1977 she had resigned in protest after the company published *Shall We Tell the President?*—a Jeffrey Archer novel centering around an assassination attempt. Now working for Doubleday, she was happy, editing several books a year (including Michael Jackson's *Moonwalk*) and living the life of any prosperous Fifth Avenue widow.

Along with six teenage companions who were also taking the seventy-day National Outdoor Leadership Course on 17,000-foot

Mount Kenya, John found himself facing dangerous challenges. During the course, he took a sixty-two-mile trek with friends through snake-infested Masai country, sustained only by dehydrated food, flour, and cheese and guided only by a sketchy map.

They spent the first week in dense bush country, with trees growing as tall as 120 feet and undergrowth as high as 6 feet. Thanks to the limited visibility and scarce landmarks, John's group lost their way, and his companions appointed him leader as they struggled through the undergrowth with no food or water, terrified for their lives.

Worried about the safety of John and his friends, course director Lou Awodey sent out an SOS and planes, as well as Masai warriors, who began combing the countryside. Meanwhile, according to one of the group, John's major worry was "how concerned his family would be if his experience ever made newspaper headlines."

At one point during the ordeal, the small group of boys stumbled into a clearing, where they encountered a gigantic rhinoceros, twenty feet away and about to charge. John froze momentarily, but didn't panic. He slowly lowered his pack, ready to run for cover as he had been trained on the course. Just as he was about to make a dash for safety, the rhino changed direction and headed back into the undergrowth.

A Masai tracker finally found the group two days later.

"They didn't eat for a couple of days," said Eric Jeffers, who had just finished the course. "When we got to them, they were in great condition and very happy they were found."

John won points for his courage from the course director. "John acquitted himself very well," Awodey said. "He really enjoyed physical challenges of all sorts. His experiences had enough danger and adventure to hold any young person's interest, and his ordeal on the hike proved he can be counted on to keep a cool head. He took a tremendous step toward maturity during this grueling course."

———··———

Registering at Brown, the university of his choice, John could not have known that the start of his college career would prove more grueling than the adventure in the African jungle. At 2 P.M. on September 10, 1979, he lined up at the registration area on the Providence campus, one of 1,305 freshmen. Within minutes, a cluster of reporters began hovering around him as he stood in line. Photographers circled him, snapping shots from various angles. For John, it was a nightmare.

He knew his arrival had already caused comment. A Brown student from North Carolina, Lars Erickson, had been quoted in a Boston paper: "If the kid's a creep, no one will want to talk to him. But if he's a regular guy, he'll be accepted."

At Andover, his classmates had had time to get to know him before the onslaught of media attention. At Brown, he was already a topic of conversation and under siege by the world press before meeting a single classmate.

John had never wanted more desperately to be a regular guy. "Come on, you guys," he said. "This is embarrassing. I know you have a job to do, I'll gladly talk to you later, but not here. This is drawing too much attention. I didn't want this ... not here ... not today."

The photographers finally dispersed, having been promised that John would pose for a photo once he had registered.

He rejoined them a short while later, next to a Brown sign he had promised to pose in front of. He stood there—smiling—while the photographers snapped incessantly. To his further embarrassment, a large crowd of freshmen created a second ring around the press.

"Who's that?" he heard off to the right.

"I don't know, maybe he's a model doing some kind of commercial."

"Don't you know?" came a third voice. "That's JFK, Jr."

"Really?"

John lowered his head and gritted his teeth, then looked up at the nearest photographer.

"This is stupid," he said. "I feel real dumb doing this."

"Just a couple more shots, okay?" one photographer said, but John headed back into the building.

"God, I wish this would go away while I'm here," he told an acquaintance who walked with him back through the registration area.

"What are you going to major in?"

"I'm not sure. Maybe American history."

The friend laughed. "That would make sense."

John grinned, his dark mood evaporating. Maybe things wouldn't be so bad. All through his school years, the kids who knew him had always understood what he was facing, and had always closed ranks around him protectively.

As nervous as he was about his impending four years at Brown, his teachers viewed his arrival with similar trepidation. Deserved or not, his reputation preceded him.

"I had heard that John was a dummy, that he was more interested in sex than in school," teaching assistant Steve Gillon said.

Brown had been an unexpected choice for John. Instead of walking to class through Harvard Yard like his father and his uncle Teddy, John had opted for Brown and strolling to class through the Green. And although his choice sent shock waves through the ranks of the more traditional members of the Kennedy clan, Brown would prove an ideal choice.

In the sixties Brown had been regarded as inferior to the other Ivy League universities, a magnet for what one Brown graduate called "bad boys." But by the seventies the college had become fashionable, much favored by wealthy families who had bright kids of college age but didn't want them to be subjected to the eating clubs of Harvard, Yale, or Princeton.

In the parlance of the day, Brown was hip and happening, with less stringent academic standards than the other Ivy League universities. With Walter Mondale's son, Billy; Jimmy Carter's daughter, Amy; and John's cousin Kerry Kennedy all in attendance, Brown was fast becoming known as the Democrats' nursery.

John's classmates would include *GQ* cover model Richard Wiese. Yet as soon as John arrived on campus, he attracted more attention than any other freshman.

"People who thought the name Kennedy was a big deal would stop and turn their heads," said fellow freshman Rick Moseley. "But people got used to him pretty quickly and they just went about their own business."

"I met John when he was a freshman and I thought he was very down-to-earth, a nice guy," said Peter Burrow, a Brown graduate. "He lived in the dorm across the street from me. He was a terrific athlete, very unpretentious, very open. A nice guy—which is surprising, given what he's been through. He was preppy in the sense that he had that prep-school nonchalance, but he wasn't very sophisticated or urbane. I think that's what made him seem so reachable, so normal."

John's mode of dress was definitely his own. A typical outfit included shorts with boxers hanging well below the hem, a frayed Brooks Brothers button-down shirt, and Top-Siders.

"He was proud of his body and his strength," Burrow said. "I lifted weights with him and at the time he must have been benching around two hundred fifty pounds, which for his weight is a lot."

A seminar on Vietnam produced evidence of his intellectual weight. "He obviously thought through the events himself and what they meant," Burrow said. "He was a major contributor to our discussions."

But more often than not, John kept a low profile. He got enough attention without calling more to himself in class.

"Had he not been a Kennedy," Burrow said, "I think he would have been class president or school president."

Socially, John had learned to hold back when meeting people, waiting to see what the new acquaintance wanted from him—and whether he or she was trustworthy. It was important to know whether someone liked him for himself and not for his name.

John's telephone number at Brown was never listed; that would have been too much of a temptation for groupies. Periodically, at a party off campus, someone might grab him and start introducing him around. That kind of unwarranted attention made him uncomfortable. He would end the conversation quickly but politely and make his exit.

On Halloween in 1979, when he was still a freshman, John went to a costume party at the on-campus house of Brown undergraduate Larry Conway. Conway's sister, Jane, a beautiful blonde who is now a model, met him as he was entering.

John and his roommate were wearing raincoats.

"What are you dressed as?" Jane asked.

"A Secret Service agent," John said.

"Are you a Secret Service agent, too?" Jane asked his roommate.

"No, I'm a flasher."

"If you're a flasher and John's wearing the same outfit you are, why is he saying he's a Secret Service agent?"

His roommate laughed. "Because he's embarrassed to tell you he's really a flasher."

"We danced together at the party," Jane Conway said. "He was a great dancer—and really sweet. By the end of the party, everyone was drunk, John included. But he wasn't a mean or messy drunk, he just got very quiet."

John applied to join Phi Psi, which one female freshman described as "full of sexy-looking guys who gave wild parties," and Richard Wiese and a group of other fraternity brothers went to tell him that he had been accepted. They found him in the theater, getting ready for a dress rehearsal.

When they entered the dressing room, John—in creased baggy pants, a Mexican jersey, and a ski cap—looked up from the mirror, where he was applying pancake base.

"Hi, guys." He reached for the lipstick. "What's up?"

Eyebrows raised, the party hounds watched John make an O with his mouth.

He caught Wiese's expression in the mirror.

"You don't think this is the right shade for me, right?"

Wiese laughed. "Just don't wear it to scut class, okay?"

"I'm in?"

"If you survive Hell Night."

John smiled.

His introduction to Phi Psi included scut class, which meant learning and reciting his alphas and betas in Greek. His summers on Skorpios served him well.

Wiese, who had won top marks the year before, became John's Big Brother according to Phi Psi tradition, which was modeled on the British public school fagging system.

"You are my slave until Hell Night," Wiese informed him. "I have a craving for a Coke; run and get me one—and make sure it's cold."

John did as he was told. When he returned, Wiese tested the can.

"Not cold enough. You need to be punished. I want you to make a paddle I can use to teach you how to properly serve your master." John bowed, exiting the room backward.

John was patently eager to be treated just like any other Phi Psi pledge, but at the same time he demonstrated ingenuity, humor, and a sharp intelligence in avoiding some of the less pleasant aspects of frat life.

Two days into that week, Wiese called John into his room.

"I want you to fold my laundry."

"Yes, Big Brother." John looked at the pile of clothing on the bed. Raised with maids and servants, he commanded few domestic skills. When he had arranged the pile into a stack that didn't look much different from the first one, Wiese shook his head.

"That's pitiful," he said. "Have you finished that paddle I told you to make?"

"Yes, Big Brother."

"Go get it."

John returned with a two-and-a-half-foot mirrored paddle with light bulbs all around it. Wiese looked at it.

"Very clever," he said.

"Thank you, Big Brother."

"Almost too clever. I think I'll save it for the right opportunity."

Kidnapping was another time-honored hazing ritual. The unlucky pledge was grabbed by his frat brothers, hustled into a car, driven to some remote spot, and deposited there with only a dime thrown after him. John's frat brothers plotted his kidnapping carefully, deciding to capture him early one morning.

By now he was living in the four-story fraternity house in an inordinately messy twenty-by-twenty-foot second-floor room, which he shared with a frat brother named Robert Littell.

He was in the shower when his would-be kidnappers burst in.

"John, you're coming with us."

"I don't have any clothes on," John called from inside the shower. "Come on, guys, at least let me get dressed."

The kidnappers looked at one another, then shrugged their shoulders.

"Okay." They left the shower area and waited.

After what seemed like ages, they broke into the bathroom—

which was empty. One of them noticed the open window and they all rushed toward it.

John was dangling from the windowsill, wearing only a towel around his waist. Beneath the window, four people were in the process of pushing a basketball net on wheels under the window so that he could jump into it.

His brothers grabbed him and hauled him back inside. After several moments spent trying to pin him down, they lost him again; his years of weight lifting prevailed. John ran to his room, grabbed a pair of shorts and a T-shirt, and hightailed it for the student union.

The kidnapping of John F. Kennedy, Jr., was never carried out—he was far too resourceful at evading his captors.

But he didn't even try to escape Hell Night.

Blindfolded and wearing just their underwear, John and twenty other pledges were locked in a bar. Each was forced to drink a huge flagon of beer. Just as John took the last swallow, a brother forced open his mouth and shoved in a live goldfish.

"Swallow it," Wiese shouted.

Gagging, John did as he was told and drank more beer to wash the fish down. Then he was led to another room.

"Crawl, you slime!"

John slithered along the floor, encountering all manner of fish and animal guts whichever direction he turned in.

"What are you going to do for the frat?" a chorus of voices shouted in the darkness. "What are you going to do?"

The brothers herded him toward the toilet, where they forced his hand into the bowl.

"Run your hand through the toilet water and grab what you find there," a voice ordered.

The brothers had put a banana down the bowl. It broke apart in his hand.

"Thank you, sirs," John said. "That was nice."

At this, Wiese pulled out the paddle.

"You must be punished for your impertinence."

"But I did what you said—"

"Silence! Bend over."

John did as he was told and Wiese paddled him lightly, following tradition—and not wanting to break the light bulbs.

"Thank you, sir," John said. "May I have another?"

"As badly as you want another, you will be denied."

Finally, covered with fish entrails and dog food, John and the other pledges were ordered out into the yard.

"Strip off your underwear," a brother shouted.

The pledges did as they were told. Onlookers hooted at the goose-bumpy recruits.

"Now streak once around the quad."

More students assembled to cheer them on. Female students shouted out ratings as each one passed. As they ran, one of the recruits tried to cover himself.

"God, I'd rather go back through the fish guts," he said.

At the end of the chilly lap, Hell Night was over. John F. Kennedy, Jr., had passed the initiation tests with flying colors and was now a full-fledged member in good standing of Phi Psi.

He was one of the boys at last. There were no Secret Service agents, and when the press showed up, they were chased off by John's frat brothers, who protected him loyally. He was finally becoming his own man, and in the process growing more and more like his father.

"We never mentioned his father to him," Peter Burrow said. "It was a no-go subject at Phi Psi, out of respect."

Away from the frat house, certain comparisons of father and son were unavoidable. Jack, for example, had been notorious for borrowing money and not being particularly quick to return it.

"Money meant absolutely nothing to him," said actress Angela Greene, who once dated Jack. "He continually charged everything and borrowed money constantly from friends and acquaintances."

John was the same. "I can recall his borrowing more money than he lent," Wiese said.

"I went to the theater to see *Waiting for Godot* with John," another student said. "He had invited me, but when it came to paying, he had forgotten his wallet."

"The notion of working at a job as if your life depended on it fascinated him," said fellow student Christa de Souza. "I remember him telling me how he planned to earn extra cash at college by standing on street corners and handing out fliers on reduced stereo system equipment."

Father and son also took pride in their bodies.

"Jack never hung up anything," said one of his roommates at Choate. "He just dropped his clothes where he was or tossed them all over the suite." John's untidiness was legendary.

"As for John, he was an exhibitionist who had a great body and knew it," said a woman who was at Brown with him. "He certainly displayed it draped in a towel often enough."

There were those who attributed John's sexual magnetism to genetics.

"John was not a philanderer like his father," Christa de Souza said. "And his taste in women ran to fresh-faced girls. In fact, if Mia Farrow were thirty years younger, there's no doubt in my mind that John would have fallen in love with her."

"He didn't just have his father's charisma, he also had his sense of humor," said Peter Burrow. "When he first moved into the frat, he bought a pig with the idea of raising it to sell for slaughter. Here's a guy with a trust fund raising pigs in the basement of Phi Psi to make money. He said he would sell it to make money for himself. That may have been a tongue-in-cheek comment, but the whole thing was rather funny at the time."

Thinking the pig was John's pet, a group of female students hatched a plan to steal it.

"We were going to grab the pig one day when John was out and then replace it with a pile of bacon," one of the students confessed. "We lost our nerve in the end, but we knew John would have loved it—he had a great sense of humor."

"It's not just a job, it's an adventure," proclaimed a popular Army recruiting commercial that showed trainees crawling through mud. Providence, Rhode Island, is known for its rainy climate, and one particular semester the rain fell relentlessly for so many days in succession that the campus turned into a muddy swamp.

John came back from a football game, his fatigues and T-shirt spattered with globs of mud. Crossing the quadrangle in front of Phi Psi, he suddenly flung himself down into the mud in full view of his frat brothers and started to crawl, shouting at the top of his voice, "It's not just a job, it's an adventure!"

Unlike the public, the fraternity members got to see every aspect of their famous brother. They both liked and respected him.

"At one point we had a basketball net set up on the front porch," Peter Burrow said. "John joined the impromptu games down there on the patio at all hours. He was an excellent athlete."

He was also known as the kind of guy who went out of his way to talk to his friends, to stop by their rooms, even just to throw a ball around. He didn't have a close circle around him, but once he trusted someone, that was it.

There was a tacit understanding with the local press that they wouldn't bother him during his time at Brown. But the inhabitants of Providence couldn't help themselves.

"When John used to wander down Thayer Street, proprietors of restaurants would see him," recalled a fellow student. "They'd offer him free hamburgers and stuff. John was always gracious and polite."

"He used to drive a gray Honda Civic, just an ordinary clinker like everyone else's," said Richard Wiese, who is still in close contact with John today. "And he had a great mix of friends. He has always had plenty of black friends and is truly color-blind when it comes to people."

Not known as a brain, John was smart nonetheless. He often surprised his friends with references to great writers and poets. When hiking, the brothers often tested each other on history and geography, subjects in which John's upbringing served him well. Outsiders often underestimated his intelligence when pestering him with questions, because he would invariably answer in shorthand to hasten his escape.

"He never liked social-register people or anyone who put on airs," Wiese said. "He's cool, and even today he does what he wants— rides the subway, whatever. He is unassuming, a good person, not at all a braggart or a show-off."

There was the constant question whether people were interested in him for himself or his name.

Once John told Wiese that a mutual friend had introduced him to his boss.

"Was he introducing you to show you off to him or to show his boss off to you?" asked Wiese.

"Boy, you really can't think about that kind of stuff," John said. "Because you could drive yourself crazy."

Even the teachers weren't immune to his charms.

"John once wandered into a course run by a teacher who was German," remembered a student in that course. "He sauntered in, his trousers at half-mast. The teacher was very beautiful and when John saw her, he did a double-take. The teacher was so nervous she could hardly go on with the class."

He tried hard to combat the impression that he was an otherworldly being who had landed at Brown from some celestial plane. He and his friends had food fights in the canteen. He also made a great point of parodying bad table manners and playing at being working-class.

Those who could see through the media creation to the real John discovered a truly charismatic person. Contrary to his tabloid image, he was neither a brooding individualist nor a spoiled brat. He was a natural leader, and people gravitated toward him. Yet he remained unaffected by all the adulation and attention. Above all, he was kind.

"I think John will goof about certain friends and stuff like that, but he'd rather be the butt of a joke than to hurt someone else," said Wiese, who often teased John as "low Irish." John just laughed. He had a good heart, and retaliation just wasn't part of his nature.

"I've never seen him intentionally lash out with malice or deliberately do anything to hurt somebody," Wiese said. "He hasn't got a vengeful bone in his body."

Once, during an abortive lunch, a student pulled down John's trousers in full view of everyone in the canteen. According to an eye-witness, John was not amused. He was proud of his body but wanted control over when and how it was displayed.

His fame, looks, and reputation ensured that during his years at Brown women constantly threw themselves at his feet.

"I remember once being virtually ordered by the supermodel Cindy Crawford to bring him to her twenty-first birthday," said Christa de Souza. "I did, and they supposedly dated a couple of times, but nothing really came of it."

"A girl turned up one day and camped in the lobby," remembered Brewster Conant, Jr. "She said John was in love with her. But he didn't know her. It took us a while to get rid of her; she obviously didn't have all of her marbles."

John played wing forward on the men's rugby team but didn't always turn up to play. His coach, Jay Fluck, echoed the sentiments of his Andover coaches: "He probably could have been a much better player had he put his heart in it."

Theater remained his great passion. Acting coach James Barnhill referred to him as "extremely talented," and the head of the drama department, Don Wilmeth, was enthusiastic about his work. "He's a very sound actor, very directable. If he had taken theater seriously, he could have been wonderful."

In some respects, the frat brothers had become John's new family. Jackie visited him in Brown, but neither she nor the other Kennedys telephoned often during the school term.

"I lived and breathed with John during the nine months he was at Brown each school year, and I was pretty aware of family visits and phone calls," said Peter Burrow. "There just weren't that many."

Jackie visited the frat house for the first time the night after a wild party. Crumpled pretzel packages, empty beer cans, and puddles of spilled wine were all over the floor. Richard Wiese, still tired from the night before, found John sitting on a wall outside the house.

"I've got to go to a professor's house and drop off a paper," John said, jumping down from the wall. "But my mother is supposed to come and meet me here. If you see her, please tell her I'll be back in a minute. She's got dark hair and dark glasses."

"I think I'll recognize her," Wiese said.

He was not surprised at John's having given him a description of the most recognized woman in the world. "John is genuinely very modest," Wiese said. "And he would not assume that you knew what his mother looked like."

When Jackie arrived, she asked to use the phone in John's room. Wiese showed her inside, and she made her call. Afterward they sat and chatted. During the conversation Peter Burrow joined them but failed to realize who was sitting across from him.

"I thought she was a Brown student or a model, because Rich knew a lot of models," said Burrow.

"Would you like to meet Mrs. Onassis?" Wiese asked.

Flustered, Burrow offered her one of the two bananas he had just brought from the cafeteria.

"Thank you," Jackie said. "But I've just eaten."

Then she started asking a lot of ordinary questions, just like any other Brown mother.

"Why shouldn't she?" said Burrow. "After all, she had a son at Brown who was just like us."

On October 20, 1979, in the Boston suburb of Dorchester, the Kennedy Library was dedicated and John F. Kennedy, Jr., made his first major speech. In front of a crowd of seven thousand, which included twenty-six cousins, his aunts, and his uncles—including Teddy, who was about to run for President—John recited Stephen Spender's poem "I Think Continually of Those Who Were Truly Great."

"This was the first time most people heard John speak," said a photographer who covered the event. "One thing that surprised us was his not having an accent. His cousin Joe and all his other cousins have Boston accents. But John didn't sound like Boston—or New York, either. His voice was flat with no accent at all. But he was gorgeous, and everyone watching that day was stunned by his looks and his charisma."

The library building, designed by I. M. Pei, stood on an undeveloped stretch of land called Columbia Point. Facing the sea, the iron and glass building was tall and dramatic.

Throughout the ceremony and most particularly during the dramatic moment when the voice of John F. Kennedy rang through the sharp Massachusetts air, asking not what your country can do for you, the eyes of his son were fixed on his widow, Jackie, with love and concern.

"John is the light of Jackie's life," said the photographer who covered this and subsequent events at the library. "I think John knows it, so he rarely brings a girlfriend with him to any of the library events that relate to his father's memory. His focus is all on his mother and he's very protective of her."

As the sky brightened, the attention of some people in the crowd turned to the *Victura*, the sailboat Jack Kennedy had loved, now displayed inside the library along with the desk under which John used to hide and then jump out at his delighted father.

The library would come to mean a great deal to John. Dave Powers, his father's aide who had once taught him to salute, had been made curator. John, now a member of the Library Foundation, would spend many hours in the library, immersed in the memorabilia of his father's life.

"He loves just to come in and walk around," said Powers. "He feels improvements should be made—that the accomplishments of his father's life should be better presented. I have nothing but confidence in John. Whatever ideas he has will be the ones we'll use."

John's favorite exhibit centered around his father's press conferences. John believed this exhibit should be expanded, as should others revolving around the President's role in the Peace Corps. As proud as John was of his father, Powers recognized that the father would feel the same pride in return.

"John is definitely his father's son. It's that special grace. When his father entered a room, it lit up. I can see that happening with John someday."

That someday became the present. By the time Teddy ran for election, John's magnetism radiated from his own personality, not just his famous name. Eminently aware of the potency of his nephew's appeal, Teddy enlisted him in his campaign.

"I first met John during the campaign," said one of Teddy's

workers. "Teddy held a clambake at the compound, and John and all the kids were there, but John kept to himself. Some of the other cousins were all over the place, in and out of the house, running up and down, throwing a football around. John was very dignified, cute, charming, and boyish. I remember thinking, 'What a nice kid.'

"Jackie was there that day as well. She never allowed him out of her sight—she watched him all the time, and he seemed very docile and obedient. I've seen them together a lot through the years, and John has always been very deferential to her. Jackie is much more tuned in to John than to Caroline. There is a real, real close relationship between the two of them. It doesn't surprise me that she's closer to her son than to her daughter—Jackie always liked men better than women."

John campaigned for Teddy in Worcester, Providence, and Fall River, Massachusetts. At a January 15, 1980, press conference held in the Providence office of former governor Dennis J. Roberts, chairman of Teddy's campaign in Rhode Island, John announced that he would make himself available to student groups.

"I want to help make my uncle more visible and to answer questions about his positions," he said. "I'm happy to do anything for my uncle."

True to his word, he even tackled the controversial subject of Chappaquiddick, following the family line: "This issue has been resolved, and I don't think it has a place in this discussion. That's all that needs to be said."

He was exhibiting all the signs of an incipient politician, but if he was gratified by his reception, he didn't voice any political ambitions of his own. He usually listened attentively to Teddy's speeches, added two or three complimentary sentences of his own, and then, flanked by security guards, made his exit.

On January 18, 1980, he made a three-minute speech for Teddy at Slavin Hall, Providence College. He was almost an hour late. An audience of three hundred fifty students listened politely as he urged them to help in Ted's primary campaigns in New Hampshire and Maine. Watching him, one reporter was disappointed.

"There were no dramatic gestures, no eloquent phrases to stir the emotions, no proud toss of the head, none of the charisma that his late father would have used so knowingly to electrify an audience."

John was low-key and intended to stay that way.

In Providence on January 21, Representative Beard welcomed him as "young Jack Kennedy." John smiled politely. He had been up most of the night writing papers for his history exam and knew he should be studying, but he didn't want to let his uncle down.

Jackie played only a small part in Ted's campaign, making a few brief appearances. In the past few years she had moved further away from the Kennedy family—even in New England, the Kennedy stamping ground. She had staked out her own territory by building a $3-million saltbox-style house on 356 acres of scrub oak tract on Martha's Vineyard. The 3,000-square-foot main house and 900-square-foot guest house boasted white oak floors, heated towel racks, brick chimneys, and a sun deck. The focal point of John's third-floor bedroom in a specially built barn was a heart-shaped bed.

Despite her spectacular beauty, Jenny Christian's romance with John sputtered out. She was away at Harvard studying psychology, and John filled the empty time with other girls.

Jackie, meanwhile, seemed to have found companionship, if not love, with Maurice Tempelsman, her financial adviser. To this day, he remains married to his wife, Lilly Tempelsman. An avuncular Belgian-born self-made millionaire, the same age as Jackie, Tempelsman controls the firm of Leon Tempelsman and Son, which buys diamonds in London and Antwerp for resale to wholesalers and dealers in the United States. He also owns the American Coldset Corporation, the world's second-largest manufacturer of petroleum drill bits, which also has global affiliations with copper, uranium, and gold mining and development companies. A financial genius, Tempelsman—unlike Onassis, of whom some whispered he was a less interesting clone—appreciates the opera, ballet, and theater. Although he failed to graduate from college, he speaks fluent French and is a gourmet and an ardent sailor, as much at home at La Côte Basque in New York as on the sixty-foot yacht he sails to Hilton Head Island with Jackie.

John soon developed an easy rapport with the new man in his mother's life, accepting Tempelsman without apparent difficulty. His mother, though, just couldn't give her blessing to the continuing passion of John's life—acting.

On March 14, 1980, he appeared as Bonario, a professional soldier, in Ben Jonson's *Volpone*. Jackie came on opening night, and after the performance he made it eminently clear to her that although this was the first play in which he had acted since arriving at Brown, it would not be his last.

The *Brown Daily Herald's* critic applauded John's performance but later publicly retracted the praise. The turnabout was humiliating.

"John doesn't move well," the critic wrote. "He's very inhibited and self-conscious on stage. And his voice is off-putting. He sounds like a rich New York preppie." Consolidating the blow to John's pride, he went on to say that he regretted having praised John's performance and that "I didn't think John was as good as I made him out to be. But I was sitting next to his mother on opening night, and I guess I was dazzled."

Undaunted, John still believed in his acting ability, as did his acting teachers. The capricious criticism hurt his pride but did nothing to weaken his intention to pursue his interest in the theater.

To smooth any maternal feathers he may have ruffled with his proclamation, John spent the summer in South Africa, working for the project development section of Leon Tempelsman and Son. Exposure to the injustices of apartheid gave John a renewed social conscience. His energy and passion for the subject when he returned impressed both Jackie and his friends.

"I've got all this knowledge, now what do I do with it?" he said to fellow Brown student Randall Poster.

Maurice Tempelsman indirectly provided an answer, paying the operating expenses for the South African Group for Education, which John created to help students understand the political conditions in South Africa. John had always wanted to work with black people, and his South African visit had intensified that desire. Passionate in educating fellow students about the real South Africa, he arranged for former UN ambassador Andrew Young to lecture on South Africa at Brown on December 16, 1980.

In May 1981, John was back in makeup and leotards, playing Antonio in *The Tempest*. Local drama critics in Providence judged his performance confident but noted that he lacked the villain's requisite malice. When asked whether he wanted to become an actor, he thought carefully before answering.

"I don't plan to make acting my profession—although I do enjoy it."

In private, however, he was far more enthusiastic. Although his mother was appalled by his attraction to the theater and had made her aversion eminently clear, John continued to act and to rebel.

"John was appearing in Shakespeare at Brown and he sent the reviews to Peter," said Patricia Seaton Lawford.

"Uncle Peter, what am I going to do?" John wrote. "I want to be an actor, but my mother has said no, and the rest of the family thinks it's a laugh."

"If a man wants to be an actor," John's uncle said, "he wants to be an actor."

Peter began to encourage John and give him advice about pursuing an acting career. Peter understood perfectly the pressure the Kennedy family could bring to bear on an actor in their midst, no matter how successful. Although an outcast, he had been devastated by the assassination, and his life had taken a downturn afterward.

"He never forgot Jack," Patricia said. "They had killed the only brother he'd ever wanted, and he saw John as this tormented little boy. I think he always carried that picture in his head of John saluting his father's coffin."

At the funeral, Peter had tried to explain Jack's death to his own daughter Sydney.

"Will we ever see Uncle Jack again?" the little girl asked.

"No, we'll never see him again," Peter said. "It's like if you lose your finger, it will never grow back again."

Fingers may not grow back, but sons eventually grow up, and Peter genuinely liked the man John was becoming. When John was a child, Peter had worried that the lack of a male influence might cause his nephew to become a mama's boy. Watching John mature, he realized his fears were groundless. But he still tried to help John as much as he could.

Jackie eventually sent Peter a stern note saying that he mustn't influence John to act because she disapproved and wanted him to be a scholar. Peter just laughed and continued to encourage his nephew.

John spent the summer of 1981 working at Terry Sanford's Center for Democratic Policy, a Washington group that was exploring the ideological reasons behind the Democratic party's November defeat. Paid just $100 a week, he stayed with the Shrivers. At Teddy's suggestion, he gave a brief press conference.

"Senator Kennedy spent hours on the phone trying to convince Jackie to let John do that interview," said a friend. "John has had nothing but bad knocks from the press, and Teddy felt it would be good to have some publicity that showed him as a serious person."

During the conference at the center's Dupont Circle offices, John nervously fingered his blue tie (decorated with white skulls), then looked down at his ink-stained white shirt.

"It's pretty wrinkled." He smiled. "Shows I'm doing my own laundry. I would wear one of those plastic pocket protectors, but they make you look like a Republican."

Asked how he spent his free time in Washington, he said, "I don't really go out much. I'm teaching myself to play the guitar." Was he considering a Washington-based political career? With typical vagueness, he said, "I'm not really thinking about careers at the moment. I'm not a big planner."

He was, however, sure of one thing. He wanted to blaze a career trail away from the shadow of his immediate family. He could have decided to work for Teddy, as had Caroline, but instead he had chosen the center.

"He worked hard," said one of his associates, "and he never asked for any special favors."

Back at Brown, he was besieged by women who wanted special favors from him—to date him, go to parties with him, to be seen with him.

"I talked to him about all that," said Larry Conway, a fellow student. "His phone rang off the hook."

"Women keep calling to invite me to dinner and I keep turning them down," John said. "That's why I usually eat early—so I don't run into the ones I've turned down."

For all the humor of the comment, John was distressed and not quite sure how to solve the problem.

"I think he was happiest in the gym working out, lifting weights with a bunch of sweaty guys," Conway said. "He liked just talking about exercise. But he didn't try that hard at anything, because any success would have led to more limelight."

When discussing the Vietnam war during a history class, the

teacher asked John some questions about his father. John remained quiet.

"He just wanted to be in the class," said Conway. "He wanted to be one of the guys."

In January 1982 John clipped his hair to a Marine crew cut for his part in the Brown University Production Workshop's presentation of David Rabe's *In the Boom Boom Room*. John played a Philadelphia street hood who is dating a go-go dancer.

"He was very good," said Chris Harty, a member of the cast. "The play had a modest budget—it was what we called a black box production, put on without faculty."

John's haircut created quite a buzz around campus. "One girl took off her top for the role," another Brown student said, "so John thought the least he could do was get a haircut."

Caroline came to opening night, as did the critic from the *Brown Daily Herald*.

"Kennedy's performance was really the high point of the evening," the critic wrote. "It's not easy to take a stereotypical part like that of macho boyfriend and to play it convincingly—without hardly ever succumbing to the characteristic Pacino-type movements and speech patterns so many actors feel obliged to take on."

On May 7, 1982, John appeared in J. M. Synge's *The Playboy of the Western World* at Brown's Fauce House Theater, playing the lead, Christy Mahon.

This was his first lead. After casting him, Don Wilmeth summoned John to his office.

"What are we going to do?" he asked John pleadingly. "I don't want to exploit you, but I don't want to ignore the fact that you are in the play, either."

John thought for a minute, then shrugged and said, "Go ahead and mention my name. But if you can do anything to minimize the press attention, I'd appreciate that."

"John did a fine job in the play," said Wilmeth. "Acting was what he did for fun and he didn't have any inflated idea of his position or his looks."

This time, at least, John's looks appeared to work against him. David Yazbek said in the *Brown Daily Herald:* "Director Don Wilmeth made a big mistake in choosing John Kennedy for the role of Christy, who requires a metamorphosis that Kennedy is incapable of producing. This is not to fault the actor for his performance, which was more than adequate. The fact is, Christy should be played by a meek-looking actor so that his transformation into a hero, which is the play's focus, is astounding and humorous. When Christy talks with wonder about the women flocking around him or boasts about his newfound athletic prowess, we are supposed to be amazed and amused. When Kennedy, with his athletic frame and good looks, says these things, we are not surprised in the least."

Though his mother was dismayed at his acting and the critics ambivalent, his fellow actors were supportive.

"I think he was drawn to acting for the usual conscious and subconscious reasons," said Chris Harty, who played his father in *Playboy.* "But he may have had less of a conscious reason than most people. After all, he didn't need to get more famous or better-looking. He acted because he was a good actor."

On April 20, 1983, John made his last major theatrical appearance at Brown, playing Longshoe, a tough Irish greaser in the Leeds Theater production of Miguel Piñero's *Short Eyes.* The play, set in a house of detention, tells the story of a child molester thrown in with a group of inmates who loathe him for his crime. *Brown Daily Herald* critic Peter DeChiara had no reservations whatsoever about John's acting abilities.

"John played his part to perfection," DeChiara wrote. "The gum-chewing, tattooed Kennedy throws his bulk around the set with infinite self-assurance and an air of stubborn defiance."

This performance surprised none of his friends. John had always been strong-willed, and acting with stubborn defiance was not exactly foreign to his nature. He had also always been fascinated not only with acting but with actors.

"Whenever I was involved with the Robert F. Kennedy Tennis Tournament, John immediately gravitated to the celebrities who came to the event," said publicist Barry Landau. "And when actors came to the Cape Cod Playhouse for summer stock, John always wanted to meet them."

John's passion for acting was so powerful that he turned down the chance to tour Ireland with the Brown rugby team because the tour coincided with a play that interested him.

"John always tried to keep a low profile," recalled Peter Burrow, "so I was surprised he got so involved in acting. Drama means pretty major exposure, and there was a real risk for John there. I was surprised he did something so open, but then he genuinely loved acting."

His eagerness to mix with actors was again evident when teenage actress and Calvin Klein model Brooke Shields came to Brown. John showed her and her mother, Terry Shields, around the campus. They strolled through the grounds, stopping for a roast beef sandwich at Matt's Sicilian Pizza parlor in Providence, which aroused a great deal of excitement. At sixteen, Brooke Shields—wearing beige corduroys, a brown wool blazer, and leather boots and carrying a Gucci shoulder bag—was breathtaking. John didn't get romantically involved with Shields, but they became friends.

In his junior year he moved off campus to a house at 155 Benefit Street, which he shared with Rob Littell, a star lacrosse player; Christiane Amanpour, who was to become a celebrated CNN correspondent; fledgling actress Christina Haag; and John Hare, captain of the tennis team. John's relationship with Jenny Christian had finally ended, although their friendship survived, and he was now involved with another student, Sally Munro.

"Sally was an unusual choice for John," said a Brown classmate. "She wasn't particularly glamorous."

Christa de Souza described Sally Munro as a "second-string type," theorizing that John wanted a woman who would trail in his wake without attracting yet more attention.

Sally was a classic New Englander who was often mistaken for Caroline. It was a pattern John would repeat with a future girl-friend, Julie Baker—a dead ringer for Jackie. From the age of three his life had been dominated by the women in his immediate family, and as he matured he gravitated toward women with familiar charac-teristics.

Sally Munro, a young woman from old Boston Irish stock, had grown up in a five-million-dollar oceanfront home in Marblehead, a Massachusetts port where her family had lived for centuries. She had grown up sheltered.

But not so sheltered that she could resist John. When he was in New York, he would play touch football in Central Park, and though none of the other players brought their girlfriends, Munro was always there, just waiting for him.

She was very bright, majoring in literature and history, and had the kind of cultured background and interests Jackie appreciated.

"Jackie really liked Sally," said a Brown student. "But John wasn't quite sure whether he was ready to commit to her."

Committed or not, his wild frat days were over.

"John was no longer a booze-guzzling rebellious slob," said a friend, charting the change in him since his involvement with Munro. The clincher came when friends noted that even his car, once filled with beer cans, was suddenly immaculate.

During the summer of 1982 John spent six weeks at the University of Connecticut, where he and cousin Timothy Shriver taught English to teenagers from low-income families. There were whispers that John was unenthusiastic about spending his summer in such a cerebral environment, but he ardently wanted to help the children and, with Timothy's guidance, applied himself to the task.

Despite the seriousness of his summer pursuits and the apparent stability of his relationship with Sally Munro, he couldn't resist sniffing out a little glamour. In December 1982 he went to Xenon, still one of his favorite late-night haunts. Without Munro to cramp his style, he attended a party hosted by the Elite model agency. No matter how sensible and intelligent Munro might be, John was far from immune to a more ostentatious type of beauty. In his T-shirt, with muscles rippling, John had his pick of any model in the club.

Despite Jackie's influence, the demands of his Kennedy heritage, and the stabilizing factor of Sally Munro, he was still something of a rebel. Although he never let himself go, there was a subtext of recklessness in his personality that growing up was not going to eradicate. He had always been accident-prone, and his driving was a subtle indication of his penchant for risk-taking.

Jackie had allowed him to drive when he was only fourteen, and according to one of his Brown classmates, "he collected tickets like confetti." Once behind the wheel of his car, he relaxed. On January 7, 1983, he was arrested by Connecticut State Police for driving eighty-one miles per hour in a fifty-five-mile-per-hour zone, and on January 29, his license was suspended in Massachusetts and New York, where his car was also registered.

About to graduate, John had reached a crossroads in his life. He was determined to become an actor, and Jackie was equally determined to stop him. She had loved Peter Lawford while despising his profession.

John was supposed to follow a more respectable career—to stay out of the public eye, which to her spelled danger.

"Jackie was always terrified that someone would make an attempt on John's life," said Leo Damore, author of *Senatorial Privilege.* "She knew acting would give him a higher profile than ever, and she totally opposed his career."

Her self-control had always been iron, like her will. She believed she was fighting for John's own good; she wanted fiercely to protect him, to steer him away from a world she considered tawdry and unworthy of him. Declaring war on his ambitions, she prepared to fight with every weapon in her armory.

"Jackie made it very, very clear that she expected John to dedicate his life to something more serious than acting," said a Kennedy family retainer. "She laid down the law: as the son of John Fitzgerald Kennedy, he had an obligation to pursue a 'worthwhile' career."

He loved his mother, admired her courage in the face of the tragedies she had endured, appreciated the love she had given him—but made one last attempt to resist her. When he announced that he wanted to attend Yale Drama School on graduation, she played her trump card.

"I'll disinherit you unless you go to law school," she said.

For John, the conflict was excruciating—and the irony inescapable. Jack Kennedy, too, had originally chosen a different destiny from the one thrust on him by his father.

"Jack didn't want to be President," said Senator George Smathers. "He wanted to be a writer, to spend his life writing books. But when his brother died, Joe Kennedy literally drafted him into politics. Jack had no choice but to do what his father wanted. I don't think anyone ever tried to resist Joe Kennedy, least of all his son."

Jackie, too, was irresistible, but for different reasons. She imposed her will on John through his love for her, not through fear. He would follow his mother's wishes and not the dictates of his heart: the theater, a vocation cast aside—the battle lost.

He was scheduled to take his Law School Admission Test at Brown in June 1983. His heart wasn't in it, but his professional future was now set in stone. On June 5, 1983, Teddy spoke at a Brown commencement forum. Beginning his talk by preaching his philosophy of arms control, his voice suddenly husky with emotion, he said, "I know how much my brother Jack cherished John's future—and how proud he would be if he could be here today."

On June 5, the night before John's graduation, Jackie hosted a dinner for seventeen in his honor at the Biltmore Plaza Hotel's L'Apogée. Lee Radziwill, Janet Auchincloss, Dave Powers, and Caroline, with the new love of her life, Ed Schlossberg, were there. At the end, Teddy presented John with some of his father's notes, framed.

After the fracas surrounding his Andover graduation, John had expressed the fervent wish that once he went to Brown, the turmoil surrounding him would finally subside. June 6, 1983, the day of his graduation, demonstrated conclusively that this hope had been in vain.

Jackie and her party arrived on the campus green more than an hour before the opening ceremony. Dressed in a purple polka-dot dress, Jackie waited under a tree, so happy that she even beamed at the photographers. Finally the procession started, with John dressed in gown and mortarboard and—a classic John touch—white chinos and cowboy boots. He was protected from the hordes of photographers by his classmates, who marched on either side of him and tried to hide him from view.

As the procession wound its way to the green, a plane suddenly materialized, skywriting the words "Good Gluck John." Jackie and her group applauded loudly. The skywriting had been their gift to him, the spelling a family joke.

As he passed her in the crowd, he waved and shouted, "Hi, Mom!"

It was a moment only John could have created. With the world press swirling around the legendary Jacqueline Kennedy Onassis, he reduced the icon and the moment to just two words—signaling to her that no matter what the world thought, no matter what the fans craved, to him, she was just "Mom."

Jackie sat in the fourth row of the audience while cameras clicked incessantly.

"It seems like the same picture over and over," said John, but he went through the morning with what eyewitness Anne Diffily characterized as "well-bred patience and courtesy throughout."

The general public would be able to catch a glimpse of him before and after services at St. Stephen's Church. Some had been waiting since eight o'clock that morning.

"I wouldn't miss it," said one.

"Took the day off work just to see young John," said another.

Reporters and photographers from as far away as France, England, and Germany fought for space outside the church, waiting with cameras poised for the arrival of the undergraduates.

When John finally appeared, press and fans alike roared their good wishes, shouting, "Good luck, John!" and "God bless." It was the fifteenth anniversary of his uncle Bobby's assassination; nineteen and a half years since his father had died in Dallas. To the crowds, John represented a past that had never been forgotten and a future that was yet to be born.

CHAPTER TEN

New York

The waves of the Atlantic churned malevolently, and John checked the swell before dropping into the water. Somewhere below lay the remains of the *Whydah*, a pirate ship that had sunk off the coast of Cape Cod in 1717. As he made his silent, slow descent through the darkness, schools of fish approached, then turned away in unison.

Moving slowly to avoid the bends, John could hear the voice of his step-grandfather, Hugh Auchincloss, spinning his terrifying tales of piracy while his grandson listened wide-eyed. As a boy, John had dreamed of the pirate Captain Kidd, whose ill-gotten loot was reputedly buried in a sunken treasure ship off this same cape. Finding the *Whydah* would not be as glamorous as discovering Kidd's craft, but it would do.

When he was seventeen, he'd met professional underwater explorer Barry Clifford on Martha's Vineyard and learned to dive with him, exploring World War I ships eighty feet beneath the New England waters.

Since then, he had dived with Clifford many times in quest of the ill-fated *Whydah*, which had been captained by Welshman Samuel Bellamy. Now, in the summer of 1983, John had joined Clifford and a team of twenty divers to search for the wreck in the treacherous Cape waters.

"John had a summer job with the team, but I wouldn't have given it to him if he hadn't taken it very seriously," remembered Clifford. "He's a good diver. The team included divers from the Special Forces [an elite branch of the armed services] who were professionals and wouldn't have tolerated John if he hadn't been their equal. But he fit in perfectly. There were times when he could have panicked, but he never did. He kept completely cool and I had the highest respect for him."

John dived nearly all day, using six to eight tanks of oxygen at a time, determined to help the team find the *Whydah*. Jackie's program to toughen him up, to put iron in his soul, had given him a kind of physical intelligence that helped him now. At Outward Bound, he had learned self-reliance, the ability to be alone and survive. His stint as a ranch hand had taught him about teamwork. In Africa he had encountered the unexpected and the ferocity of the wild. All these lessons had molded him into a man who could hold his own with the more experienced divers.

This summer, he would learn that hard work doesn't always pay off immediately. The goal of finding the ship wasn't nearly so important as what he discovered about himself during the search. The *Whydah* was found the following year, when he was no longer on the team. Nevertheless, he had made his mark. He had enjoyed his summer, relaxing after work with drinks at waterfront bars.

"John wasn't a rich dilettante," Clifford said. "He was someone we all liked and appreciated."

In August Bobby Kennedy, Jr., was arrested for heroin possession. The following year, his brother David was to die of a drug overdose after years of battling his addiction. Patrick Kennedy and his cousin Chris Lawford would both grapple with drug dependency, but they and Bobby would be luckier and overcome it. All four had been born to pain, privilege, and too much money—as reliable a setup for addiction as poverty and deprivation.

John flirted with drugs, acquiring a taste for marijuana and sampling cocaine. Despite those experiences, and the reckless seam that ran deep through the Kennedy nature, he had a powerful inner compass that ultimately steered him away from excess.

November 22, 1983, marked the twentieth anniversary of the death of John F. Kennedy. Caroline, Teddy, Stephen and Jean Smith, Eunice Shriver, and Patricia Lawford knelt to pray by the grave. A generation had been born and had grown up since Jack's death. At a memorial Mass at Holy Trinity Church, Teddy reaffirmed his brother's legacy:

"As the torch is passed to each succeeding generation, I believe that those who seek peace and justice, those who join the forward march of the human pilgrimage on earth will say of John Fitzgerald Kennedy that he has never left us, and he never will."

John did not attend the memorial; he was not even in the country. After seeing his graduation turned into a media circus, he wanted no part of the attention surrounding the anniversary and had left for India a month earlier.

His cousins Kara and Teddy threw a farewell party for him at Manhattan's Rockabout Disco, where he and Sally Munro danced the night away before he left for London. During his layover, he escorted Caroline to a party at the American Embassy celebrating the premiere of her BBC-WNET documentary, "New Visions: American Art and the Metropolitan Museum."

While his relatives knelt by his father's grave, John was in the land of Gandhi, completely removed from the Kennedy orbit. Jackie had always loved India, had been able to find solitude and privacy there, and hoped John's six-month stay would provide the same experience. That hope was realized. Free of the press, John was able to immerse himself in study and social work.

His time in India was the quietest interlude of his entire life up to that point. No cameras pursued him, no reporters hurled questions at him; he was at liberty to investigate this other culture, applying to it a curiosity and lust for information that sometimes rivaled his father's. After a few months he asked Sally Munro to join him in India.

Anyone who spends a long period in India understands the adjustment required on returning to the West after the intensity of the crowds and the poverty. When John and Sally Munro returned, they eschewed the pristine, manicured lawns of the exclusive Kennedy homes to spend the Fourth of July amid the volatile crowds celebrating in Central Park.

John had always been a New Yorker, riding the city streets on his bike and watching videos on his Betamax. *Broadway Danny Rose* was a favorite. At that point he could wander the streets largely unrecognized, taking Sally to King Karol on Third Avenue, where they browsed through the adult titles in search of their evening's entertainment.

"I showed John the list," remembered a sales clerk. "John asked Sally to pick one out. She closed her eyes and pointed to a film called *Bodacious* and that was it."

He had his own apartment, a co-op he had sublet on West Eighty-sixth Street, and was free to indulge his youthful taste. Not that he had much spare time. In October 1984, he took a $20,000-a-year job as assistant to the New York Commissioner of

Business Development. He had his own office—a cubbyhole—and worked with local businesses to encourage the growth of public-sector jobs in New York.

"He's unpredictable in a good way," said the corporation's president. "He was both orderly and passionate—a rare combination."

John arrived for work each morning dressed in bicycle shorts and T-shirt. Even after changing into a suit, one small clue to his real personality was likely to remain: his shirttail hanging out from beneath his jacket.

John flew to California on December 26, 1984, to attend the memorial service for his uncle Peter Lawford, who had died a gruesome death on Christmas Eve, induced by drugs and alcohol. A broken shell of a man, Peter had been racked by guilt about not having been able to save Marilyn Monroe, and consumed with terrible sadness over losing Jack.

"As soon as I got home from the hospital, Jackie called me," remembers Patricia Seaton Lawford, Peter's widow. "She knew all about the moment of his death and how he had hemorrhaged. She had obviously arranged for the hospital to let her know when and how he died. She was gentle, kind, and understanding of the horror I had witnessed. She talked of Jack and for a moment we were united in our grief. She sent acres of flowers to the funeral, but couldn't come to the service. All the other Kennedys did—including John, who looked gorgeous and came to the memorial dinner at La Scala."

Uncle Peter was the only one in his family who had supported John's acting. Once the memorial dinner was over and he returned to New York to face law school, there was no one left in his family who understood his unrealized dream.

Once he started law school, there could be no such thing as a casual date for John F. Kennedy, Jr. His status as an American prince, whose every move unwittingly helped to sell the very tabloids he despised, meant that every woman he encountered, no matter how briefly, became a momentary media princess.

In 1984, Sally Munro was still a part of his life, but with the prospect of three years of law school ahead of him, the future loomed dull and conventional. At heart he had always been a rebel, but his only rebellion to date had involved the theater. With that avenue blocked by his mother's threat to disinherit, and his days filled with legal studies, there was only one outlet left for his energetic creativity: women.

He had never been drawn to society girls or debutantes, though the women he had romanced up to this point were primarily safe, proper girls like Jenny Christian and Sally Munro. They were nice, bright, well-bred girls from good backgrounds with intellectual ability and college degrees—young women molded in the image of his sister and, more important, those who may have won his mother's approval.

Suddenly, in the throes of a new rebellion, John smashed the mold and turned to quite another type, a woman after whom his father might well have lusted, but surely would have found too aggressive for his tastes.

Madonna Louise Ciccone's story is well-known, as much a part of modern American mythology as is the story of Marilyn Monroe. An attention junkie who described losing her virginity as "a career move," by 1985 she had just completed the climb from downtown New York rock star to international celebrity. With the release of her "Material Girl" video, she conquered MTV, while her *Like a Virgin* album sold 3.5 million copies in just twelve weeks.

But while her music was skyrocketing in popularity, Madonna's real self was just beginning to surface. Deep within her was a volcanic ambition for stardom that far surpassed that of any woman who preceded her—including Marilyn Monroe.

In the public's mind, Madonna was little more than a Marilyn

Monroe emulator who slavishly re-created her idol's famous *Diamonds Are a Girl's Best Friend* sequence for the "Material Girl" video. But in her own mind, Madonna was not just Marilyn emulated but Marilyn reincarnated, sent here to fulfill her psychic destiny. She had an ongoing friendship with rock star Prince, who was also obsessed by Marilyn and filled his house with posters of the dead star. Brat pack actor Sean Penn had even taken her on a date to Marilyn's grave site.

Absorbing Marilyn's image into her own was a strategic move. It was almost as if she felt she could transcend Marilyn by literally consuming the legend. Once she had completely ingested the image and made it part of hers, then she could move on and become more herself—with Marilyn receding into the background.

"I will be a symbol of something," she explained. "Like Marilyn Monroe stands for something. She became an adjective."

After the *Like a Virgin* tour, Madonna did a photo shoot for *Life* magazine. Photographer Bruce Weber shot her in a parody of Marilyn's role in *The Seven-Year Itch.*

At every step, Madonna continued her consumption of the Marilyn mystique, but she craved something more. John F. Kennedy, Jr., was just the dish to finish off the meal—the ultimate Monroesque experience.

"She had read every Marilyn Monroe biography in print," said Christopher Anderson, Madonna's biographer. "She knew the details of the affair with the late president. She considered herself to be the heiress to Marilyn Monroe and confided to friends she felt fated to consummate a relationship with Kennedy's son."

Preppie JFK Jr. was not normally her type. She was then toying with Sean Penn, wondering whether to consolidate their relationship. Like John, she was confronted by a multitude of erotic possibilities. At the moment she was drunk with her newfound success in *Desperately Seeking*

Susan and was shuffling all manner of sexual cards in the romantic deck available to her.

Major stars were besotted by her combination of sluttiness and cuteness. Instead of succumbing to many a big name who was courting her, Madonna spent part of her time throwing wild parties in her Upper West Side apartment, all of them well documented in the tabloids.

"She ran a Puerto Rican stud farm up there," said her ex-lover, deejay Mark Kamins. "Madonna and this other girlfriend of hers fooled around while me and the other guy watched," said one of her regular guests, Bobby Martinez. "Then we *all* had a good time. I think she likes women as much as she likes men." Nothing sexual was beyond her. She liked women, men, orgies, sado-masochism, and any other perversion of which her sexually inflamed imagination and marketing sense could conceive.

She fed the press with outrageous quotes. "I've got the most beautiful belly button in the world," she boasted. Every word—and then some—was printed. She reveled in leaking sensational details of her libidinous antics to the media, openly indulging her taste for anonymous sex, and punctuating the stories with erotic poses and saucy smiles.

Throughout her campaign to transcend Marilyn's iconography, Madonna increasingly dominated and manipulated any man within her reach. Whereas the idol was known for her vulnerability, Madonna was invulnerable. She demanded control of her own destiny, flexing her sexual muscles to achieve that self-mastery, using sex to further her career. Madonna recognized that adding John F. Kennedy, Jr.'s scalp to her sexual belt would be another publicity coup.

In a sense, sex to Madonna was a similar tool to Joe Kennedy's public use of his family. Whereas John's grandfather marketed his family's beauty to penetrate America's consciousness, she lived to flout convention, to spit in the face of respectability, and to shock the normally unshockable. Whereas Joe sought the presidency for his family's scrapbook, Madonna sought John to enhance her mythology.

John's every move would be reported in every supermarket tabloid in the country. Madonna would make sure of that.

Not one to be shy about her desires, Madonna had initially pursued John, leaving countless messages on his answering machine.

"Why don't we meet?" she suggested. "You can come see my show and we'll get to know each other."

John agreed to the date, finally meeting up with someone who loomed as large in the minds of the public as himself. He was definitely curious. Her openness about her private life must have both shocked and titillated John, who himself sought anonymity from the press.

The date was set and he arrived at Madison Square Garden to find thousands of Madonna wannabes screaming hysterically at their idol. They writhed to the sexuality of her *Like a Virgin* and gazed at her in wonder as, breaking the mood of the act, she told of her days of living in a derelict apartment just across the street from the Garden.

"I used to look out at the Garden and say, 'I wonder if I'll ever get in there,' " she told the crowd.

While Madonna had been starving in a slum, eating out of garbage cans, clawing her way to success, John had grown up on Fifth Avenue, cruising on Onassis's yacht, privileged and above the fray. She was unabashedly more interested in herself than in him, yet she seemed to fascinate John, as a snake might fascinate an apprentice snake charmer who knew that he was secretly planning to become a concert pianist instead. They were universes apart, and Madonna knew it and behaved accordingly, taunting him.

In her dressing room after the show, she held court to a group of admirers that included the graffiti artist Futura 2000, *Miami Vice* star Don Johnson, dancer Erika Belle, her closest friend at that time. When John walked into the room, Madonna completely ignored him, instead concentrating wholly on Futura. The shy artist had been briefly involved with her, but it was obvious to him that the attention she was giving him was directed at someone else. He realized that Madonna was trying to make John jealous, to pique his interest in her, to excite him. He played along with her game, almost out of habit. He had seen her play it so often before.

Colluding with Madonna, Futura stood with her in a corner, giggling and holding hands. Across the room, by the door, John watched, uncertain what to do next. In the opposite corner, Don Johnson, media sensation of the moment, leaned haplessly against the wall, holding twenty-four long-stemmed red roses, looking like a hurt puppy who had drunk too much.

After being ignored by his hostess for a few minutes, John finally walked over to Erika.

"Hi, my name is John. John Kennedy, Jr."

"Oh, Rica, this is John Kennedy," Madonna said, then laughed.

John remained nonplussed. He shook hands with Erika and made small talk about her career, her relationship with Madonna, the state of her champagne glass.

"How ya doing, John?" Madonna asked every once in a while, before returning to Futura.

She had scripted the moment well. Begging John to meet her, then leaving him to dangle in a corner of the room, she was surrounded by the evidence of her power. There was Don Johnson, at the height of his popularity, lingering soulfully in one corner of the dressing room. On the other side of the room, her real target for the evening: John F. Kennedy, Jr.

After playing her hand to the maximum, she left Futura and swooped up John, suggesting they leave together. She was about to fulfill her psychic destiny. She smiled at John angelically—well aware of the irony of the moment.

Another woman in John's life was aware of the same irony. It was clear that this Madonna was no angel and that she definitely was not the kind of girl Jacqueline Kennedy Onassis wanted for her beloved son.

According to Erika Belle, in whom Madonna confided every detail of her relationship with John, it was no surprise that there was a frantic message from Jackie on John's answering machine when he and Madonna came back to his apartment after their first real dinner date, wanting to know what was going on and begging John to call her.

It must have seemed to Jackie as if the ghost of Marilyn was returning to steal away another of her men. Twenty-two years had passed since her rival had sung "Happy Birthday, Mr. President," and now her son had begun dating her doppelganger. Jackie was determined to monitor the depth of the relationship.

Madonna's version of the story, according to Erika, was that Jackie wanted to know where they went. When he called her back, he patiently described their date, secretly amused that she wasn't ashamed to show her curiosity by calling.

Erika claims that when Jackie discovered John and Madonna had gone out for dinner a second time, Jackie called his apartment, obsessively, finally reaching him at two in the morning.

After a brief conversation, John turned to Madonna and told her that his mother wanted to know what she was like and wanted to meet her.

Madonna laughed until it hurt.

"Can you imagine how far I've gone," she exulted to Erika. "Jackie O wants to know all about me!"

John's attraction to Madonna was a radical departure from his normal taste in women—as much as he was a departure for her.

Unfortunately, their lovemaking proved to be less than dazzling. Madonna wanted her men to perform sexually. She was a queen bee, demanding unlimited amounts of honey. This was the same woman who would humiliate Warren Beatty, make mincemeat out of Kevin

Costner. She believed that every straight man should have a gay encounter in order to understand what a woman feels.

"John was far too straight for Madonna sexually," said a close friend. "She told me that going to bed with him was like going to bed with an innocent."

"John and Madonna basically just had a series of one-night stands," said another close friend of Madonna.

"John is absolutely gorgeous, but he's not the man for me," Madonna told Erika.

"And Madonna wasn't right for John," said Erika after being with them on four occasions. "She comes on far too strong for him. Blatant sexuality really embarrasses John. He is very gracious, chivalrous, shy, gentle, and well bred, and he really doesn't like aggressive women." Erika witnessed John's aversion to blatant sexuality one night in the Mike Todd VIP room at the Palladium in Manhattan.

Madonna was meeting John and the others at the party later. The guest list included Duran Duran and Julian Lennon. Sultry Brazilian actress Sonia Braga was there, sitting at the table next to John. She was all over him, like fly paper, flashing her legs, really intimidating him. Suddenly he saw Erika and gave her a desperate look that said, "Help, get me away from this woman." He peeled himself away from Sonia and moved quickly toward Erika, who was smiling at him encouragingly.

"Hi, do you remember me?," he said, then put his hand on his rescuer's shoulder and got a drink.

Beyond sex, something else happened on Madonna's first date with John. While Madonna wanted more aggressive sex play, she discovered a part of John's private personality that was much stronger than she imagined. That morning the two agreed to see each other again.

In addition to being objects of intense media scrutiny, both John and Madonna were very attuned to their bodies. They worked out together at Plus One, a private gym in Soho, jogged in Central Park. While totally incompatible on a sexual level, they were comfortable together and felt strangely drawn to each other.

In the end, while the tabloids speculated about the famous couple, an unexpected irony surfaced. Whereas Marilyn had projected sexuality and longed for a relationship, Madonna flaunted sex and normally had no interest in such a partnership. Yet with John her normal pattern dissolved. While Jack Kennedy could never have endured a platonic friendship with Marilyn, that was exactly how John and Madonna's relationship evolved. She eventually married Sean, and John, much to his mother's relief, began swimming in calmer waters. He and Madonna remained living proof of the classic phrase, "just good friends."

At the end of April 1985, John chipped his ankle while playing football. Jackie went with him to Lenox Hill Hospital, where he was fitted for a cast. By May 9, he was able to walk on crutches and slipped into Charivari on Fifty-seventh Street, wearing a Hawaiian shirt and shorts, and tried on a Perry Ellis jacket. He was hampered by his crutches, and started hopping around the store on one leg. He had already attracted attention, and the sight of him hopping around was too much for the store's female customers. Plucking up courage, one customer approached meekly.

"Can I sign your cast?"

"Sure," John said good-naturedly.

The other female customers rushed toward him to add their signatures, covering the cast right up to his thigh. They were a mob, but a gentle one. But the incident was a sign of things to come.

Instead of relaxing during the summer before starting law school, John played the male lead in Brian Friel's *Winners*. On August 14, 1985, he made his professional acting debut at the seventy-five-seat Irish Arts

Center in Manhattan. Any hopes he might have cherished of softening his mother's attitude toward acting by ending his relationship with Madonna were dashed.

"Jackie was terrified that the critics would come and see John in *Winners*," her cousin John Davis said. "Since rave reviews might encourage him to continue a career in acting, she tried to leverage the critics into ignoring the play."

But the press monitored every aspect of the production, covering John's arrivals and departures at the theater. On opening night, a security guard protected the premises from press intrusion. Admission to the play was by invitation only, and friends and family flocked to see John's performance.

"This is definitely not a professional acting debut by any means," John said. "It's just a hobby."

Jackie's attempt at a media blackout having failed, she and Caroline boycotted the six performances.

John's costar in the four-character play was Christina Haag, his former housemate from Brown, who was now studying acting at Juilliard and seeing John offstage as well as on. Jackie much preferred Haag, the Catholic daughter of a retired businessman, to the scarlet Madonna.

John's cousins Kara Kennedy, William Kennedy Smith, Tony Radziwill, and Bobby Kennedy, Jr., all came to the play and cheered him on.

"John was stupendous," Bobby said. "He's been a very talented performer all his life—with an incredible ear for mimicry. When we were little he used to tell stories in an Irish brogue or in a Russian accent. He was only nine or ten and he would have all of us—even the older cousins—in stitches. He's really funny."

But there was no comedy in *Winners*. Friel's play was somber, John's role that of an Irish Catholic teenager engaged to his pregnant girlfriend, played by Haag. The ninety-minute drama ended with the lovers drowning.

Since the play was set in Northern Ireland, John's role called for a very particular accent—which he delivered respectably.

"He hung around someone with that accent and picked it up," said the Irish Arts Center's executive director, Nye Heron. "His accent was specific, right down to a county. He's one of the best young actors I've seen in years."

Joseph Daly, who has acted in avant-garde and regional theater for thirty-five years and who appeared on Broadway in *Mastergate*, played the narrator. "John definitely had talent," Daly said. "He didn't seem the least bit flustered like most amateurs. He did his job and he worked hard. He wasn't a dilettante. I don't think he ever thought of himself as a celebrity—he just happened to be a Kennedy and that was that. He had a great time during rehearsals and he was just one of the cast."

Surrounded by his friends from Brown, John was able to relax and have fun doing what he liked best. When other performers were nervous, John was there to support them or make them laugh. He helped several cast members get over their preperformance jitters.

At one of the cast parties he got the chance to discuss favorite roles and different plays with Daly.

"Are you going to pursue acting, John?" Daly asked.

John thought for a moment, then shrugged. "I don't know."

"Well, you should. You seem to enjoy yourself so much. That's half of what acting is about."

John didn't say anything, resisting the urge to suggest that the veteran actor repeat his advice to Jackie.

John's appearance in *Winners* captured enormous interest and countless offers to produce the play on Broadway with the same cast. The offers were rejected and the play closed, but John's relationship with

Christina Haag continued. She was stylish, enterprising, and between jobs, though not above working as a hat-check girl at Elio's Restaurant or as an assistant to Seventh Avenue designer Christine Thomson. Haag was serious about her career, playing Ophelia at Center Stage in Baltimore and appearing on television in *The Littlest Victim*, playing the part of a hospital public relations executive.

If John couldn't be an actor, he could at least stay in touch with the theater through Christina.

"John always wanted the appearance of a steady girlfriend and the respectability of having a steady girlfriend," said a source. "But he would upset Christina very much and make her extremely jealous.

"Without warning, John occasionally just disappeared—but never alone. During a rafting trip with the Kennedys he met a girl who was not part of the official group. After a brief conversation, John and the girl disappeared for two days. There was a little motel on the side of the river and they were gone.

"While he was involved with Christina, he would be spotted in a small restaurant or club with other girls. But Christina always stayed with him despite the tension, probably because the relationship was important to her."

Jackie liked Christina Haag, and when her father died in 1992—long after her breakup with John—Jackie paid a personal condolence call to her apartment.

In September 1985, John returned to India. His mother was there at the same time, working on a book about Indian costumes, and the two did some sightseeing together in Hyderabad.

John studied health care, adult education, and food production at the University of Delhi. He met Rajiv Gandhi, Andhora Pradesh, India's minister, and M. J. Akbar, a noted journalist and politician, and explored the country. As on his previous visit, there was virtually no media coverage. Villagers were often surprised to find the unpretentious young man arriving via rickshaw, unescorted.

He was especially taken with the unique landscape of the Deccan Plateau and spent several evenings walking around the Jubilee Hills, whose stunning rock formations date back thousands of years. The ravages of time and industrialization have eroded some of the ancient monuments; Jackie arranged for grants and used her contacts to initiate a plan for restoration.

Immediately on his return from India, John was thrown back into his official role as the son of JFK, officiating at various events commemorating his father's life. On November 5, 1985, he went to Cambridge for the dedication of John F. Kennedy Park. When he came back from the ceremonies, he found his car gone.

Anne Marie Rowan, publicist for the Charles Hotel, lent him the cash to bail it out. As always, John was penniless. He repaid her with a check. She took months to cash it, saving it as a souvenir.

At a ceremony celebrating the twentieth anniversary of the founding of the Brooklyn Restoration Project, John donned roller skates and went skating with a group of children involved in the program. A little boy, struck by his friendliness, shyly tugged at John's sleeve.

"Yes?"

"What's your name?"

"John Kennedy."

"John Kennedy!" the boy cried. "He was one of our Presidents."

"Yeah, I know," John said with a smile. "He was my dad."

In 1986, ten thousand members of Manwatchers voted John (along with Don Johnson) one of the most eligible bachelors in America.

"He has the Kennedy magic," said Suzy Mallery, president of

the Los Angeles-based organization. "He has the style and the cha-risma."

John's response on hearing the news was typically understated. "I don't know what to say."

He was left speechless again when, on June 16, *People* named him "America's Most Eligible Bachelor," complimenting him for his "self-effacing charm." Other bachelors chosen included Mikhail Baryshnikov and David Lee Roth.

Three days later, as John's stock as a bachelor headed off the chart, Caroline married Ed Schlossberg at Our Lady of Victory Church in Manhattan. The bridegroom was Jewish, but they were married in a Roman Catholic ceremony. The bride was twenty-eight and the groom forty-two, and to many it seemed that Caroline had chosen a father figure as a husband.

The son of a Manhattan businessman, Schlossberg had earned a Ph.D. in literature and science from Columbia. He wrote poetry and designed T-shirts; he was more of a conceptual artist than a scientist. He seemed an unusual choice for the ostensibly conventional Caroline. Certainly his artistry and intellect made him the antithesis of Caroline's Kennedy cousins, but John liked him.

There were fireworks that night, songs by Carly Simon, and champagne toasts offered to the bride and groom in the glow of Japanese lanterns. Perhaps his sister's marriage made John reflect on his own lifestyle; he became more attached to Christina Haag. But that didn't change the fact that he was still a desirable commodity.

In September 1986, John started at NYU Law School, where he quickly made friends with fellow student Faith Stevelman. Most Eligible Bachelor and first-year law student are not necessarily compatible tags, but John kept his head down and threw himself into his studies. Once again, those who got to know him could see through the media fog to the real person beneath.

"The press makes him out to be a narcissistic celebrity brat, but he's not," Faith Stevelman said. As for John's plan to become an assistant district attorney when he completed his studies, she believed he was making the right choice.

"It takes someone who really wants to get down and deal with real people's needs," she said. "I don't think John likes things easy—or false."

He won high marks from most people he met, but not from his landlord. He moved out of the sublet West Eighty-sixth Street co-op for another apartment in the West Nineties, leaving the co-op in "an obnoxious condition." For all the self-control and perfect manners he displayed in his academic and social life, it seemed that in the privacy of his own home, John could let loose.

"Somebody put a fist through the wall," said the owner of the complex.

John had, of course, grown up with servants, and the state of the apartment reflected his lack of domesticity and indifference to his surroundings. "He doesn't give a shit," said one of his few detractors. The floor of the co-op had to be sanded, the carpet (which had been burned) replaced, the walls patched. Apparently John had come within inches of eviction, and his beleaguered landlord took legal action. John's lawyers settled the case out of court, keeping unanswered the interesting questions the incident raised about his private life, the source of his hidden anger.

During the summer of 1987 John worked in Washington as a law clerk with the Justice Department, doing research in the civil rights division. Having won one of eighty places normally awarded to the top law students in the country, he was paid $353 a week to be an intern in the attorney general's summer program. Brian E. Meyers, deputy director of the Office of Attorney General Personnel Management, fiercely denied that nepotism had played any part in John's selection.

"I remember his application coming across the desk," said Meyers. "John came from a very good law school and had excellent qualifications."

John's time in Washington proved uneventful. He spent most of his lunch hours in the office, eating out of a brown bag. Christina Haag was with him part of the time, while pursuing her own acting career. But now that John had clearly rejected the theater, the media's interest in him subsided.

He attracted only a modicum of attention every now and again. A gossip column reported that he'd been seen dancing to "Mack the Knife" at a downtown bar; another time he had flown down to Palm Beach for Easter, booking two coach seats (one for his guitar) since first class was sold out. Christina Haag was still his official girlfriend; Robin Saex, a close mutual friend, noted, "They bring out the best in each other."

In July 1988 he was flung back into the limelight. When he rose to introduce Teddy Kennedy at the 1988 Democratic National Convention in Atlanta, it seemed to one reporter that the dome of the arena would collapse under the force of the simultaneous intake of breath from the women in the audience. John's speech introducing his uncle was brief, but the audience was mesmerized by his charm, his good looks, and his name. Afterward, the Omni echoed with thunderous applause for two solid minutes. Even NBC's Tom Brokaw was captivated by John, declaring, "He is as charming and handsome as a movie star."

John had been nervous before the speech, but he had made it for Teddy. The result was pandemonium that would never subside. The following night, when he walked into Rupert's, Atlanta's most fashionable club, for a benefit for Atlanta's Task Force for the Homeless, it was as if Elvis had come back to life. Dressed in a tan suit, lavender shirt, and purple tie, John was immediately besieged by women wanting to meet him and men eager to shake his hand. Two girl singers, backed by a sixteen-piece live band, sang to a throbbing disco beat, and cocktail waitresses served drinks to celebrities like Rob Lowe and Ally Sheedy. But the attention of the entire room was focused on John. He took a swig of beer, then ducked out the club's back door and away from the madness.

In some ways, he remained ambivalent about the constant media attention. A girlfriend from Brown went to a downtown Manhattan disco with him. The paparazzi had been tipped off that John was going out on the town and trailed his taxi to the club. When the taxi screeched to a halt, John and the girl dashed to safety, crouching behind a bush.

As the photographers craned their necks, trying to snap his picture through the leaves, the girl turned to John and said sympathetically, "How awful for you, having to put up with this all the time."

"That's half the fun," John said.

At the end of his first year at law school, John took a $1,100-a-week summer job as an intern at the Los Angeles law firm of Manatt, Phelps, Rothenberg, and Philips. He lived in Venice, where Christina Haag was a frequent visitor.

One of the firm's partners, Charlie Manatt, had been Teddy Kennedy's roommate at Harvard. Before John arrived, there was resentment that he had won his internship through nepotism. Internships at the very Democratic and very glitzy Manatt firm usually lasted for three months. The positions were highly sought by law students across the country, and the students chosen were usually leaders in their schools—which John definitely was not.

When the administrators announced that he would be joining the firm for the summer, they asked that the other employees welcome John without bothering him in any way. But at the big party thrown to welcome all the interns, scores of young women who worked for

Manatt were so excited about the prospect of meeting John that they charged into the conference room before he actually arrived. The door finally opened and John walked in, cutting through the sea of people like a clipper ship. A Hollywood PR agent couldn't have designed a better entrance, but the sight of so many women staring at him as if they were hungry jackals set John searching for male attorneys he knew.

"Hey, how's it going?" John said to one of them. While they chatted, he avoided women's attempts at making eye contact.

"Mr. Kennedy, it's a pleasure to meet you," a tall redhead said.

"Nice to meet you," he said, then turned back to his colleagues.

The women kept trying. John answered their questions with customary politeness, though each left him a little hotter under the collar. His frustration wasn't eased by his awareness that the party had been thrown to show him off to the other employees.

Years of public attention had made John adept at reading others. He could tell whether a woman was interested in him or his celebrity status—and in either case he resented being besieged by so many of them on his first day on the job. Then, of course, there were the male attorneys who were jealous of his looks and his very presence in the firm.

"Isn't it just peachy to have John-John working with us this summer?" one disgruntled lawyer said loudly. "A guy who looks like that can't know how to write a good brief."

"I'd like to study his briefs," said a woman lawyer, peering at John over her wine glass.

Once he started working, John hoped the scrutiny would ease. But the competitiveness of the young lawyers precluded their rallying around him. He worked quietly and steadily on the cases assigned to him, but the griping continued. And Manatt was smart enough to channel high-profile cases that were within John's abilities his way.

"They give him all the easy work," one lawyer said over coffee. "Shit, I just worked my ass off on a fifty-page brief that bored me to tears, and he gets to iron out a minor contract dispute for that rap group, Process and the Do Rags."

"He's so dumb, they can't afford to give him anything important," another lawyer explained. "But what are you going to do? Manatt himself assigned him that Laker contract."

The firm represented only a few entertainment clients, and interns normally weren't allowed near the sports and entertainment accounts. Some of the interns saddled with the heavier work complained.

"I've seen his work and he's not so great."

"You're just jealous because you haven't been able to score since he got here."

"Well, hell—they're all saving themselves for John-John!"

As womanizers, none of them could compete with John. Sometimes it seemed as if the less effort he made, the more he was pursued.

Every morning as he arrived at his office, he was greeted by one of the firm's female attorneys.

"Good morning, John."

"Good morning."

She stood waiting for him to speak; John busied himself at his desk.

"Need some help with anything?"

"No, thanks. I'm fine."

"If you do need anything—anything at all . . ."

"I'm fine."

Her crush was so obvious that the others in the office began to make jokes behind John's back. They didn't dare say anything to her face because of her powerful position in the firm.

"It wouldn't hurt you, John," one young lawyer said. "It might take the pressure off."

"I'll be okay."

"If she gets mad ..."

But John was not about to become a trophy. He didn't approach women that way and didn't think he should be treated any differently. Nor was he worried about any potential damage she might do to his legal career. Whenever he failed, it was big news, and anything he did right was written off. What could be worse than that? Eventually the lawyer gave up on him, but there were plenty of other women lined up with equally shallow pretenses to take her place.

"Did you get that memo?"

"Yes."

"What do you think they meant at the staff meeting?"

"I'm not sure."

"Were you looking for this file?"

"Not my case. I'm not sure who's working on it."

"Some of us felt very sorry for him," said one employee at the firm. "The women were throwing themselves at him and the men resented him, tried to compete. I was hoping that he would be smart and show everyone, but when I saw his legal briefs, they were badly done and his spelling was terrible."

The professional pressures on John were intense, and it didn't help matters that everyone in the firm was aware of the avalanche of calls from women wanting to talk to him.

It became almost comical because of the number of girls that were calling up. Most of them were girls who could barely string a sentence together.

"Please, I know you don't believe me, but I'm a friend of John's. Please put me through."

"Who shall I say is calling?"

"He's expecting my call."

"Your name?"

"I'm returning his call."

"Is he expecting *your* call, or are you returning *his?*"

"He's expecting me to return his call."

After a while, the receptionists began trading the best excuses.

"I'm his sister."

"She lives in England."

"Don't we have a great connection? I tell you, these fiber-optics ..."

"What firm did you say you were with?"

"Um——" there was the sound of a phone book being opened. Then, "Manatt, Phelps, Rothenberg and Philips."

"You work for them?"

"Yes, would you put me through to Mr. Kennedy? It's very important."

"Why don't you just walk down the hall?"

"Excuse me?"

"This *is* Manatt, Phelps, Rothenberg and Philips."

"It is?"

"That's right."

A former employee said, "They seemed like girls he had met once who had found out where he worked and were desperate to talk to him.

"One afternoon he came in to pick his papers up and he was with two guys and they were all going to bike home," remembers the employee. "He got his papers from another woman in the office and then he shrugged his shoulders and, in a croaky voice, began to sing, 'I'm bringing home the bacon, I'm a working man.' Then he sashayed out of the door."

After hours he did his best to relax, working out at the Sports Club, dancing at L.A.'s Flaming Colossus—where an eyewitness described him as looking out of place—and going to parties with or without Christina Haag.

The switchboard was lit up by female callers attempting to bluff their way past the operators, but some who called did know him. Madonna was one. When her stormy marriage with Sean Penn reached the breaking point, she began calling incessantly.

"She was really after him and he seemed to really enjoy her, but in the end, they didn't get very involved," said a Manatt employee.

Ironically, Madonna was calling John for solace. While piqued by her new interest, he had no intention of getting involved with her, though he did play the knight by inviting her to Hyannis in an attempt to distract her from her marital woes. Madonna signed the guest book as "Mrs. Sean Penn," as if to reassure Jackie that she had no real designs on her son.

A Manatt secretary noticed John doodling on the back of a legal brief one day. He had drawn exaggeratedly pointed breasts, rather like the Gaultier bras Madonna wore in her concerts, as well as the face of a man who was crying large tears, surrounded by knives and daggers.

On September 12, 1988, on what would have been his parents' thirty-fifth wedding anniversary, *People* published the cover story naming him "Sexiest Man Alive."

"In the mid-eighties, John could go around New York City fairly anonymously," said his friend Richard Wiese. "But when *People* awarded him that title, there was a big change in media attention."

Another friend said, "John was flattered by being named Sexiest Man Alive and we all teased him about it and told him he shouldn't believe his publicity. Part of him still liked being the Prince, but he knew there was a major down side to the *People* cover."

Until then, the public's interest in John had resembled the interest of fond family friends in a child whom they lovingly observed as he grew up. He had been treated tenderly, revered more for the memory of his father than for himself, pursued more because of his mother's tragic glamour than for his own abilities or charm. Now, however, he had been projected as a hunk, a sex symbol, accorded movie-star status without ever having appeared in Hollywood. In many ways, for John the whole thing was a tremendous irony. He had wanted to pursue a theatrical career, to accept some of the Hollywood offers flung his way. But he had relinquished his ambitions for the sake of his mother, who was afraid of the exposure, afraid for his safety and for the dignity of his name.

Now that he had been hailed as a sex symbol, his status as a Kennedy had in the eyes of many been undermined. Worse, he was now fated to live with all the negative elements of stardom and none of the artistic benefits. Photographers camped outside his apartment, vying for his picture; television crews followed him with hidden cameras; teenage girls pinned his picture on their walls. Privacy, for John, was as remote a dream as Camelot.

Meanwhile, his destiny was about to be transformed yet again. In many ways actress Daryl Hannah resembled Jackie; ethereal yet determined, manipulative yet shy, spacey yet frighteningly focused when she set her heart on something. She had a powerful ally in the shape of her stepfather, Jerry Wexler.

"Jerry Wexler adored Daryl," said best-selling novelist, Chicago socialite Sugar Rautbord. "He was the kind of man who controlled his family like Joe Kennedy, and he was very upset that she was unhappy with Jackson Browne. One day he sat Daryl down and said, 'I don't understand. You are a beautiful woman, you are an actress, you have all the money in the world, what are you doing in this unhappy relationship?' "

Tremendously shy, Daryl looked downcast, then said, "Nobody asks me out. They are afraid to. And I'm afraid that if they do, they won't like me. I'm a basic girl and I like swimming and skin diving and natural food, and no one will ask me out."

Wexler, a man who prided himself on being able to move universes, turned to Daryl and said, "In your wildest dreams, who would you like to go out with?"

Daryl didn't answer at first. Then she looked up and said straightway, "J.F.K. Junior."

Jerry phoned Teddy Kennedy that instant.

"I don't care what happens, but let them meet each other," Jerry told Teddy. "They could hate each other, but let them meet."

Fortuitously, Jackie's sister, Lee, was marrying film producer Herb Ross, and Daryl was invited to the September 1988 wedding reception, held at Jackie's apartment. John and Daryl liked each other immediately.

They hadn't met since La Samanna, when Daryl had been only eighteen, and John was once more struck by her unique combination of waif-like beauty and sexy athleticism.

A leggy five-foot-ten blonde, Daryl was childlike, street smart, was a year younger than John, and came from a background that he found far more interesting than the *vitae* of the usual Social Register debutante. Her parents, Sue and Don Hannah, were Midwestern, Old Guard society, and Daryl had grown up amid rusticity on a farm with miniature ponies in a world where wearing thirty-two-year-old polo shirts under tuxedo jackets was *de rigueur.*

"I withdrew into myself to the point where I was semi-autistic and an outcast," she recalled after her parents divorced when she was seven. "I was terribly thin—my legs were like pins, with knobs for knees. Kids called me broomstick."

Daryl decided to become a movie star when she was about eight and saw *The Wizard of Oz.* She lived in a dream world, populated with invisible friends.

"I'm still like that a lot of the time," she says. "I often tried to infuse my real life with the magical qualities of my fantasies, and it got me into a little trouble. I crashed down to reality a few times before I realized that there were no such things as my fairy tales."

She escaped into sports as well.

"Daryl was always a real jock," said Sugar Rautbord, who hired Daryl to baby-sit her son Michael. "She was never a rocket scientist, but she was a lovely girl with a great sense of humor."

When Daryl was thirteen, her mother, Sue, married Jerry Wexler, a colorful and wealthy tycoon whose brother was Haskell Wexler, one of the most celebrated cinematographers in Hollywood. While Jerry prepared his four children for his remarriage, Daryl and her mother, brothers, and sisters spent a year living in a luxury hotel suite.

Daryl moved to L.A. when she was seventeen and, through Wexler's connections, stayed with Susan Saint James until moving into an apartment with Rachel Ward. At twenty-two, she met singer Jackson Browne at a concert in Chicago when he pulled her up on stage and dedicated a song to her. He was ten years her senior and divorced from second wife, Lynne Sweeney (his first wife, Phyllis, committed suicide in 1976). Jackson and Daryl became deeply involved, even buying a house together in Santa Monica, but their stormy relationship was punctuated by a number of separations.

Daryl dedicated herself to achieving success. From the start, it seemed as if only an act of God could stop her. She had a feisty attitude to life, and at one point in her evolving career sued Coca-Cola for using her name and picture in a commercial without her permission. She didn't back down even though at that time Coca-Cola was the parent company of Columbia Pictures—a powerful Hollywood entity.

Her persistence paid off and she carved out a unique niche for herself in Hollywood as the last of the waif-like blondes, starring in *Splash*, *Roxanne*, and *Steel Magnolias*.

She was wealthy but loved to play at poverty, very much as John always had. When they first met, she drove an old Buick and had a fondness for flea markets and going out in an old baseball cap and jeans without being recognized. She and John shared a similar attitude to fame.

"There are two kinds of actors," she said once. "Some just thrive on the extrovert life. Others love acting because they can hide behind the characters and feel emotions and express themselves through people who don't really exist."

Daryl and John belonged to the second kind.

She was an instinctive actress who played roles, but her closest friends were able to detect the real Daryl underneath the facade.

"Part of her appeal is that childlike quality, and she'll have it in her nineties," noted her friend Elise Paschen. "And that's what's charming, alluring—even compelling about her. But that's a role she plays; it's a smoke screen. She appears to be ethereal and ephemeral when she's actually strong and courageous."

"Daryl is perfect for John; she is soft-spoken (her voice is like Jackie's, but she has this patina of Marilyn)," explained Sugar Rautbord. "She bicycles, skis, skin dives, she's an animal conservationist, and she's not afraid to get her hair wet. She is gracious and sweet and perfect for John."

But for all their similarities, and their many telephone conversations and meetings, Daryl and John kept their relationship low-key. Jackson Browne was still a fixture in her life, and John was still seeing Christina Haag.

On October 4, 1988, just a few weeks after the *People* profile, although still involved with Haag, John took Daryl Hannah out on a date. Every detail was recorded in the New York papers, from their visit to a West Village club to their stop at a bar called Automatic Slim's, to the pool games played until closing time at the TriBeCa club S.T.P., where they heard the Danny B. Harvey Band and High

Ground. Three thousand miles away in Los Angeles, Hannah's live-in lover, Jackson Browne, made no comment.

At the end of November 1988, John was confronted by the full force of the mania the *People* title had unleashed. He made a lunchtime appearance at Bloomingdale's in Manhattan to help sell Christmas ornaments made by disabled artists in aid of Very Special Arts, a charity funded by the Joseph P. Kennedy Foundation.

Hundreds of women screamed and pushed, desperate to see or touch the object of their obsession. John fought desperately to stay calm as television lights flared in his face, intrusive reporters jostled one another in their eagerness to talk to him, and autograph seekers lunged at him. For a moment he looked like a hunted deer.

"I hope you'll all buy a few boxes," he said, leaning into the microphone. "I'm here to sell boxes and that's what I want to get to do."

He signed a few boxes, scrawling his left-handed signature with a red pen, and managed to sell $50,000 worth of ornaments. But having his efforts to raise money for charity met with the hysteria normally afforded rock stars left him thoroughly demoralized.

"It was very obnoxious from the second John walked in," said Very Special Arts executive Kathy Walther. "John hoped it would be more substantive."

At the end of the year, he did manage to make a more concrete contribution to charity, appearing on the television program "Christmas Party for the Special Olympics," on which fifteen disabled athletes shared their Christmas celebrations with the Kennedy family. Eunice Kennedy Shriver had founded the charity, and part of the program was filmed during a Mass in the Kennedy chapel at Hyannis Port. John read a Christmas story during the broadcast.

In January 1989 he escaped from Manhattan and went skiing in Aspen, at that point overrun by celebrities but not yet by paparazzi. He went shopping at the Aspen gift store, Curious George, where he bought an antique sheriff's badge. True to form, he was without cash or credit cards.

"Can I write you a check?" he asked.

"It's against store policy," replied the clerk.

Finally the manager appeared, recognized him, and authorized his check.

John worked out at the Aspen Club, where he was spotted by writer and television personality Couri Hay, who runs the club Tatou.

"I worked out with him and discovered John is a major exhibitionist," said Hay. "He loves to walk around in the nude. He is in great shape and eager for everyone to see it. He walks around in the gym with his bathrobe open, and when he takes a shower he leaves the curtain open. He could have been a porno star. . . .

"I remember there was a big party at Hyannis Port when John emerged from the house dressed in only a towel—and then, completely naked, went swimming. Afterwards, he swaggered out of the water, real slow. Some of the waiters at the party were gay, so they couldn't take their eyes off him.

"I watched him work out. He's almost like a bodybuilder, he works really hard. And the girls at the gym really react to him. You'd think he was a movie star.

"When John is at the club, girls never take their eyes off him. He has a quiet charisma but attracts a tornado of attention. I went to a party with Tama Janowitz, but when John came into the room everyone deserted us for him. The entire room turned its attention on him. He's the center of attention wherever he goes."

On May 17, 1989, John switched gears and went to New Rochelle to appear on WVOX-AM and WRTN radio with Andrew Cuomo. The son of Governor Cuomo was the head of HELP, Inc., a group that builds housing for homeless women with children. The show was a phone-in, and during one call John blurted out that he wouldn't complain if someone sought to build housing for the home-less in Hyannis Port.

"You can start in my house," he said.

After the show, an embarrassed Gene Capoccia, housing devel-opment director for Barnstable, Massachusetts, which has jurisdiction over Hyannis Port, said, "I've never been to the Kennedy home, but I don't think he meant it literally. He couldn't have meant it. He's an in-telligent man, so I don't think he means Hyannis Port."

John made no further comment.

On May 19, 1989, John graduated from New York University Law School. Jackie, Caroline, and Christina Haag were on hand at Madison Square Garden to see John, dressed in purple and black robes, receive his degree. Maurice Tempelsman and Ed Schlossberg also attended. After the ceremony, John obligingly posed for photo-graphs in the press room.

"How do you feel, Jackie?" asked one reporter.

Smiling her slow, enigmatic smile, she looked up at John and said, "I want to let the man in the family speak."

That evening John, Christina Haag, Jackie, Maurice Tempelsman, Caroline, and Ed Schlossberg all celebrated over dinner at the River Cafe in Brooklyn. John kept jumping up from the table and using the pay phone outside the restaurant. He dialed over and over again until he got through. Then he spent forty-five minutes talking animatedly on the telephone, although his entire family was waiting for him in-side.

Haag was his official consort, but Daryl Hannah remained a vibrant secret element in his life. They had spent Memorial Day weekend of 1989 together on a forty-six-foot yacht at Smith Mountain Lake in Virginia. There, in what the tabloids described as a floating love nest, Hannah confided in John that she planned to move to New York, and he suggested they move in together. Not long afterward, Jackson Browne and Daryl made up. According to all accounts, John was desolate.

"He's very capable of having his heart broken," said a woman close to him. "And I think, for a time, Daryl broke it. He really fell hard for her."

The impact of his shattered romance with Daryl bled over into his career. In July 1989, he took the New York State bar exam with 6,853 other lawyers. He and 2,188 of them failed. John said he was very disappointed, adding, "I have to give it everything I've got next time so I don't go through this again."

CHAPTER ELEVEN

Real Life

On the morning of August 21, 1989, John left his apartment to find a group of reporters and photographers waiting for him. He seemed calm enough; then one of the reporters yelled, "How d'ya feel, John?"

"I felt relaxed until I saw you guys," John said with a quick smile.

He headed for the subway, which would take him to the office of Manhattan District Attorney Robert Morgenthau—where he, along with sixty-eight other recruits, would be sworn in as assistant Manhattan district attorneys. The press followed him right into the Manhattan Criminal Court building and waited while he was photographed and fingerprinted before the ceremony.

Being assigned to the special prosecution bureau meant John

would be prosecuting cases of consumer fraud, low-level political corruption, and landlord-tenant disputes. Cases which normally went unnoticed would now capture media attention.

"How do you feel about the assignment?" one reporter called out.

"I feel good," John said with just a touch of irony. He wasn't likely to complain about the cases offered to a fledgling A.D.A.

Inside the building at One Hogan Place, a number of the female A.D.A.'s were excited about his arrival. "I'm looking forward to seeing how good-looking he is," one of them said.

His hopes of starting the job like any other new employee were dashed in the frenzy of media representatives, hungry for any tidbit. At lunch John went to a Chinese restaurant at 40 East Broadway with a group of other A.D.A.'s. Just as he took off his jacket and rolled up his sleeves to dig in, reporters demanded a comment on his first morning at work. He shook them off at first.

"Come on, John," cried one newshound. "Give us *something!*"

"Please, this is embarrassing," John said, struggling to remain polite. "I have to work with these people."

The press dogged his every step in court—both professionally and as a private citizen. He had been stopped for speeding on July 9, 1989, and now, on August 25, 1989, he was scheduled to appear at the State Department of Motor Vehicles in Corona, Queens. His car had been uninspected, uninsured, and unregistered. He had pleaded guilty by mail to speeding and inspection violation and was at risk of having his license revoked for a year. He had been stopped for driving an unregistered car in 1988 and, absent-minded as always, hadn't bothered to register it.

He pleaded guilty to the charges, then disappointed the journalists who had gathered at Queens Traffic Court by sending a lawyer, Richard Halloran, to appear on his behalf. Halloran arrived bearing copies of John's insurance papers, and the charges were dismissed.

Real Life

His family and the memory of his father continued to exert a strong influence on John's life and mind. In November 1989, Caedmon Records (a division of Random House) released a tape of John reading his father's Pulitzer Prize-winning *Profiles in Courage*. John had agreed to do the reading on the condition that Caedmon make a generous donation to the Kennedy Library. With Caroline and Teddy, he had also launched the Profile in Courage Award, to be presented annually to an individual for public service.

"Throughout my life, people have come to me and said, 'I got into government because of your father,'" John said. "I feel a great pride in that. So, as my father tried to do in his book and in his life, we want to recognize and encourage not only excellence in public service but also rare courage: people who have sacrificed something, taken a position that is politically unpopular and stuck to it because it's the morally right thing to do."

On the surface, at least, he seemed set on consolidating a more serious image. "All I'm going to do in my free time between now and February is study," he said, but he continued to juggle his romances. He took Christina Haag to a romantic supper at the River Cafe, and the next morning was observed leaving his apartment arm in arm with Daryl Hannah.

At work, he operated out of a small office with two old desks, four chairs, and, in one corner, a miniature basketball backboard and hoop. He often rode to work on his bicycle or traveled by subway. One of his close female friends said, "You're rich, John, but you don't live like a rich man."

In January 1990, John worked on his first major case, in which five travel agency workers went on trial for laundering drug money. In February he took the grueling twelve-hour New York bar exam again and was optimistic about his chances of passing on his second try. Through it all, he continued to devote himself to family causes.

For the past two years he had been helping develop Mental Retardation and Developmental Studies, a program designed to train 125 students to work with the handicapped. The Joseph P. Kennedy, Jr., Foundation provided $100,000 to fund the program, and on March 16 John went to City University in New York to present grants to the first Kennedy Fellows. As always he was deluged by photographers, but this time he was pleased to be winning publicity for the program.

On May 1, 1990, in a headline that was to be repeated worldwide, the *New York Post* trumpeted, "The Hunk Flunks."

John had failed the bar for a second time, falling just 11 points short of the passing score of 600. Faced not only with the prospect of being asked to resign his $30,000-a-year post but also with legions of press outside his office clamoring for a comment, John tried to put on a brave face.

"I'm very disappointed. But you know, God willing, I'll go back there in July and I'll pass it then. Or I'll pass it the next time, or I'll pass it when I'm ninety-five. I'm clearly not a major legal genius. I hope the next time you guys are here will be a happy day."

"John is very bright," says his college friend Peter Burrow, "but he has had so much attention and has always avoided getting boxed in. I think on the bar exam he did get boxed in. The whole world was watching, and the pressure mounted, so he started playing against himself. But that wasn't a reflection on his intelligence."

"John just didn't study hard enough for the exam," said a confidante. "He didn't care enough. He isn't really all that much into being a lawyer."

John's failure to pass the bar became such an object of discussion that Dr. Joyce Brothers came up with an opinion: "I think he wants it [to pass the bar] desperately. I think there is a certain amount of distraction in his life. He's a young attractive man who has women throw themselves at him, and there is an enormous amount of pressure just being a Kennedy."

Daryl Hannah was still vacillating between Jackson Browne and John when she went with John on August 29 to celebrate Timothy Shriver's thirtieth birthday at a family party at Lola's in downtown Manhattan. They spent the evening with thirty-five Kennedys and Shrivers. Daryl, in blue jeans and cotton shirt, was relaxed, fit in with the family, and seemed to be happy with John.

On September 30, he escorted Madonna to a PR party for her younger brother, Chris Ciccone, who was promoting his artwork. According to witnesses, Madonna coiled herself all over John, who was polite but distant, leaving as quickly as possible.

Daryl was not jealous. Jackson Browne was still a vital part of her life, and she knew that until she made a choice between the two men, she had no basis for possessiveness.

With no real commitment forthcoming from her, John was at a crossroads. It seemed as if any woman he wanted could be his.

Jackie was smart enough to stay out of the fray. She watched from the wings but, according to an old family friend, "Jackie never tried to introduce him to girls or to find suitable wives for him. She had introduced the 'right' kind of men to Caroline but was extremely careful not to intrude too much in John's romantic life."

Madonna was safely out of the running; his acting career had been successfully sidetracked; but there was still one area in which John defeated his mother: the way he dressed.

Jean Claude Baker, at whose restaurant, Chez Josephine, mother and son often dined, remembered one exchange between the two as they met for dinner. John was dressed in jeans and carrying a backpack; Jackie was very chic, very elegant, very discreet, as always.

"Oh, John," she said softly. "Just look at the way you're dressed."

He laughed and took her arm as they walked into the dining room.

"He always makes it clear he wants to be treated like a regular customer," said Baker.

Of course, none of the other customers carried backpacks.

On one Saturday night in May, around the time of his second bar failure, John took Christina Haag to the 10 P.M. showing of *Miami Blues*. Cousin Willie Smith accompanied them.

"John practically ignored Christina all night," said one witness. "At one point, he and Willie were so deep in conversation that they seemed to forget Christina was with them."

As they crossed the street by Lincoln Center, Haag was left stranded on a traffic island in the middle of the street for about five minutes. Whether it was Smith's company or John's distress over failing the bar that caused the lapse in manners, to many the incident was typical of the way Kennedy men treat women. On a deeper level, however, John wasn't a typical Kennedy man; he was capable of tenderness and chivalry.

"He stays friends with most of his girlfriends long after they break up with him," observed a female acquaintance, "and he's extremely careful not to hurt their feelings by going on in detail about new women in his life. He is very sensitive about not hurting other people."

John flew out to Los Angeles near the end of May 1990, ostensibly to study for his third attempt at the bar. A security guard at the Four Seasons Hotel spotted him at a poolside lunch with *Pretty Woman* star Julia Roberts. Although Roberts later denied ever having met John, the guard was adamant that they had lunched together.

A few days later, John met a twenty-two-year-old Santa Monica sophomore, Stephanie Schmid, on Venice Beach. A tall, willowy

Texas-born blonde, Schmid was physically similar to Daryl Hannah. John later wined and dined her at the Four Seasons. According to a source close to Stephanie, John treated her like a princess and during their two-day affair complained of being distracted from his studies by his addiction to beautiful women.

In July, the month when he was due to take the bar, he accompanied Daryl Hannah to Raoul's Brasserie on Varick Street in Manhattan. To onlookers they seemed deep in conversation and extremely affectionate. Yet even she couldn't hold his attention entirely. When she left him to go to the rest room during a party in Manhattan that same month, he sidled up to Irish singer Sinead O'Connor and asked for her phone number.

O'Connor took John's pen as if to write her number down for him, then snapped it in half and stuffed it into his pocket.

John was becoming adept at juggling his women, much as his father had once done. One evening he took Christina Haag to the Russian Tea Room, only to plead a headache and take her home early. He returned to the Tea Room forty minutes later with a statuesque blonde.

He was unmarried and flawlessly handsome; the world was his oyster. It was inevitable that he would harvest pearl after pearl.

His life in Manhattan was, on the surface, relatively normal. He finished work around 5:45 every day and rode his black mountain bike to the Downtown Athletic Club in Wall Street, where he worked out until dinner. He spent Saturday mornings shopping in D'Agostino's on the Upper West Side, buying such items as cereal, eggs, mangoes, and an Entenmann's Danish Ring. On Saturday afternoons, he usually Rollerbladed in Central Park without attracting attention.

He devoted more time to working out at the three different Manhattan clubs of which he was a member than to studying for the bar. As a child he had always been hyperactive, and traces of the trait still remained.

"What really struck me was his restlessness. He couldn't sit still for more than ten minutes at a time," recalled a New York City corporate lawyer who took a bar review course with him. "The classroom had a door that opened onto a little deck, and every day he'd get up and open the door three or four times for no reason."

In an attempt to focus on the July bar exam, he took a two-week vacation and an additional unpaid two weeks just to study. But his time was still consumed by the two primary pulls in his life: his Kennedy heritage and what those around him were beginning to term his Casanova complex.

On June I, 1990, he attended the $1,000-a-plate JFK Foundation banquet at the Kennedy Library, but arrived too late to change into a tux. That, of course, didn't prevent his ardent fans from nearly swooning as Teddy introduced him and he ascended the podium to speak a few words.

He steadied himself in the eleventh hour and knuckled down to his law exam, signing on for the $1,075 Bar Bri Course, studying with tutor Erica Fine—with a sixty-five percent chance of passing.

"He's not going to give up. He isn't a quitter," said Fine, a thirty-three-year-old lawyer and assistant director of the course. "He's a really nice guy. I think he's very intelligent. He may have a problem with the standardized exam, but this is doable for him. My guess is that the pressure on him was too intense. He is under much more pressure than the average person."

His took his third crack at the bar exam at the Jacob K. Javits Convention Center in New York on July 24, 1990. Three separate sources confirmed that John was given a private room in which to take the examination, which consists of 250 multiple-choice questions and 6 essays. Many of the other candidates, who had taken the test in the crowded general area, were incensed that John had been given preferential treatment. The rules of the bar allowed for those with health problems to take the test in a separate room, but according to a disgruntled fellow candidate, "Kennedy didn't look sick that day. In fact, he was playing Frisbee in the park afterwards with some girls."

Daryl Hannah was taken dangerously ill while filming *At Play in the Fields of the Lord* in the Brazilian jungle. She was rushed to a hospital, where she spent a week recuperating from a mysterious fever. Hearing of her illness and unable to take time away from work, John arranged for 1,000 red roses to be flown to her bedside via chartered plane.

"John has a very chivalrous side to his nature," said a former girlfriend. "He is very drawn to the damsel in distress. He has so much sweetness and tenderness that he wants to save her."

On August 29, 1990, Hannah flew from San Francisco to Boston to spend the weekend with him. Despite her continuing attachment to Jackson Browne, it appeared she was leaning toward becoming Mrs. John F. Kennedy, Jr.

"Daryl is incredibly sweet, but she's also an unbelievably ambitious operator," said a source who had many in-depth conversations with her. "She's well-packaged, bright, and knows how to make herself seem like a victim, rather like a bird with a broken wing.

"She hasn't been involved with many men, but she's really hot and sexy and she communicates that with a kind of animal intelligence. I don't think she's a threat to Jackie, though, because all she really wants to do is take care of John. She's a fun girl who likes to Rollerblade and is very antistyle, rather like Diane Keaton. She is ideal for John—loyal, rich (she isn't marrying him for the dough) and wonderful with children. Jackson's children love her. I'd say she's a perfect Kennedy wife because she is already an abuse collector—which is perfect because John is unlikely to be a faithful husband."

On November 7, 1990, John received the news that he had at last passed the state bar. When he arrived at work he was mobbed by reporters and, walking briskly past them in the chilly weather, paused just long enough to say, "I'm very relieved. It tastes very sweet at the moment."

On November 25, 1990, John turned thirty, and Jackie threw a birthday party for him at the Tower Gallery in Manhattan. George Plimpton escorted Jackie. Christina Haag made an appearance but didn't spend much time with John.

"The party was really boring," said Manhattan events publicist Norah Lawlor. "It wasn't the least bit hip or happening. They had a bad band, a cheese table, very low-key. Everyone seemed preppy and privileged. Christina wore a simple summer dress, and John wore suspenders and just stuck to people he knew."

If John's thirtieth birthday party seemed boring to onlookers, other aspects of his life were suitably adventurous. He traveled to the French West Indies and spent a brief vacation on the fashionable island of St. Barthélemy, one of his mother's favorite escapes. Her friend Rudolf Nureyev owned a house there.

John went swimming in the nude on the very public Governor's Beach. A New York travel agent recognized him and quickly snapped a picture of the assistant Manhattan district attorney, stark naked.

This was standard reckless and impulsive behavior for John, according to a close friend. "He doesn't always plan everything he does," she said.

Proud of his body, he felt secure in St. Barts, normally a stronghold of the wealthy and privileged. Despite his mother's experience years ago when her nude sunbathing photographs had been published throughout the world, he still risked swimming sans suit. Luckily for him, the travel agent who took the full frontal shot rejected all financial offers from the media. She kept the photograph to herself and a few friends who, now and again, were granted the privilege of gazing upon the Adonis-like body of John F. Kennedy, Jr.

While John's nudity at St. Barts was a mild curiosity, another situation arose that would force him to relive the most painful period of his life and to grapple with a whole new set of revelations which threatened to focus still sharper scrutiny on an already overexposed family.

Jackie had been right to steer him away from acting and Hollywood. Instinctively she knew that the movie industry would never give up mining the Kennedy legend for potential profits. While the rest of the country and world waited with anticipation, Jackie, John, and the Kennedys braced themselves for the September opening of a new film by Oliver Stone, *JFK*.

"I think it was difficult for John when *JFK* came out. He couldn't even watch TV without seeing his father being assassinated," said Richard Wiese. "He loves his mother and is very respectful of his father's memory."

"I haven't seen the film and I don't intend to," John told the press. "How I feel about my father's death is a personal, family matter."

For most young children, the circumstances surrounding a parent's death are usually obscured by the fog of innocence. Some family members may offer a few details over the years, but rarely the entire picture.

For John F. Kennedy, Jr., not only were the details of his father's murder exhaustively rehashed as he grew up, but wild and less wild assassination theories sprang up continually all over the world.

John was developing an assertive attitude toward the press and becoming more willing to confront his enemies. When paparazzo Victor Malafante stalked him for days in a van, making a documentary centering around a day in the life of John F. Kennedy, Jr., John sneaked up behind the van, flung open the doors, and jumped inside.

"What do you want?' " John yelled, then left without waiting for an answer.

"He seemed upset," Malafante said. "I got the feeling that he was fed up with all the press attention."

Another photographer, Angie Coqueran, also stalked John relentlessly. "I often spend twenty-four hours a day trailing him around," said Coqueran. "I've seen him exercising on his roof at one thirty A.M. and I've seen him work out for two hours and then smoke a cigarette."

His smoking, however, was judicious.

"John only smokes one cigarette a day," confirmed one of his girlfriends. "Even when the pressure to pass the bar was at its height, he stuck religiously to his one daily cigarette."

He had self-control and he wasn't afraid of anyone. Angie Coqueran once spent hours covertly following him, only to have her cover blown by a jealous rival.

Unaware that she had been exposed, she sat in her car outside John's downtown apartment until she heard a tap on her window. Looking up, she saw that her prey was right in front of her.

Slowly she rolled her window down.

"What are you doing here?'" asked John in a tone that mingled anger and curiosity.

"Just what the other photographer told you," said Angie.

John smiled. To Angie, it seemed that he had a strong dislike for rats.

"Why are you so keen to photograph me all the time?" he asked.

"Photographers have been photographing you since you were a kid," she said. "And I think you are going to be President."

John laughed.

John may have defended himself against intrusions on his life, but he was friendly to anyone who was kind to him. Carolyn Neal, who cleaned his sixth-floor office at the Manhattan Criminal Courts, teasingly asked him not to Rollerblade along the corridor, as it left marks. On Valentine's Day she was rewarded with a box of candy and a card that read "Be my Valentine. Love, John Kennedy."

"We hit it off immediately," said Carolyn, who was in her fifties. "He's always smiling, he always had a warm word for me. I've got a crush on him."

While the press focused on John's after-work intrigues, there was still a job to be done. On June 14, 1991, he took the witness stand in a Manhattan federal courtroom to testify for the government in a case involving an immigration officer who had made illegal raids on bodegas and pocketed some of the confiscated money. John's testimony was brief, but his appearance elicited blissful sighs from some female courthouse employees who had jammed the courtroom just to catch a glimpse of him.

Sarah Jessica Parker, an actress who appeared in *L.A. Story* and starred in *Honeymoon in Vegas*, had a short fling with John.

"The body's beautiful," she said. "But I said to him, 'What you have is wrong. It's not right.' It's unfair, as a woman, to have to stand next to him."

Parker found John much brighter than his image had led her to expect.

"When he talks about things he cares about, he's extremely fluent and very impassioned," she said. "He's someone who has a lot of passion that's waiting to be expressed."

Sarah's own passion for John was brief. She had been living with *Chaplin* star Robert Downey, Jr., when she met John; she went with him to Hyannis and to various New York parties. When she flew to Las Vegas to start filming at the end of July 1991, John failed to return her calls, and the romance was over.

His brief affair with Madonna had meant little to either of them, but Sean Penn still harbored a grudge against John. At a party held at the TriBeCa Grill in honor of Robert De Niro, Sean snubbed John when he tried to introduce himself.

"I know who you are," Sean said. "You owe me an apology."

John walked away. News of the encounter reached Madonna, who sent John a funeral wreath the next day, white roses garlanded with a black and gold ribbon emblazoned with the words "In deepest sympathy," and a card that read "Johnny, I heard about last night," signed "M." John joked that he would put the wreath under glass.

On August 30, 1991, John tried his first case for the Manhattan district attorney's office. The case against alleged burglar David Ramos, who had broken into an apartment and stolen jewelry and cash, was almost watertight. But during his cross-examination of Ramos, John was visibly nervous. Once or twice he seemed to stutter, and to informed onlookers he appeared to be afraid of losing what in essence was a sure conviction.

"They don't usually give hard cases to young assistants," said *New York Post* reporter Mike Pearl, who covers the Manhattan courts. "And this one was particularly easy—the burglar was caught in the apartment, asleep in the bed of the young woman whose apartment he was burglarizing.

"John did fumble a couple of times in summation, but overall he was quite good. I've seen assistant D.A.'s down here faint on their first summation."

If his first case aroused a great deal of media interest, his career in general gave rise to much comment among members of the legal and law-enforcement professions.

"When John goes into court, the defense attorney will always want to have his scalp under their belt—to be able to say, 'I beat John F. Kennedy, Jr., in a court case,'" observed Detective Joe Keenan, who worked in the district attorney's office with John. "So they're more ag-gressive in going up against him.

"I've had a couple of cases with him and I've always found him to be a regular fellow. I worked on a case with him involving an art thief who had AIDS. John was very understanding about it and gave the thief a lot of leeway. He wasn't afraid to talk to the guy or go near him.

"At work you never get the feeling you have to treat him differ-ently from anyone else. He can give and take, horsing around and ki-bitzing. He doesn't come on like gangbusters or strut around in any way. He's a man's man and he gets along well with his colleagues."

A twist of fate with the flavor of Hollywood occurred just two weeks after John tried his first case as an assistant district attorney. On Sep-tember 13, 1991, *A Matter of Degrees* opened at the Bleecker Street Cin-ema. Originally made in 1988, the film had been produced by John's friend from Brown, Randall Poster. Christina Haag and Norman Mailer's daughter Kate were in the cast. The film was a coming-of-age saga set at a college radio station, and John had traveled to Providence to see Haag while she was on location there. When he arrived, his friends persuaded him to take the small role of a guitar player and to sing Elvis Costello's "Alison." Although the film was funded by the Sundance Institute, the rights for the song were never obtained, and John's cameo was reduced to ten seconds.

His relationship with Haag was also over. It ended in 1991, and today she describes the split as "amicable."

At the end of November 1991, John flew to Palm Beach and spent five days at the Kennedy compound during his cousin Willie Smith's rape trial.

"John came down to support Willie because they were damn close," said Jim Connor, a Kennedy employee. "There was talk that

Jackie had forced him to come, but that wasn't true. John is his own person and he came down because he wanted to help Willie."

Through the years, the Kennedys regularly celebrated Christmas and Easter at the compound, almost eliminating the rest of Palm Beach from their consciousness—at least until the fateful Easter of 1991, when Teddy Kennedy suggested to his nephew Willie that they spend the evening at Palm Beach's Au Bar, where they met Patricia Bowman.

Despite the severity of the charge and the public's seeming disgust with the Kennedys, John was spared the brunt of their anger. When he went to lunch with his cousin and the defense team during a break in the proceedings, he was greeted by calls of "You're cute!" This pixilated adoration didn't distract him from the seriousness of the moment and his reason for being in Palm Beach.

"He's helped me out in the past and I was glad to come and be of assistance," John said. "Willie is my cousin. We grew up together. I thought I could at least be with him during this difficult time."

To anyone who knew all the details of Willie Smith's case— including the five other women who had alleged rape but whose evidence had not been admissible—it was clear that his innocence was very much in question. But if John had any doubts about his cousin's innocence, they were eclipsed by his family loyalty and the bond he had formed with Willie through their childhood years.

Despite his mother's battles to insulate him from the negative Kennedy influences, he was proud to be part of the family. He was especially proud of his Irish heritage, which he wore on his sleeve: in the summer of 1991, he had a shamrock tattooed on his forearm and displayed it proudly, not just at touch football games but at dinner parties.

If there was any doubt about John's loyalty to his family, it was dispelled when celebrated attorney Raoul Felder commented on the TV show *A Current Affair* that the Willie Smith rape trial symbolized "the fall of the house of Kennedy." John immediately telephoned his mother's favorite Madison Avenue florists and sent Felder a large bouquet of yellow chrysanthemums. The accompanying card read "Still standing, baby. Best, The House of Kennedy."

Over Christmas 1991, Rose Ganguzza, manager of Xuxa, a Brazilian superstar whose children's TV program made her a billionaire and who once dated soccer star Pele, sent her client's video and photograph to John's office.

"Soon afterwards, John called me and said he would like to get to know Xuxa," said Ganguzza. "She came to New York and we set up a lunch date for the two of them at TriBeCa Grill."

Xuxa went directly to the restaurant, and Ganguzza went to the D.A.'s office in a limousine to pick John up.

"Do you have a limousine outside?" John asked when she got up to the sixth floor.

"Yes."

John frowned. "I'd feel really funny getting into a limo in front of my work."

She sent the limousine away and the two walked to the restaurant, where she had requested a quiet table. People kept asking Xuxa for her autograph, but no one asked John. During their conversation, Xuxa discovered that John knew very little about Brazil.

"I own an island off the coast of Brazil," she said. "Why don't you come down for Carnival?"

John seemed to like the idea—and her.

After lunch, Xuxa was walking toward the car when John said, "I want to show you around my neighborhood."

He lived in TriBeCa now, in a duplex loft decorated rather like the inside of a ship, and he felt safe and at ease in his own territory. They walked through the streets, and Xuxa was dazzled by his easy charm.

"He was wearing a Versace suit," says Ganguzza, "and Xuxa told me she thought he was sexy but shy."

John's relationship with Daryl Hannah continued to simmer on the back burner. Jackson Browne was still important to her, and John, for his part, was still juggling romances. In February 1992, Daryl was in New York, promoting *Memoirs of an Invisible Man* and staying at her newly purchased and remodeled apartment on the Upper West Side.

"Right before Valentine's Day, about one in the morning, John and Daryl were seen having an argument," said journalist Frank di Giacomo.

John stood by his bike, and Daryl straddled the wheel.

"So, why did you come back?" he asked her repeatedly.

"I want to make my relationship with Jackson work," she said after a while. "I can't see you anymore."

John tried to console himself by dating a sultry Wilhelmina model named Julie Baker—a brunette who bore more than a passing resemblance to Jackie.

"Julie and John did date," confirmed Julie's roommate, Christy Orr. "They didn't go out too much but spent most of the time in our apartment in the Village, watching TV or just talking. He took her to some avant-garde shows downtown and was sweet and romantic and bought her flowers. He was also really nice to me. I was going on a trip to Latin America, and he told me what vitamins I should take while I was down there."

John and Julie tried to keep their relationship a secret, but when they did venture out to a Manhattan party they were inseparable. "They hardly mingled," a party guest reported. "The touching and French-kissing shocked people."

Like Daryl, Julie didn't have a monopoly on John's affections. Richard Wiese had introduced him to six-foot-tall *Sports Illustrated* cover girl Ashley Richardson, and they dated for a while. He was still playing the field and seemed open to meeting any number of beautiful women of all types.

Then, on Valentine's Day, 1992, *A Current Affair* broadcast every detail of John and Xuxa's date. They had been filmed from the moment the stretch limousine parked in front of the D.A.'s office until their stroll through the streets of Manhattan. Although Xuxa vehemently denied having cooperated with *A Current Affair,* John was convinced he had been set up.

"I wrote a letter to John saying Xuxa had no idea what was happening and that she didn't need publicity," insisted Rose Ganguzza. "I don't know how they found out about the lunch date. Her driver had noticed the van following them but thought it was just John's security detail."

John never replied to the letter, and Xuxa never heard from him again.

Mortified by the infringement of his privacy, infuriated by the knowledge that millions of viewers had spied on his date, he was becoming increasingly disgusted with life in New York. He would not, however, boycott the press completely. In May 1992, *Prime Time Live* aired an interview with John and Caroline in which they discussed the Profiles in Courage Award.

Reporter Jay Schadler, who talked to Caroline for forty-five minutes before the meeting at the Kennedy Library, found her highly nervous. John, too, was nervous. He had spent time preparing for the interview, reading his father's speeches and replaying his press conferences.

When the camera light flashed on, most of his nervousness disappeared. And from the start he seemed to enjoy the thrust and parry of the interview.

"How have you managed to keep your life as private as you have?" asked Schadler.

"Well, I haven't talked to people like you very much," John said.

His answers at first were a little strained. He was choosing his words carefully.

But he quickly relaxed. "He was bright, witty, and knowledgable," Schadler said.

Realizing that John was far more approachable than he had been led to expect, during the filming of a short walk they took together Schadler asked John whether he could ask additional questions.

"Sure. That's fair game. You can ask anything," John said. Then he added, "I'm not necessarily sure I will answer everything."

Schadler proceeded to broach the delicate question of what he referred to as "the stories about your father."

"I think the real question," John said, "is whether or not, given the tenor of the times, my father would have gone into politics at this point."

Schadler's questions were incisive, and John balked at none of them. After the interview aired, John sent Schadler a note saying it had been a pleasure.

He was, of course, aware that his mother might not feel the same way. Watching the interview on television with friends, he predicted her reaction.

"She's gonna be outta control," he said.

John was beginning to feel the same way. Despite his *Prime Time Live* honeymoon, his disgust with the media erupted again when Teddy remarried in June 1992. The paparazzi immediately saw the difference in attitude between the young man they'd photographed several years ago and the angry subject they now faced.

"John flew in for the wedding and I caught him at the airport, trying to get a cab," said one photographer. "He used to be easy with the press, would pose for one or two shots, but he has changed. This time he ducked down, hid his face, and dived into a cab. The cabdriver gave me the finger and roared away, so I couldn't get my picture. A couple of days later I was back at the airport and I saw that cabdriver and said, 'Well, did you enjoy being the big hero and saving John?' And the driver admitted to me that after all that, John had tipped him only fifty cents."

During the summer of 1992, John went kayaking with three friends around the Aland archipelago, a chain in the Baltic Sea between Sweden and Finland. He had kayaked before in Maine and Alaska, but on this trip was relegated to being navigator and cook—specializing in spaghetti. Afterward, he wrote of their expedition for the *New York Times* travel section as "four desk jockeys in search of manageable danger." He was paid just $600 for the account, which was written in lyrical terms: *"The western winds rose and fell with the sun, and so we slept by day and paddled at night through still water, marveling at the extravagance of a sky where sunrise, sunset and moonrise occur almost simultaneously."*

When one of the desk jockeys failed to negotiate a rough patch of water, John went in after him. When he had dragged his friend through the raging waters to the shallows, they discovered that the friend's legs were so numb he couldn't walk.

"We carried him on shore and wrapped him in a sleeping bag," John wrote simply.

The national press played up the story, using John to bring back the memory of his father's heroism during World War II, when, as commander of *PT-109*, he tirelessly swam rough waters to save injured members of his crew.

In Manhattan, the political machine began buzzing about John's potential. He was young, handsome, and well-spoken. He was already known around the world. Could it be that Camelot was not forever lost?

When Manhattan congressman Ted Weiss died, Democratic party leaders saw their opportunity and approached John, asking him to run for the seat.

He had never voiced a desire to go into politics, although it was clear that the political universe was his for the asking. Perhaps it was his mother's efforts to distance him, as a boy, from the family, or his own recognition of his limitations, or just the dangerous resonance of the Kennedy name in politics—but John turned down the offer to enter the race.

When the politicians tried to change his mind, he stopped them. "I feel very good about my job as Manhattan assistant district attorney," he said. "There's still a lot of work to do. Right now I haven't given politics much thought. It is way, way down the road."

"We've bandied about the idea of him going into politics," says Richard Wiese. "I think he's almost embarrassed by the subject. It's one of those things he would harbor a feeling about secretly. I can see him going into politics. It could also be very difficult—he's avoided the press his whole life and he would have to embrace it. And he has a tough act to follow."

He was treated like a star wherever he went now, and he responded like a polished politician. "In the context of 1992, at almost any party or social event, someone will come up to him and say 'Wow!' and shake his hand," says Richard Wiese. "And John will say, 'Thank you.'"

Daryl was back in John's life again. She spent Memorial Day 1992 at Hyannis, staying at Jackie's Gay Head house. Then, in July, she and John dined and danced at Raoul's on Varick Street, Daryl in T-shirt, jeans, and a floppy hat, and John in green fatigue pants and a black T-shirt. They kissed their way around the dance floor to the sound of Loup Garou, a zydeco band.

They spent Labor Day weekend together at Martha's Vineyard, where Daryl and John, Jackie, Caroline, Maurice Tempelsman, Teddy, and his wife, Vicki, had a clambake. The family approved of Hannah, and she resolved to sever her ties with Jackson Browne forever.

She flew to Los Angeles on September 23 to pack up her belongings and tell Browne their relationship was over for good. But things didn't go as planned. Her serene farewell erupted into a vicious fight that ended only when the police were called, some say by an irate Browne.

"When our officers arrived, other people were there besides Browne and Daryl Hannah," said Santa Monica Police Sergeant Gary Gallnot. "All parties said there was no problem—it was a misunderstanding that had already been resolved. Miss Hannah did not appear to be injured."

But the actress's friends told another tale: that when she told Browne their relationship was over, he threatened to call the police if she left. She yelled, "Go ahead," and he promptly made good his threat. By the time the police arrived, she was bruised and hurt. Her normally Sphinx-like spokesperson, Alan Nierob, confirmed that she had sought medical treatment due to "serious injuries." Browne's manager, Donald Miller, called her claims "absolutely untrue. The incident didn't happen. Jackson says it's absolutely untrue."

She did not press charges.

John had become adept at stepping in to save damsels in distress. He had provided a shoulder for Madonna to cry on during her separation from Sean Penn, even though his involvement with her had never been as intense as his relationship with Daryl. Now he flew to Daryl's side. Wearing dark glasses, combat boots, and a baseball cap, she met him at Los Angeles Airport. They spent two days together before flying back to New York on MGM Grand Airlines on September 28.

The next few days were spent hidden away in Manhattan, John treating Hannah as gently as he might a bird with a broken wing. They emerged when he took her to dinner on October 1 at Cucina Stagionale Restaurant, near his loft.

Photographer Russell Turiak, who saw them there, said, "Her eye looked awful. There was a horrible purple bruise that extended from under her left eye up the side of her nose. She also had two fingers taped together as if they had been injured."

She kept fingering the petals of a red rose during dinner; John kept touching her gently, solicitously. A week later, his protectiveness was immortalized on film when an ever intrepid *A Current Affair* film crew captured them nuzzling on the stoop of her Upper West Side apartment.

By giving him the opportunity to play a role he relished, that of knight in shining armor, Hannah bound him closer to her than ever. It appeared that she was on the threshold of winning America's greatest romantic prize. Certainly millions of women throughout the country dreamed of fitting her glass slipper.

On October 26, 1992, Larry David, *Seinfeld* scriptwriter, gave television life to the secret dreams of the American woman. In an episode of the show titled "The Contest," David featured John at the heart of the plot.

They were together all the time now, and John's Casanova complex appeared to have subsided. He flew to Chicago for the November 24 memorial service for Daryl's stepfather, Jerry Wexler, who had died on November 7. The service was held at the Drake Hotel in Chicago; a thousand spellbound guests watched Calvin Bridges and his Chicago Praise Band belt out "My Guy" in memory of Wexler, whose joie de vivre had made him a legend. The Gold Coast Room of the Drake Hotel rang with poetry, songs, jokes, and recollections, while chocolate telephones were given out in memory of Wexler's addiction to the same.

It was a long way from the somber rites with which the Kennedys were familiar. The service mixed Hollywood (Sharon Stone, Faye Dunaway, Susan Saint James) with the Chicago Old Guard and the wealthiest real estate developers in the country. The atmosphere was closer to Las Vegas than Hyannis Port, the tribute a lovingly irreverent one to a man who had lived life to the fullest.

John stood by Daryl's side.

"John walked in behind Daryl and her sister Page like part of the family," said Sugar Rautbord, who attended the service. "Daryl looked about fourteen years old. Her hair was brown, she wore no makeup, and she had on knee socks. She and all the family carried roses. Her sister Page had just given birth to a baby, Manny Jerrold, and during the ceremony she handed the baby to John. He held it, just as if he were Page's brother-in-law and married to Daryl."

Early in 1993 he took her to the Los Angeles club Dragonfly. He was dressed in old sweats, Daryl in a baggy dress. Glancing across the dance floor, she noticed a man wearing an unusual denim jacket, broke away from John, and sidled up to the man.

"I just love your jacket," she said.

The man slipped off the jacket.

"Here, wear it for a while."

She was thrilled.

John saw her childlike delight, looked at her tenderly, pulled out a $100 bill from his pocket, and offered it to the dazed man. Within seconds, the denim jacket belonged to Hannah. She was a woman who knew what she wanted, and John was the man to give it to her.

On March 13, 1993, Daryl Hannah went to the Rose Bowl Flea Market in Pasadena and for $50 bought a triple lace-on-lace off-the-shoulder wedding dress. Dressed in plaid baggy shorts, a peasant blouse, and sunglasses, she looked like the embodiment of grunge.

News of Daryl's purchase spread like wildfire. From that moment on, the media held its collective breath for an engagement announcement.

Rumors persisted that Jacqueline Kennedy Onassis despised Daryl, but that is not the truth. A source close to the family confirmed, " All Daryl wants is to love and take care of John, and that's is exactly what Jackie wants."

In July, John left his job in the D.A.'s office. His four years there had won him friends and the admiration of his co-workers. Despite unparalleled media attention, he had won five jury trials. In the words of his boss, District Attorney Robert Morgenthau, "He's done a very good job and I do wish him well."

Yet although John was sighted in Washington touring the Justice Department, by August no appointment had been announced and his professional future was still in question.

On the personal front, he and Daryl spent a six-week holiday in the Far East. Their trip began without any media intrusions or fanfare. On the flight from Los Angeles, as an eyewitness commented, "they hugged and kissed quite openly. As they island-hopped to this scuba diver's paradise they made no secret of their love for each other.

Arriving in the South Pacific island of Micronesia, John switched from romantic to athletic mode. Away from the glare of the media, he exhibited the kind of frenzied activity that has caused some of his friends to label him hyperactive. His day began with a fishing expedition, followed by eight hours of diving, and then ended with an evening volleyball game.

Unaware that the media was, in fact, recording his every move, John and Daryl spent an idyllic few days in the Koror resort in the republic of Palau. Eating only fruit and vegetables, they stayed in a $200-a-night hotel suite equipped with a king-sized bed and a dramatically romantic view of the Pacific.

Soon their trip was to degenerate into a desperate game of hide-and-seek, with the media dogging their every move. But here, in Koror, watching John and Daryl stroll hand in hand along the beach, it seemed clear that their wedding was imminent.

Some Kennedy watchers may have been taken by surprise at the intensity of his relationship with Daryl Hannah, but those who had been aware that John had granted her the ultimate accolade of accompanying him to the Inauguration understood the immensity of his commitment to her.

Daryl had stood next to John at the January 1993 Inauguration and watched with him as a Democrat was sworn in as the forty-second president of the United States.

A staunch Clinton supporter, John had attended the Democratic convention in New York and helped boost Clinton's campaign.

John watched the Inauguration enthralled. Observing the son of the thirty-fifth president stand with shining eyes, watching as the forty-second president of the United States was sworn in, some who had been close to John F. Kennedy remembered the president they had loved and lost. And watching John—so close to Bill Clinton, who had so often evoked the name and image of Jack Kennedy during the campaign and who had the previous day kneeled, and prayed, before the eternal flame at their hero's Arlington grave—some of the older Democrats who had seen the birth and death of Camelot looked at John F. Kennedy, Jr., and wondered: Was he a bittersweet relic of the past or a vision of a future yet to unfold?

He was the Prince of Camelot, and his birthright was undeniably political power. Yet he continued to sidestep his destiny, to delay the choice, to avoid the commitment.

"I think both of us have a strong sense of my father's legacy and how important it is—and we both respect it enormously," John once said of himself and Caroline. "But at the same time, there is a sense of—a realization—that things are different and that he would have wanted us to go on with our own lives and not reenact his. I think everyone finds their own messages in their own time."

He has not found his own messages yet, at least not in a public sense. Nor has he tried to reenact his father's life, although there are strong parallels. Instead of fleeing from his father's fascination with blond temptresses, John has embraced quite a few. Instead of indulging his fascination for the theater, he has bowed to his mother's wishes and relinquished his ambitions—just as his father once bowed to his father's wishes and relinquished his dream of becoming a writer. Instead of rejecting a life of public service, John is hovering on the edge, his political future uncertain.

Yet he is just as much the child of Jacqueline Kennedy Onassis as of John Fitzgerald Kennedy. Like his mother, he is subtle, sensitive, mysterious, has a love-hate relationship with the press, craves privacy yet sometimes courts publicity, and is far more creative than most Kennedy family members. Yet his greatest creation is a tentative, unheralded one. For all the tragedy that has shadowed his life, he was born with looks, charm, heritage, good fortune—blessings so lavish that in a nation that values the self-made above all, he has seemed doomed to remain merely an heir.

Yet out of all of that, John F. Kennedy, Jr., has finally excelled in re-creating himself. From being the most famous child in America, who bears the country's most famous name, John F. Kennedy, Jr., has become America's Prince Charming, more worshipped and desired than the most desirable of Hollywood stars. But while the rest of the world remains populated by frogs who hunger to be princes, America's most charming prince has spent a great deal of his life striving to be a frog.

Out of all the glamour and radiance of who he is and what he represents, John's most triumphant creation may be his very ordinariness. Seeing him, even his father might well have approved. When John was born thirty-two years ago and Jack Kennedy saw him for the first time, a reporter asked him whether he wanted his son to be President. Kennedy paused for a moment. Remembering the dreams his father had thrust upon him, unaware of the tragedy and destruction that lay ahead, Jack Kennedy made a simple reply:

"I just want him to be all right."

Source Notes

Many of the sources are included in the text. The following notes are intended to give the reader an indication of some of the research and interviews upon which the book is based.

Prologue

This is based on author interviews with Jim Seymore and Carol Wallace. John's selection as Sexiest Man Alive led to tremendous razzing from his friends. The story, written by Joyce Wadler and reported by Victoria Balfour, provided a valuable portrait of John at this time.

CHAPTER ONE

Fort Atkinson story based on Steve Karten interview with Dave Powers, with further background from his book, *Johnny, We Hardly Knew Ye.*

Dorothy Turbridy, Dinah Bridge, and Fletcher Knebel material comes from their oral histories, made available to the author by the Kennedy Library, Boston, Massachusetts.

Jackie and N Street from Janet Auchincloss' oral history at the Kennedy Library in which Janet talks with great amusement of Jackie's obsession with decorating.

Birth details from the archives of the *New York Times* and other published reports, as well as author interview with Helen Thomas of UPI, who covered the birth.

Luella Hennessy material from Kennedy Library oral history.

Georgetown University Hospital details from author interview with doctor who was interning there at the time, as well as C. David Heymann's *A Woman Named Jackie* and Kitty Kelley's *Jackie Oh!*, both of which were helpful volumes.

Details of 1095 North Ocean Boulevard from author interview with Agnes Ash, former editor of *Palm Beach Daily News*, who frequented the house, and other Palm Beach sources.

No-air-conditioning information from author interview with workmen who recently installed air conditioning in the house. At the time this book was completed, it was reported that the compound is currently for sale.

Rose as a grandmother from author interviews with Barbara Gibson, her former secretary, and Rita Dallas, nurse to Joe Kennedy. A Palm Beach source confirmed that Rose was so determined not to use her pool unnecessarily that she would regularly visit the home of Palm Beach socialite Mary Sanford and use her pool instead.

Curtain dividing Joe and Rose's living room from author interview with Senator George Smathers, who saw it.

John's letter to Rose from her memoirs, *Times to Remember.*

Gloria Swanson details from her memoirs.

Peter Lawford introducing Kennedy to Marilyn from author interview with Patricia Seaton Lawford, his last wife.

John's first photo session from Rose's memoirs.

CHAPTER TWO

A great deal of the information in the chapters covering the White House years come from details contained in Secret Service files, released to the author by the Department of Treasury under the Freedom of Information Act. Further background was obtained from Stephen Karten interview with Paul Fay, from Janet Auchincloss' oral history.

Inauguration Eve gala from author, who was afforded a private screening by Patricia Seaton Lawford of never-before-seen segments of the film her late husband and Frank Sinatra made of the gala. The film is rich with the promise of Camelot and provided a dramatic and poignant record of the birth of the Kennedy presidency.

Details of White House and White House routine from oral histories of French teacher Jacqueline Hirsh and White House usher J. B. West. Also from author interviews with Evelyn Lincoln, President Kennedy's secretary, and Mary Gallagher, Jackie's secretary. Tish Baldridge, Jacqueline's social secretary, confirmed certain details, but did not consent to an interview because "Mrs. Kennedy does not like us to give interviews."

Senator George Smathers in interview with author gave more background.

Cecil Stoughton's memoirs were helpful, as were those of Pierre Salinger, White House press secretary, entitled, *With Kennedy.*

Princess Grace information from oral histories from the John F. Kennedy Library.

Further details came from the oral history of Janet Auchincloss.

Hyannis Port details from author interviews with Rita Dallas and Barbara Gibson, who worked there. The author visited Hyannis Port and explored the surrounding areas.

Cordenia Thaxton material from oral history from the Kennedy Library.

CHAPTER THREE

This chapter is based mainly on author interviews with Evelyn Lincoln, Mary Gallagher, George Smathers, Patricia Seaton Lawford, Bill Haddad, Stephen Karten interview with Dr. Janet Travell, author interviews with Hyannis neighbors Dick Gallagher and Larry Newman.

Pierre Salinger, J. B. West (*Upstairs at the White House*) and Cecil Stoughton's memoirs (*The Memoirs of Cecil Stoughton, the President's Photographer and Major General V. Clifton, the President's Military Aide*) were all useful.

Edward Gallagher's material comes from his oral history at the Kennedy Library.

The memoirs of Maud Shaw, *White House Nanny*, contain valuable information about John's upbringing. Evelyn Lincoln, during an interview with the author, credited Maud for the greater part of John's upbringing. Her methods seem, to this British-born author, to be uniquely British and have left their distinctive mark on John, who, in the face of immense provocation, seems consistently able to maintain a very British stiff upper lip.

Ben Bradlee material comes from his book *Conversations with Kennedy*.

The oral history of Janet Lee Auchincloss, released after her death to the Kennedy Library, provided a unique insight into Jackie and her relationship with Jack, as well as his visits to Hammersmith Farm.

White House policeman Kenneth Burke's material is from his oral history at the Kenendy Library.

Author interview with Tish Baldrige on background.

Helicopter story from author interview with Rita Dallas.

President's grief at Patrick's death from Janet Auchincloss oral history and Ralph G. Martin's book, *A Hero for Our Times.*

Descriptions of the tenth wedding anniversary evening come from author interviews and conversations with Hugh "Yusha" Auchincloss, Ben Bradlee, Toni Bradlee, Sylvia Whitehouse Black, Jamie Auchincloss, and the oral history of Janet Lee Auchincloss.

Stanley Tretick oral history from the Kennedy Library provided details of his memorable session with John and Jack.

CHAPTER FOUR

The assassination and its aftermath have been extensively documented, and the author and a team of researchers consulted the archives of the *Washington Post* and the *New York Times* among other publications.

John Jr. and the assassination from author interviews with Helen Thomas, Evelyn Lincoln, and Stephen Karten interview with Dave Powers.

Jackie's initial reaction from Nancy Dickerson's memoirs and the oral history of Janet Auchincloss from the Kennedy Library.

Joe Kennedy's reaction from author interview with Rita Dallas.

Lyndon Johnson's letter to John is reprinted by courtesy of the Lyndon Johnson Presidential Library.

John and Caroline's outing to Manassas was described to the author by Jamie Auchincloss.

Jackie leaving the White House comes from J. B. West memoirs.

John's birthday party from Stephen Karten interview with Dave Powers and author interview with Jamie Auchincloss, as well as John Davis' detailed account in *The Kennedys, Dynasty and Disaster.*

John Jr. leaving the White House from Stephen Karten interview with Dave Powers.

The author also repeatedly viewed the documentary *Three Days in November*, which contains extensive footage on every aspect of the assassination.

Details of Jackie at Georgetown come from the memoirs of Maud Shaw and Mary Gallagher.

Caroline after the assassination from Jacqueline Hirsh oral history.

John and Mrs. Lincoln comes from Stephen Karten interview with Evelyn Lincoln, as well as the memoirs of Maud Shaw.

Michel Bouvier details come from his relative John Davis' book.

Billy Baldwin's from his memoirs, *Billy Baldwin Remembers*.

Bill Hadadd described John's "Are you a daddy?" reaction in an interview with the author.

CHAPTER FIVE

A great many details of St. David's were provided to the author by Malachy Cleary, a former St. David's teacher, as well as by classmates of John and two St. David's employees who talked to the author on condition of confidentiality.

Letters regarding John's haircuts were released to the author by the Kennedy Library.

Background on John in London from Maude Shaw memoirs and from British newspaper archives.

The Rita Dallas helicopter story comes from her book, *The Kennedy Case*.

John's plane comes from Stephen Karten interviews with Kurt Wagner and Gordon Donald.

The Hawaii trip and Peter Lawford background from author interview with Patricia Seaton Lawford.

Background on the trip to Hawaii from Stephen Karten interviews with John Spierling and Cecily Johnson.

Patricia Kennedy Lawford's fury at trip comes from Patricia Seaton Lawford (who had access to Peter's private papers) and was confirmed by Milt Ebbins interview with James Spada, author of *Peter Lawford: The Man Who Kept the Secrets.*

Joe Kennedy's letter to Patricia Kennedy Lawford was recalled to the author by Patricia Seaton Lawford.

Jackie switching place cards at the wedding of Sydney Lawford comes from Patricia Seaton Lawford.

Details of John at his aunt Janet's wedding come from author interview with Jamie Auchincloss.

CHAPTER SIX

Jackie and publicity were provided to the author in an interview with Agnes Ash.

Ethel Kennedy's attitude to Jackie comes from author interviews with Patricia Seaton Lawford, Rita Dallas, and from a confidential source who has observed them together.

The volumes that proved most helpful for background on Onassis are Peter Evans' book *Ari: The Life and Times of Aristotle Onassis* and Arianna Stassinopolous, *Maria Callas: The Woman Behind the Legend.*

Zsa Zsa Gabor (for whose mother, Jolie, Maria's mother worked and who moved in the same circles as Lee Bouvier and Ari) told the author about Rose's reaction to Jackie wanting to marry Ari and also described the evening Maria and Ari had at Maxim's to the author (who also visited Maxim's for background).

Personal interviews with Lilly Fallah Lawrence and Lynn Alpha Smith provided crucial information regarding Ari.

The material regarding Lee Radziwill's attitude as a child toward the truth comes from Janet Auchincloss' oral history.

Bobby's reaction to Jackie marrying Onassis comes from Patricia Seaton Lawford.

Ari and John material from a transcript of a "Now It Can Be Told" interview with John Davis.

Ari and Rose material from author interview with Barbara Gibson.

Background on the wedding came from *New York Times* reports, as well as Stassinopolous' and Evans' books.

Chapter Seven

Lengthy details of John's life during this period were obtained from the Secret Service files.

John's life at Collegiate was described to me in great detail during personal interviews with Paul Smadbeck, Peter Cohan, and Wilson McCray, as well as two sources who requested anonymity. Further information was provided to Stephen Karten in interviews with Marjorie Dobkin, Jim Balinson, John Mosler, Sr., and John Mosler, Jr. Extensive Jackie and Ari background came from personal interview with Lynn Alpha Smith.

Ari's experiences at Peapack are recounted in Ron Galella memoirs.

Ari's largesse to Jackie (the communion wafers inscribed with her initials) can be found in the memoirs of Christian Carafakis, *The Fabulous Onassis: His Life and Loves.*

Rose Kennedy and Ari from Rose Kennedy memoirs.

John on the *Christina* comes from author interview with Eleanor Lambert and with confidential source who was on the yacht with him.

Peter Beard's recollections of life on the *Christina* come from *Hype* by Stephen L. Aaronson.

John's relationship with Ari comes from author interview with Dick Gallagher.

John in *Oliver!* comes from author interviews with Peter Cohan, Mrs. Cohan, and a photographer who covered the event.

John and Bob Cramer on Skorpios comes from author interview with Bob.

Details of Androscoggin were told to the author by Mr. Stanley Hirsch, principal, and Tom Lane, maintenance, at Androscoggin.

Ari and Jackie's marital problems have been described in various accounts, and details were given in author interviews with Lynn Alpha Smith and Lilly Lawrence.

Jackie clashing with Rose's guard from author interview with Jim Connors.

Jack Kennedy and boredom can be found in Nancy Dickerson memoirs, *Among Those Present.*

Jamie Auchincloss spoke in detail to Kitty Kelley for her book *Jackie Oh!* regarding John's reaction to his father's infidelity and, during an interview with the author, discussed the subject further.

John Davis' comments were made during the "Now It Can Be Told" interview.

Background on Jackie and money is from author interview with Jack Anderson.

Ari's loneliness was described to the author in an interview with John Kessanis.

Ethel and Carol Channing story can be found in Nancy Dickerson's book.

John being called mama's boy from author interview with David Horowitz. Collier and Horowitz' book, *The Kennedys,* provided important background for this book.

Bobby Kennedy, Jr., quotes from taped interview made available to author by the interviewer.

Jackie keeping John from the cousins from author interview with Barbara Gibson.

Ethel Kennedy's children from author interview with Rebecca Michael.

Jackie's upbringing from author interviews with Jim Connors and Dick Gallagher.

Jackie letting John drive from eyewitness.

John and drugs from author interviews with Barbara Gibson and Wilson McCray.

John stealing a car from author interview with Wilson McCray, who was in Switzerland with him.

CHAPTER EIGHT

The author visited Phillips Academy in Andover and received considerable help from archivist Ruth Quattlebaum.

Background on John's relationship with Teddy Kennedy was given to the author during interviews with Dick Gallagher and Rick Burke.

Background and details of John's life at Andover came from author interviews with Wilson McCray, Skip Owen, Harold "Holly" Owen, Elizabeth Melaragno, Andrew Gibbon Nyhart, Brian Crull, Dickie Thieras.

Stephen Karten interviewed John's classmates Heather Trim, George Dix, Douglas Creedon, and John Dabney.

Although Jenny Christian did not grant a comprehensive on-record interview to the author, two lengthy conversations with the author supplied a great deal of background and psychological insight into John.

Back issues of the *Phillipian* (the school newspaper) and the Andover yearbook also provided background and details.

John's eighteenth birthday party comes from Andrew Gibbon Nyhart and confidential source.

Source Notes

Jackie and Bob Colacello from Bob Colacello's book *Holy Terror: Andy Warhol Close Up.*

CHAPTER NINE

Repeated lengthy personal interviews with John's "big brother" and college friend, Richard Wiese were invaluable. According to Wiese, John was aware that he was talking to this author and, while not authorizing the book, made no attempt to deter Wiese from granting a series of interviews.

Further background was obtained from the Brown archives, the *Brown Daily Herald*, and the Brown yearbooks.

John's frat brother Ron Czarnetsky provided information and background in personal interviews, as did Peter Burrow, Larry Conway, Jane Conway, and Brewster Connant, Jr.

John's acting teacher, Don Wilmeth, provided Stephen Karten with insights into his acting career.

Details of Hell Night and John's frat initiation came from Richard Wiese, a confidential source, and Ron Czarnetsky.

Angela Greene and Inge Arvad comments on Jack Kenendy can be found in *A Question of Character*, by Thomas C. Reeves.

Christa de Souza's article on John published in the London Sunday *Times* was very helpful in portraying his time at Brown.

John and Peter Lawford from author interview with Patricia Seaton Lawford, who recalled their correspondence for her.

John and acting at Brown from author interview with Larry Conway and Stephen Karten interview with Chris Harty.

John's attraction to acting from author interview with Barry Landau. Landau, a leading publicist who was involved in the Clinton campaign, tells of how, when John attended a Clinton event, he made a beeline for the actress Shelley Winters and spent much of the evening talking to her about acting.

Jackie's reaction to John's acting from author interview with Leo Damore.

Joe Kennedy forcing Jack into politics from author interview with Senator George Smathers conducted in his Miami office. Smathers also talked about John's political chances and expressed the opinion that time was running out if he planned a career in politics.

The author viewed video footage of John's Brown graduation.

CHAPTER TEN

Wydah expedition from author interview with Barry Clifford, who led the expedition and found the ship.

Kennedy cousins and drugs from author interview with David Horowitz and published sources including the archives of the *Palm Beach Post.*

John and cocaine from three confidential sources.

Jackie and Peter Lawford's death from author interview with Patricia Seaton Lawford.

John and Madonna from author interview with Erika Belle, a confidential source, and from Stephen Karten interview with Futura 2000. Madonna's publicist, Liz Rosenberg, denied that Madonna and John had a relationship but confirmed that he was at her Madison Square Garden concert.

Jackie's phone calls to John regarding Madonna were revealed to the author by Erika Belle, who was then her best friend and was party to intimate details of the relationship. A second source in whom Madonna confided told the author further details of her opinion of John.

The Sonia Braga incident comes from Erika Belle.

John's experience in "Winners" from author interview with Joseph Daly, Bobby Kennedy, Jr., tape, "Now It Can Be Told" interview with John Davis.

Source Notes

Details of Christina Haag's employment on Seventh Avenue from Christine Thomson and details of her career from her agent.

Background to John's visit to India was provided by researcher Ayesha Attari, who interviewed sources there.

Full details of John's time at Manatt were supplied by a former employee who observed him during that period, took extensive notes, and gave the author lengthy extracts.

People magazine details from author interviews with Jim Seymore and Carol Wallace.

John and Daryl Hannah from author interview with Sugar Rautbord and confidential sources.

Jesse Kornbluth's *Vanity Fair* profile of Daryl Hannah provided background information and insights.

Michael Gross' *New York* magazine article "First Son" and Aaron Latham's *M* magazine profile of John were both valuable.

John at the Aspen Club comes from Stephen Karten interview with Couri Hay.

CHAPTER ELEVEN

John failing the bar has been reported in various publications. The psychology behind John's failure comes from author interviews with Peter Burrow and Richard Wiese (who is still in touch with him and sees him in Manhattan).

John and Jackie's relationship from Jean Claude Baker interview.

John's thirtieth birthday party from author interview with Nora Lawlor.

The naked picture of John in St. Bart's were taken by travel agent, Shelby Shusteroff, who confirmed their existence in a conversation with the author. The pictures were seen by one of Shusteroff's friends, Stuart Schectman. According to Shusteroff, the pictures were not taken for financial gain, but on impulse, when she recognized

John at the beach. Nude sunbathing is accepted in St. Bart's, where families as well as singles sunbathe on Governeur's Beach and Le Saline.

Details of John's work in the D.A.'s office were given to the author in an interview with Detective Joe Keenan, who worked there with him.

John's friendship with William Kennedy Smith was confirmed to the author by Jim Connor and Richard Wiese.

John sending flowers to Raoul Felder from Stephen Karten interview with Raoul Felder.

John and Victor Malafante from Stephen Karten interview with Victor Malafante.

Details of the Palm Beach rape case have been widely published. The author also talked at length to Michele Cassone, who was at the compound with Patricia Bowman just three days after she and Bowman met Willie Smith.

Details of John's date with Xuxa come from author interview with her manager, Rose Ganguzza and *Current Affair* producer Jeremy Spiegel.

John and Julie Baker material from author interview with Christie Orr, her roommate.

The background to John's appearance on *Prime Time Live* was provided to the author in an interview with Jay Schadler.

John and Oliver Stone's *JFK* from author interview with Richard Wiese.

John and politics from author interview with Richard Wiese.

John and Daryl from author interviews with Sugar Rautbord and Russell Turiak.

Jerry Wexler's memorial from Sugar Rautbord and Joanne Bon Giorno.

John's quote on his father's legacy from *Prime Time Live* interview.

John and the press from author's interviews with Angie Coqueran and Paul Steiner.

Jack Kennedy on wanting John to be all right from author interview with Helen Thomas.

Bibliography

ADLER, BILL. *The Kennedy Children: Triumphs and Tragedies.* New York: Franklin Watts, 1980.

ANDERSEN, CHRISTOPHER. *Madonna, Unauthorized.* New York: Simon & Schuster, 1991.

ARONSON, STEVEN M.L. *Hype.* New York: William Morrow, 1983.

BALDWIN, BILLY. *Billy Baldwin Remembers.* New York: Harcourt Brace Jovanovich, 1974.

BIRMINGHAM, STEPHEN. *Jacqueline Bouvier Kennedy Onassis.* New York: Grosset & Dunlap, 1978.

BRADLEE, BENJAMIN C. *Conversations with Kennedy.* New York: W. W. Norton, 1975.

BROWN, PETER HARRY AND PATTE B. BARHAM. *Marilyn: The Last Take.* New York: Dutton, 1992.

BRYANT, TRAPHES, WITH FRANCES SPATZ LEIGHTON. *Dog Days at the White House.* New York: Macmillan, 1975.

BURKE, RICHARD E., WITH WILLIAM AND MARILYN HOFFER. *The Senator: My Ten Years with Ted Kennedy.* New York: St. Martin's Press, 1992.

CALLAS, JACKIE. *Sisters.* London: Macmillan, 1989.

CARAFAKIS, CHRISTIAN, WITH JACQUES HARVEY. *The Fabulous Onassis: His Life and Loves.* New York: William Morrow, 1972.

CASSINI, OLEG. *In My Own Fashion: An Autobiography.* New York: Simon & Schuster, 1987.

CHELLIS, MARCIA. *The Joan Kennedy Story.* New York: Simon & Schuster, 1985.

COLLIER, PETER, AND DAVID HOROWITZ. *The Kennedys: An American Drama.* New York: Summit Books, 1984.

COLACELLO, BOB. *Holy Terror: Andy Warhol Close Up.* New York: HarperCollins, 1990.

DALLAS, RITA, WITH JEANIRA RATCLIFFE. *The Kennedy Case.* New York: G. P. Putnam's Sons, 1973.

Bibliography

DAMORE, LEO. *Senatorial Privilege.* Washington, D.C.: Regnery Gateway, 1988.

DAVID, LESTER, AND IRENE DAVID. *Bobby Kennedy: The Making of a Folk Hero.* New York: Dodd, Mead, 1986.

DAVIS, JOHN H. *The Kennedys: Dynasty and Disaster: 1848–1984.* New York: McGraw-Hill, 1984.

DAVIS, L.J. *Onassis, Aristotle and Christina.* New York: St. Martin's Press, 1986.

DICKERSON, NANCY. *Among Those Present.* New York: Random House, 1976.

EISENHOWER, JULIE NIXON. *Pat Nixon: The Untold Story.* New York: Simon & Schuster, 1986.

EVANS, PETER. *Ari: The Life and Times of Aristotle Onassis.* New York: Summit, 1986.

GALBRAITH, JOHN KENNETH. *Ambassador's Journal.* Boston: Houghton Mifflin, 1969.

GALLAGHER, MARY BARELLI. *My Life with Jacqueline Kennedy.* New York: David McKay, 1969.

GALELLA, RON. *Jacqueline.* New York: Sheed & Ward, 1974.

GARDINE, MICHAEL. *Billy Baldwin: An Autobiography.* Boston: Little, Brown, 1985.

GIBSON, BARBARA, WITH CAROLINE LATHAM. *Life with Rose Kennedy.* New York: Warner, 1986.

GOODWIN, DORIS KEARNS. *The Fitzgeralds and the Kennedys.* New York: Simon & Schuster, 1987.

HALBERSTAM, DAVID. *The Best and the Brightest.* New York: Random House, 1969.

HAMILTON, NIGEL. *JFK: Reckless Youth.* New York: Random House, 1992.

HEYMANN, C. DAVID. *A Woman Named Jackie.* New York: Lyle Stuart Book, Carol Communications, 1989.

KELLEY, KITTY. *Jackie Oh!* Secaucus, N.J.: Lyle Stuart, 1979.

KENNEDY, ROSE FITZGERALD. *Times to Remember.* New York: Doubleday, 1974.

LASKY, VICTOR. *J.F.K.: The Man and the Myth.* New York: Macmillan, 1963.

LEIGH, WENDY. *Arnold.* Chicago: Congdon & Weed, 1990.

LINCOLN, EVELYN. *My Twelve Years with John F. Kennedy.* New York: David McKay, 1965.

MARTIN, RALPH G. *A Hero for Our Time.* New York: Macmillan, 1983.

MENEGHINI, G.B., WITH RENZO ALLEGRI. *My Wife Maria Callas.* Milan: Rusconi Libri, 1981.

Bibliography

MILLS, JUDIE. *John F. Kennedy.* New York: Franklin Watts, 1988.

O'DONNELL, KENNETH P., DAVID F. POWERS, AND JOE MCCARTHY. *Johnny, We Hardly Knew Ye.* Boston: Little, Brown, 1970.

PARMET, HERBERT S. *JFK: The Presidency of John F. Kennedy.* New York: Dial Press, 1983.

RAINIE, HARRISON, AND JOHN QUINN. *Growing Up Kennedy: The Third Wave Comes of Age.* New York: Putnam, 1983.

REEVES, THOMAS C. *A Question of Character.* New York: Prima, 1992.

SALINGER, PIERRE. *With Kennedy.* Garden City, New York: Doubleday, 1966.

SAUNDERS, FRANK, WITH JAMES SOUTHWOOD. *Torn Lace Curtains.* New York: Holt, Rinehart & Winston, 1982.

SHAW, MAUD. *White House Nannie: My Years with Caroline and John Kennedy, Jr.* New York: New American Library, 1966.

SHULMAN, IRVING. *Jackie!* New York: Trident Press, 1970.

SLEVIN, JONATHAN, AND MAUREEN SPAGNOLO. *Kennedys: The Next Generation.* Bethesda, Maryland: National Press, 1990.

SPADA, JAMES. *Peter Lawford: The Man Who Kept the Secrets.* New York: Bantam, 1991.

SPARKS, FRED. *The $20,000,000 Honeymoon: Jackie and Ari's First Year.* New York: Dell, 1970.

STASSINOPOULOS, ARIANNA. *Maria Callas: The Woman Behind the Legend.* New York: Simon & Schuster, 1981.

STOUGHTON, CECIL. *The Memoirs of Cecil Stoughton, the President's Photographer, and Major General Chester V. Clifton, the President's Military Aide.* New York: Norton, 1973.

SUMMERS, ANTHONY. *Conspiracy.* New York: McGraw-Hill, 1980.

TETI, FRANK. *Kennedy: The New Generation.* New York: Delilah, 1983.

THOMAS, HELEN. *Dateline: White House.* New York: Macmillan, 1975.

WEST, J.B., WITH MARY LYNN KOTZ. *Upstairs at the White House: My Life with the First Ladies.* New York: Coward, McCann & Geoghegan, 1973.

WRIGHT, WILLIAM. *All the Pain That Money Can Buy: The Life of Christina Onassis.* New York: Simon & Schuster, 1991.

Index

Index

Index

Index

Index

Index

Index

Index

Index

Index